**IF YOUR LIFE IS NOT W̶~~~~~~~ K̶E IT TO BE,
YOU MAY BE FIGH̶~~~ YOURSELF . . .**

Every person is different—but psychologists around the world agree that all people can be divided into sixteen basic personality types. In *LIFETypes* consultant Sandra Hirsh and psychologist Jean Kummerow bring you a complete, step-by-step system for discovering and recognizing:

- why you may be drawn to being a teacher or a writer rather than a doctor or an accountant
- how your personality type reacts to specific situations—using actual case histories
- the ways different LIFETypes interact with each other—even when they're in love
- the inner-dynamics that go into every decision you make.

By knowing and understanding your personality preferences—and those of the people around you—you can make the right choices for your life.

LIFETypes

SANDRA HIRSH is the author of five books on career, organizational, and personality development. As the principal of Sandra Hirsh Consulting, a career and management consulting firm, she has worked with clients that include Honeywell, 3M, Pillsbury, Lockheed, Texas Utilities, Unisys, and the National Association of Women Business Owners.

JEAN KUMMEROW, Ph.D. is a Licensed Consulting Psychologist and principal of Jean Kummerow & Associates in St. Paul, MN. She works with a wide variety of organizations assessing individuals for specific positions, advising managers on concerns relating to human resources, and providing individual career counseling.

LIFETypes

Sandra Hirsh
Jean Kummerow

WARNER BOOKS

A Time Warner Company

The Myers-Briggs Type Indicator™ and MBTI™ are registered trademarks of Consulting Psychologists Press, Palo Alto, California.

Warner Books, Inc., 1271 Avenue of the Americas, New York, NY 10020

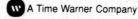 A Time Warner Company

Printed in the United States of America
First Printing: June 1989
10

Library of Congress Cataloging-in-Publication Data

Hirsh, Sandra Krebs.
   LIFETypes / by Sandra Krebs Hirsh & Jean M. Kummerow.
      p. 288
   Bibliography: p.
   ISBN 0-446-38823-8 (pbk.) (U.S.A.)
   ISBN 0-446-38824-6 (pbk.) (Can.)
   1. Typology (Psychology)   2. Myers-Briggs Type Indicator.   3. Self evaluation.   I. Kummerow, Jean M.   II. Title.
BF698.3.H57   1989   88-33635
155.2′64—dc19   CIP

Book design by Giorgetta Bell McRee
Cover design by Dean Morris

To my husband, Roger Schmidt;
to our children, Katherine, Andrew and Elizabeth Hirsh;
Barbara and Rick Schmidt; and to my mother, Sophie F. Krebs.

SANDRA HIRSH

To my husband, John Loban
and our children, Elizabeth and Rob Loban.

JEAN KUMMEROW

Acknowledgments

We are indebted to the following people for their careful reading of the chapters and their insight into personality types. Their individual stories and suggestions enriched our book.

Wm. Scott Anchors, Paul Anderson, Robert Bella, Charles Breer, Susan Bidwell, Edwin Braman, Thomas G. Braman, Susan Brock, Helen Bruant, John Buchanan, Ruth "Susie" Burke, Amanda E. Carlson, Hal Chader, Sue Clancy, Charles Clark, Nicki Davidson, Lynn Davis, Sandra Davis, Larry Demerest, Michael Deis, John K. DiTiberio, Pat Eickmeier, Jeanne Exline, Binnie Ferrand, Peter L. Flint, Penny Pilgram George, Heather R. Gross, Allen Hammer, Carolyn Anita Hartmann, Karen J. Hemphill, Katherine, Andrew and Elizabeth Hirsh, P. William Kirkpatrick, Kay Kummerow, Bonnie Laumb, Rick Laumb, Gordon Lawrence, Lorin Letendre, Lila Lewey, Dr. Charles Lewis, Fiona Lindsay, John Loban, Willy Madsen, Loring W. McAllister, James F. Martin, Mary M. Melbo, Dwight Moore, Terri O'Dowd, Barbara Olson, Jane Cabak Phipps, Naomi L. Quenk, Ph.D., Rachel Quenk, Connie Reyes, Terry Reyes, Susan Scanlon, Roger Schmidt, David Shores, Kelley A. Sillers, Marj Steele, Carol Stuart, SueLynn, Suzanne M. Swanson, Ann C. Thomas, Alice Toso, Sondra Van Sant, John J. Witek, and Robbin Derksen Walker.

One particular individual, Mary McCaulley, deserves special attention for the foundation in psychological type that she gave to both of us.

Our gratitude is immense and heartfelt for the help of our assistant, Bonnie Laumb, who contributed to every phase and detail of the manuscript preparation with patience, thoroughness, and emotional support.

Finally, to our editor Leslie Keenan, a special thank you for her gentle, yet firm guidance—her collaborative approach with us was appreciated.

LIFETypes

Contents

LIFETypes

Part One

THE PREFERENCES

Introduction

This is a book about you. Although you are unique, you have probably noticed that you have some behaviors in common with other people. Conversely, some people have behaviors different from yours. Patterns exist in your behavior, and they are not random. You have a particular type of life because of these patterns—your LIFEType. Other people with patterns similar to yours share your LIFEType. Learning more about your patterns can lead to understanding yourself and others better.

Throughout history, people have developed systems and categories in order to understand one another and to help explain the obvious similarities and differences in people. You may have developed your own way of labeling the patterns you see. Astrology, through the use of birth signs, has long been a popular way of categorizing people. The ancient Greeks had a four-part system by which they characterized individuals: the label "sanguine" described the cynical person; the label "choleric" described the mystical and/or idealistic person; the term "phlegmatic" was applied to the skeptic; and "melancholic" described the pessimist. American Plains Indians categorized people according to the directions of the compass. Each direction was related to a specific behavior type: North meant innocent; South meant wisdom; East meant imagination and new ideas; and introspection was the quality of the West.

In this book, you will be introduced to still another system. This system is based on a theory about personality types developed by Swiss psychiatrist Carl Jung. Two American homemakers, Katherine Cook Briggs and Isabel Briggs Myers, expanded and elaborated on Jung's theory and developed an inventory to help people determine their psychological type. The Myers-Briggs Type Indicator,™ which had a humble beginning in the 1920s, is today the most widely used psychological inventory in the world. It is that psychological type theory that we will explain here.

Psychological type is based on the idea that people have preferences. On a very simple level, some people prefer chocolate ice cream and others, vanilla. To get a bit more complex, within each one of us, physical and mental preferences are present. Our physical preferences include such things as our preferred hand, our dominant eye, or the foot with which we generally lead.

To illustrate this graphically, conduct the following simple experiment. Write your name on a piece of paper, first with your preferred hand and then with the other. Compare your thoughts, feelings, and impressions as you carry out these two simple tasks. What differences did you note in your writing?

Although you have two hands, you do prefer to use one over the other. When you used your preferred hand, most likely you found that your writing was easy and natural, and took little effort. Chances are that the resulting writing was what you expected. Writing with your nonpreferred hand most likely was awkward, and took more effort, concentration, and time. Perhaps the result was not what you would have desired. Note, however, that you were able to write your name with either hand when you wanted. If something were to happen to your preferred hand, you probably would begin to use the nonpreferred hand. Through the use of concentration and greater time and effort, the writing could eventually approach that achieved with your preferred hand.

In a similar way, we have mental or psychological preferences for performing certain tasks. The four basic preferences, or psychological dimensions, are:

> *Energizing*—how and where you get your energy
> *Attending*—what you pay attention to when you
>   gather information
> *Deciding*—what system you use when you decide
> *Living*—what type of life you adopt

There are two possible choices for each of the four preferences, for a total of eight preferences. While we use all eight, we generally favor only one from each of the four basic preferences. The combination of these four preferences results in our psychological type. While these four psychological preferences were intuited by Jung, Briggs, and Myers, four-part frameworks describing the differences in human behavior have been found in many cultures in their myths and religious symbolism. For Jung, the interest in the differences between people came about when he was trying to understand the breakup in his personal and professional relationship with Sigmund Freud. Part of the Briggs' family interest in individual differences came when Isabel Briggs introduced her young suitor, Clarence Myers, to her parents. Clarence Myers was fascinating to the Briggs' because his behavior was quite different from theirs.

Thus, the work on psychological type came about because these curious people, quite independently of one another, had a need to understand some of the personal differences which existed in their own important relationships. Briggs and Myers, upon reading Jung, found that his framework encompassed their work. They adopted his terminology and added to it as they continued their studies for the next forty years.

In this book, the preferences, which are based on the work of Jung, Briggs, and Myers, have their own psychological meanings and are even spelled according to psychological understandings rather than customary usage. Let's examine some of these meanings.

The Energizing Preferences: Extraversion and Introversion

There are two ways a person can be energized. Extraversion is the preference that relates to drawing energy from outside of oneself in the external world of people, activities, and things. Introversion is the preference that relates to drawing energy from one's inner world of ideas, emotions, and impressions.

The Attending Preferences:
Sensing and Intuition

The two preferences for attending are Sensing and Intuition. Sensing relates to the preference for paying attention to information that is perceived directly through the five senses and for focusing on what actually exists. Intuition refers to the preference for paying attention to information that is taken in through a "sixth sense" and for noticing what might or could be, rather than what actually exists.

The Deciding Preferences:
Thinking and Feeling

The deciding preferences are Thinking and Feeling. Thinking is the preference that relates to organizing and structuring information to decide in a logical and objective way. Feeling is related to the preference for organizing and structuring information to decide in a personal, values-oriented way.

The Living Preferences:
Judgment and Perception

Judgment and Perception are the two preferences that relate to how one likes to live one's life. Judgment is the preference that relates to living a planned and organized life, while Perception refers to the preference for living in a more spontaneous and flexible way.

According to psychological type theory, you are born with your particular psychological preferences. You generally rely on your preferred preferences, which you use almost automatically. Your family background and work environment may affect how you use those preferences. When situations demand, you can choose to use those preferences that come less naturally. All eight preferences are available for your use, but four of them will be more accessible and comfortable for you.

Psychological preference does not represent an all-or-nothing concept. Remember that you were able to write with both hands. Similarly, you have all eight of the psychological preferences within you, four of which you use more naturally. Although these four preferences come more easily, this does not necessarily imply that you have more skill or ability in the use of those preferences. It will be important to remember that your preferences are dynamic and fluid, not cast in concrete. They relate to your selected way of behaving in most situations.

You are probably curious about your LIFEType. In the first four chapters of this book, you will determine your favorite four of the eight psychological preferences. Once you have identified your four preferences, you can turn to the specific chapter in Part Two that describes your LIFEType. For further confirmation of your type, you may wish to take the Myers-Briggs Type Indicator,™ a well-respected and documented psychological tool which measures Jungian personality types. The MBTI™ has carefully researched questions and word pairs which are arranged in a forced-choice format that asks one to choose between mutually viable options. A listing of type-related organizations can be found on page 277.

In each of the next four chapters, you will learn about the eight preferences and determine the four that best describe you. Each preference chapter gives a general description and includes information about communications, relationships, and work styles. There is also information about careers and the percentages of each preference that might be found in the United States population.

At the end of each preference chapter, there is a space for you to note the preference that best describes your pattern of behavior. Using the following letter codes, you will come up with the four letters that describe your personality type. E is used for Extraversion, I for Introversion; S stands for Sensing, N for iNtuition (because the letter I has already been used for Introversion); T stands for Thinking, F for Feeling; J stands for Judgment, and P for Perception. All possible combinations of the preferences result in sixteen personality types. The letters that you select will indicate your type and will guide your reading through the chapters in Part Two on the sixteen types. By determining which four of the preferences describe you best and by reading about your LIFEType, you will gain much self-awareness and understanding of your own behavior. Once you understand yourself better, you can go on to learn about others in your life, gaining considerable insight on how they think and how you can get along with them.

People have used this knowledge of psychological type to:

- determine their life mission,
- follow an educational and occupational path which provides the most interest, enjoyment and satisfaction,
- help them learn how to relate to other important people in their lives—their mates, families, employers, and colleagues, and
- most importantly to understand themselves and their LIFE-Types.

Chapter One

THE EXTRAVERT AND INTROVERT PREFERENCES

This chapter focuses on the first set of personality preferences, Extraversion (E) and Introversion (I). The Extraversion and Introversion preferences have to do with how people are energized. Extraversion is the preference that relates to gathering energy from the world of action and interaction. An Extravert (a person who prefers Extraversion) gets energy from people, activities, and things. Extraverts look for stimulation outside of themselves. They tend to have a breadth of interests and to keep an active involvement with people and things. Extraverts talk about what is on their minds, and if you want to know what they are thinking, just listen.

Introversion is the preference that relates to getting energy from internal sources. Introverts (people who prefer Introversion) get energy from inside themselves, using their internal world of ideas, emotions, and impressions. Because of their internal focus, they are inclined to keep their thoughts and ideas to themselves. If you want to know what an Introvert is thinking, you may need to ask, because Introverts prefer to keep their thoughts inside. Introverts function best when they have time for themselves and for reflection. As a rule, they like to think carefully before acting on their thoughts.

Extraversion and Introversion have specific meanings (and even spellings) in the context of this book—meanings related to how people get energy. While the word *extravert*, in popular understanding, often means that one is outgoing, this meaning reflects only a part of the understanding of Extraversion as presented here. The word *introvert*, in popular language, generally means a person who is withdrawn; however, the concept of Introversion is more widely defined in this book.

At their worst, Extraverts may act superficially and make "off the cuff" statements without thinking about their implications. If Extraverts take more time to reflect—that is, to introvert—these wayward remarks might not happen. At their worst, Introverts may defend themselves against the external world and withhold their contributions, thus missing the appropriate time for stating their ideas. They may need to extravert their thoughts more.

GENERAL CHARACTERISTICS

In order to gain further understanding of the general characteristics of Extraversion and Introversion, read through the following lists of paired statements and select those that apply to you.

I am more likely to act like an Extravert and:	I am more likely to act like an Introvert and:
Project my energy outward, making my actions easy for all to see.	Keep my energy inside, making it difficult for others to know me.
Absorb myself in activities.	Absorb myself in thought.
Focus outwardly toward activity and action.	Focus inwardly toward thoughts and ideas.
Speak freely and vocally.	Hesitate before speaking and proceed cautiously.
Tolerate crowds and noise.	Avoid crowds and seek quiet.
Be distracted easily.	Concentrate well.
Meet people readily and participate in many activities.	Proceed cautiously in meeting people and participate in selected activities.
Enjoy a public arena with lots going on.	Enjoy a private arena where I can be alone.

Get restless without involvement with people or activities.	Get agitated without enough time alone or undisturbed.
Skim the surface and act quickly, in an expedient way.	Reflect and act in a careful way.

What others might say when you've overused your Extraversion:

"Can't you be still and be quiet!"

"Mind your own business!"

"Shut up and listen!"

"Slow down! Give me a minute!"

"Stop! Next time, think before you speak!"

What others might say when you've overused your Introversion:

"I never hear from you about anything. What's going on?"

"Why don't you come out of your shell?"

"Let's get busy and talk this over now!"

"Let's get on with it!"

"Don't just sit there; do something!"

Here are two vignettes to illustrate further the difference between Extraversion and Introversion. Which individual seems more like you?

Free Time

One Extraverted woman is always busy and forever "on the go." She has many friends with whom she talks as often as possible. When she is not at work, the phone at her house rings "off the hook." She spends long periods of time talking to her friends, going to parties, and discussing work events. When she is at home alone for longer than an hour, she gets restless for company. She has lots of interests—sports, politics, bicycle trips, music, and dancing. Her friends describe her as outgoing, friendly, and talkative. Sometimes her friends complain that they "can't get a word in edgewise," and her boss worries that she'll wear herself out to the detriment of her work with her continual round of social activities.

An Introverted woman has a sense of deliberateness about her. She has two close colleagues, one of whom she has known since grade school. When she is home from work, she enjoys being away from all the demands of the office. Home is where she is able to relax, read, think, and listen to her favorite classical music without interruption. These activities rejuvenate her. She enjoys jogging in the quiet countryside and has been a runner for as long as she can remember. She dislikes attending most parties, especially large and noisy ones, even when they are occasionally required by her work. She feels drained when she spends too much time in those situations. Her colleagues describe her as pleasant, reserved, and quiet; however, they complain sometimes that they do not really know what she thinks about things. Her boss worries that she may not be spending enough time interacting with others, to the detriment of her career.

Home Alone

An Extravert and an Introvert are happily married to each other. Both have busy schedules, which include independent travel. This often leaves each of them at home alone with time on their hands.

The Introvert finds that when the Extravert is "on the road," the house becomes serene and quiet. He likes having this alone time to reflect and appreciate the wooded setting where they live. This time also gives him an opportunity to tinker with his computer or to watch an entire football game without interruption. Because he enjoys being alone, he seldom invites anyone over, nor does he venture far from home base when his Extraverted spouse is out of town.

Things change, however, when the Introvert takes a business trip and the Extravert is home alone. Very little time elapses before the Extravert begins to feel lonely and in need of activity. She finds all the quiet and solitude uncomfortable. Because of this, she typically arranges to be with friends—going to the movies, to dinner, or to exercise. She enjoys the time "alone" because it gives her a chance to be with her friends, whom she sees less frequently when the Introvert is in town.

The Introvert comments that when he is away on business, it is hard to reach the Extravert by telephone because the Extravert is usually out on the town. On the other hand, the Extravert knows that when she is away on business, she can count on reaching the Introvert at home at almost any time of the evening because he enjoys being at home alone. The Introvert may not define it as being alone because he is his own best companion.

Now that you have read something about the general characteristics of Extraversion and Introversion, which preference seems to be more like you?

_____ Extraversion   _____ Introversion

COMMUNICATION STYLES

The Extraversion and Introversion preferences are revealed in the way people communicate with each other. In general, Extraverts communicate readily and are at home in the outside world. They are less comfortable keeping their thoughts to themselves, preferring to talk matters over with others. In general, Introverted types do not have the need to communicate as much with the external world and are more interested in "the life of the mind." Introverts want privacy. They prefer having time to think and reflect before speaking.

As you read through the following statements about the preferences, choose the preference that better matches your communication style.

I am more likely to communicate like an Extravert and:

Communicate outwardly with energy, excitement, and enthusiasm with almost anyone in the vicinity.

I am more likely to communicate like an Introvert and:

Keep my energy, enthusiasm, and excitement to myself, unless I am sharing it with someone I know well.

Respond quickly to questions and outward events.	Take time to think before responding to questions and outward events.
Communicate one-to-one or in groups with equal ease and enjoyment.	Prefer communicating one-to-one.
Need to moderate myself in order to allow others a chance to speak.	Need to be drawn out and invited by others to speak.
Prefer face-to-face, verbal communication over written communication.	Prefer written communication over verbal, face-to-face communication.
Think out loud, interact with others, and in the process reach my conclusions.	Reflect and think for a time before presenting my conclusions to others.
Need to share my experiences with others almost as soon as they happen, in order to make them come alive.	Need to internally review my experiences before sharing them with others.
Share personal information easily.	Hesitate about sharing personal information.

Here is a vignette that illustrates the differences between the communication styles of Extraversion and Introversion. Which individual in the vignette, the Extravert or the Introvert, seems more like you?

Technical Writers

Two Extraverts and two Introverts were assigned to work together on a writing project announcing a new product for their company. They decided to split into two teams, the two Extraverts focusing on the external market, the two Introverts concentrating on an internal marketing announcement.

In the beginning of their project, the Extraverts talked about it extensively. They decided that they would visit and interview as many marketing people as possible. They would also talk to customers to find out what they needed to know about the new product. The team's information would be checked out with the engineers. Only after doing these steps would they begin their writing project. They would talk through their ideas before writing them down, and once their ideas had jelled, they would "write" their first draft, together, by talking into a dictaphone.

The team of Introverts, on the other hand, met initially and briefly shared their thoughts on how to begin the project. Because they each felt more comfortable working alone, they planned to each individually draft an outline. They would then meet to compare their outlines before beginning on the assignment because they wanted their thoughts to be well organized, even in the early stages. Each would first work on the project alone. Only after they each had completed a draft and had their own ideas clarified would they meet again to discuss each other's work and to merge their separate ideas into a unified announcement.

Now that you have read something about the communication styles of Extraversion and Introversion, which preference seems to be more like you?

_____ Extraversion   _____ Introversion

RELATIONSHIP STYLES

The Extraversion and Introversion preferences also apply to the way people behave in relationships. Extraverts tend to relate to a number of people in a general and sometimes superficial way. Introverts tend to relate to a few selected people and gradually build an in-depth relationship over a longer period of time. As you think about your relationships, read through the following statements and select the preference that better matches your relationship behavior.

I am more likely to relate like an Extravert and:	I am more likely to relate like an Introvert and:
Like having many acquaintances and friendships in addition to my primary one.	Like knowing a few select people and favor relating to only one individual deeply.
Enter a new relationship easily and throw caution to the wind.	Show caution in beginning new relationships.
Talk about my relationship to others.	Keep my thoughts about my relationship to myself.
Feel in my element in the dating process.	Feel out of my element, needing to push myself to date.
Make contact with almost everyone at social events.	Stick with a few people at social events.
Discuss any and all of my thoughts readily with my partner.	Sort through my thoughts first, before sharing my conclusions with my partner.
Become lonely quickly when my partner is absent.	Tolerate my partner's absence well.
Share my personal space and time easily with others.	Require my own personal space with plenty of private time.

Here is a vignette about an Extravert and an Introvert in a relationship, and the way that they prefer to spend their Friday nights. Which person in the couple more closely resembles you?

Friday Nights

After a tiring and busy week, an Extravert and an Introvert separately thought about their "ideal" Friday night. The Extravert, who raced home, was very anxious to tell her partner, the Introvert, about her plans for them for Friday night. Her plans included dinner and some dancing with another couple from her office. The other couple were newly engaged and were looking forward to questioning her and her husband about the secrets of happily married life.

At the end of his work week, the Introvert often felt "washed out" and in need of time to "recharge his batteries." On this particular Friday, he gave a presentation on a new line of computers to a group of insurance agents. He was looking forward to relaxing in his favorite chair, with time to unwind and think. He wanted a quiet dinner and expected to watch television or putter around in his shop; he hoped that his Extraverted wife would become interested in telephoning friends or visiting neighbors.

On hearing the Extravert's plans, the Introvert wondered to himself why anyone would want to spend Friday evening out running around instead of relaxing at home. He gave his wife a pained look that implied that they needed to discuss their different plans.

Now that you have read about the differences in relationship styles of Extraversion and Introversion, which preference seems more like you?

_____ Extraversion   _____ Introversion

WORK STYLES

The Extraversion and Introversion preferences are applicable to the work that people choose, the work setting that maximizes their strengths, and the kinds of workers with whom they feel most congenial and productive. Extraverts enjoy a work setting that is activity oriented, has variety, and allows for frequent interactions with others. Introverts enjoy a work setting that is quiet and private, and that allows for concentration on the task.

As you read through the following paired statements, choose the one that better matches your preferred work style.

I am more likely to work like an Extravert and:

Become impatient and bored when my work is slow and unchanging.

I am more likely to work like an Introvert and:

Become impatient and annoyed when my work is interrupted and rushed.

Seek a variety of action-oriented tasks.	Seek quiet to concentrate.
Be focused equally on what is going on in the work site as well as with my work.	Be focused more on the work itself than on what is going on in the work site.
Respond quickly to requests and spring into action without much advance thinking.	Think through requests before responding, even to the point of delaying action.
Enjoy phone calls as a welcome diversion.	Find phone calls intrusive, especially when concentrating.
Develop my ideas through discussion.	Develop my ideas through reflection.
Use outside resources to complete my tasks.	Use myself as my basic resource to complete my tasks.
Need frequent changes in pace and seek outside events.	Get caught up in my work and disregard outside events.

Here is a vignette to illustrate further the differences between Extraversion and Introversion. Which individual, the Extravert or the Introvert, seems more like you?

Ideal Job

An Extravert has what he considers to be an ideal work situation. His job duties include many current marketing projects that involve relaying information between the home office and the field. In addition, he has a wide variety of assignments relating to training new sales representatives, interviewing customers, and discussing marketing reports with senior management. He describes his work as a whirlwind of activity, with many chances to interact with all levels both inside and outside of the corporation. His workday consists of frequent interruptions and discussions with co-workers, which he finds stimulating. His office is located next to the reception desk where he can see customers and co-workers entering and leaving. The Extravert feels in the "thick of things" at work. He feels fortunate to have a job that allows him as much variety as this one does.

An Introvert feels he has the perfect job. He was hired by a large company to do a long-term, in-depth analysis of their educational programs. He was to develop criteria for evaluating the overall results of these programs. In order to accomplish this major task, he was given a copy of a corporate file that listed employees' names, their educational history, and their accomplishments over a three-year period. He was told that he need not interact personally with nor interview any of the employees on the list; he need only study and generalize from the file about the effectiveness of each employee's training from that person's three-year history. He could, however, reach them by electronic mail, if this proved necessary. He preferred this approach since he did not like interacting personally with many people in a short time period.

In addition to his job duties, the Introvert's work setting allowed him to meet his needs for quiet and concentration. His office was located away from the "beaten track" and was closely guarded by a secretary. There were few other people in this wing of the building; the researchers each had their own offices. His telephone rarely rang, and drop-in visitors were minimal. He felt lucky to have the necessary space and solitude to research the project. Even at lunchtime, he chose to interact only with a select few of the other researchers and employees.

Now that you have read something about the work styles that relate to Extraversion and Introversion, which preference seems more like you?

_____ Extravert   _____ Introvert

CAREER INFORMATION

To perform well at work, individuals may need to use all of the eight preferences at the appropriate time and when required by the situation. Knowing this, people tend to select occupations

that allow them to use the preferences that are most natural to them.

Extraverts frequently choose occupations that encourage activity and interaction with others on a regular and frequent basis. Introverts frequently choose occupations that encourage reflection and in-depth concentration on concepts and ideas.

While Extraverts can and do enter all occupations, some are more appealing to them than others. According to available research,[1] some occupations (in alphabetical order) seem to be especially attractive to Extraverts: consultant, dental assistant, food service worker, home economist, insurance agent, marketeer, receptionist, restaurant manager, sales manager, sales clerk, and other occupations in which they can put their energy to active use. These occupations are not meant to be an exhaustive list but serve to illustrate some areas that an Extravert might enjoy.

While Introverts can and do enter all occupations, some are more appealing to them than others. According to available research, some occupations (in alphabetical order) seem to be especially attractive to Introverts: chemist, computer programmer, electrical engineer, lawyer, legal secretary, librarian, math teacher, mechanic, surveyor, technician, and other occupations in which their energy is focused internally on facts or ideas. These occupations are not meant to be an exhaustive list but serve to illustrate some areas that an Introvert might enjoy.[2]

If your specific occupation or one that you are interested in is not listed here, think instead of its general characteristics and ask yourself how those fit the profiles we've drawn of Extraverts and Introverts.

POPULATION STATISTICS

Based on the best current research available, there seems to be a predominance of Extraverts to Introverts in the United States population, with possibly 70 percent preferring Extraversion and 30 percent preferring Introversion. There also appears to be more females who are Extraverted than males.[3]

IN A NUTSHELL

ENERGIZING
(Orientation of Energy)[4]

Extravert (E) . . . . **Introvert (I)**

External . . . . Internal
Outside thrust . . . . Inside pull
Blurt it out. . . . . Keep it in
Breadth. . . . . Depth
Work more with people   Work more with ideas
and things . . . . and thoughts
Interaction. . . . . Concentration
Action. . . . . Reflection
Do-think-do . . . . Think-do-think

MY PREFERENCE

Now that you have sorted through your preferences for Extraversion and Introversion as they relate to general characteristics, communication styles, relationship styles, and work styles, it is time to summarize what you have discovered so far. Indicate with a check mark the preference that you have selected in each of the sections.

General Characteristics   —————Extravert   —————Introvert
Communication Styles   —————Extravert   —————Introvert
Relationship Styles   —————Extravert   —————Introvert
Work Styles   —————Extravert   —————Introvert

Overall my preference seems to be for _____.
Write in "Extraversion (E)" or "Introversion (I)."

If your check marks do not indicate a clear preference for Extraversion or Introversion and you are still undecided about your preference, keep track of your need to replenish your energy over the next few weeks. See whether you are more likely to be energized by activity and interchange with others (Extraversion) or by solitude with time for reflection (Introversion).

Chapter Two

THE SENSING AND INTUITION PREFERENCES

This chapter focuses on the second set of personality preferences, Sensing (S) and iNtuition (N).* The Sensing and iNtuition preferences have to do with what people pay attention to or what kind of information they gather and how they gather it. Sensing is the preference that relates to paying attention to information received directly through the five senses. For a Sensor (a person who prefers Sensing), it is the actual facts and details of situations that are noticed and believed. Sensors rely on information that is practical and has useful applications. Sensors are oriented to the present and focus on living life as it is.

INtuition is the preference that relates to paying attention to the world through a "sixth sense," "gut feel," or "hunch." For an iNtuitive (a person who prefers iNtuition), it is the possibilities of a situation and its various meanings that are noticed and believed. INtuitives pay attention to their insights and look for underlying meanings or relationships. INtuitives are future oriented, and they focus on making changes. Both Sensing and iNtuition are equally valid and necessary ways for taking in information.

Sensing and iNtuition have specific meanings in the context of this book. The Sensing preference is best understood as gathering information directly, via the five senses. The iNtuition preference is best understood as gathering information indirectly, via inspiration and interpretations.

While Sensors have and may pay attention to their insights, these insights are used to support the data gathered through the

---

*We use the capital N for *iNtuition* because I has already been used for the word *Introversion*.

five senses. When iNtuitives pay attention to the facts and details, it is because these facts and details primarily support an iNtuitive understanding. Sensors use a realistic, pragmatic, and exact standard for the information they accept. INtuitives use an imaginative, insightful, and approximate standard when accepting information.

Using only Sensing or iNtuitive information can lead to inaccuracies. Sensing information may be inaccurate when Sensors concentrate only on the details; for example, the Sensor who "can't see the forest for the trees." INtuitive information may be flawed when iNtuitives focus only on the big picture and ignore the details; for example, the iNtuitive who "can't see the trees for the forest."

GENERAL CHARACTERISTICS

To gain further understanding of the general characteristics of Sensing and iNtuition, read through the following lists and select those statements that most apply to you.

I am more likely to act like a Sensor and:

Use direct observation and first-hand experience.

Learn new things through imitation and observation.

Value solid, recognizable attainments, achieved in a step-by-step manner.

Focus on actual experience, discounting information that comes through the imagination.

Trust my five senses and my own experience to know what is, and be governed by that.

I am more likely to act like an iNtuitive and:

Use "intuitive flashes."

Learn new things through general concepts.

Value different or unusual attainments, achieved via inspiration.

Focus on possibilities and inferences, discounting information that comes through direct observation.

Trust my inspirations and hunches to reveal what might be, and be governed by that.

Be content, accepting life as it is and making changes as reality dictates.

Be restless, seeing how life can be different and trying to modify it.

Get annoyed when things are left too much to chance, preferring precise and exact information.

Get annoyed when things are too clearly defined, preferring approximations and generalizations.

Appreciate and enjoy traditional and familiar ground.

Appreciate and enjoy new and different experiences.

Behave practically.

Behave imaginatively.

Become creative through effort and perspiration.

Become creative through insight and inspiration.

What others might say when you've overused your Sensing:

What others might say when you've overused your iNtuition:

"Didn't you catch the overall meaning?"

"Didn't you read the fine print?"

"You're a stick in the mud!"

"You've got your head in the clouds!"

"Why do you always want to do it the same way?"

"Why do you always want it done differently?"

"You need to look beyond the obvious!"

"You need to be more realistic!"

"Don't give me: 'If it ain't broke, don't fix it'!"

"Don't give me: 'It will all work out, trust me'!"

Here are two vignettes to further illustrate the differences between Sensing and iNtuition. In each vignette, which individual, the Sensor or the iNtuitive, seems more like you?

House Hunting

A Sensor and an iNtuitive were house hunting. The iNtuitive spotted a house that came close to being her dream home.

Although it was in bad need of repair, she could see its many possibilities and challenges. She was intrigued by the home and saw its potential for being a beautifully restored Victorian. She knew that her Sensor husband would see the house in its unimproved state and would therefore be very reluctant to purchase it.

In order to achieve her goal of purchasing the house, the iNtuitive used the following tactics. She decided to orient her husband toward the few features of the house that were currently in good shape—the lawn and garden, the beautiful woodwork that would not require any stripping nor staining, the fourteen beautiful stained glass windows, and the formal staircase. She also pointed out the large kitchen, where he would be able to do his gourmet cooking. However, she knew that a major selling point to her Sensor husband would be practical cost considerations.

She gathered general estimates about the costs for the necessary remodeling, told him what the square footage of this house would cost when compared to new houses that he favored, and emphasized the resale value of property in this historic part of town.

In doing this, she engaged his Sensing in a positive way, allowing him to minimize the negative parts of the house, such as the poor heating and plumbing. She appealed to his sense of tradition and history as she conjured up stories of the types of Christmas celebrations they could have in this old house. She ultimately convinced him to go ahead with the purchase over his desire to buy a new house in a suburban development. Over the years, through her inspired remodeling, the couple have achieved a house that meets the traditional and practical needs of the Sensor and the iNtuitive's creative and inventive needs. In the intervening ten years, the iNtuitive still has not run out of dreams and plans for their house.

Children at Play

A Sensor and an iNtuitive child are observed playing, each going about it in different ways. The Sensor child takes her play rather seriously and often imitates real-life events. She behaves with her dolls just like her mother does with her baby brother. The iNtuitive child, on the other hand, takes real-life things and turns them into something completely different. He does not imitate life, but rather makes up fantasy worlds full of alien languages and customs that only he understands.

Playing with his blankets and pillows, this iNtuitive will construct battlegrounds of hills and valleys where he can place his army figures. To his Sensor sister, however, his construction looks like a mess. She needs him to point out how the blankets and pillows could be a battlefield.

In their drawings and art work, the difference between the two children is very apparent. The Sensor draws objects exactly as they are in life. She lets her mother know if she puts an extra blossom on a flower that she is copying from a real flower in their kitchen. The iNtuitive son has rarely drawn anything that his parents could easily recognize. Nothing is depicted exactly as it is in real life; he always embellishes it. In their drawing styles, the Sensor child resembles Norman Rockwell, and the iNtuitive child resembles Picasso.

Now that you have read something about the general characteristics of Sensing and iNtuition and have read some vignettes that illustrate the differences, which preference seems to be more like you?

_____ Sensing   _____ iNtuition

COMMUNICATION STYLES

The Sensing and iNtuitive preferences are revealed in the way people communicate with one another and the subjects that interest them. In general, Sensors focus on what is real and communicate easily about actual facts and practical matters. They are less comfortable in communicating theoretically. In general, iNtuitives focus on their insights and on what might be possible for a person, situation, or idea. They have less need to communicate accurately about actual facts and details.

As you read through the following paired statements relating to the differences between the Sensing and iNtuition communication styles, choose the preference that better matches your behavior as a communicator.

I am more likely to communicate like a Sensor and:	I am more likely to communicate like an iNtuitive and:
Present my evidence, facts, details, and examples first.	Present my insights, concepts, and ideas first.
Want to know the practical and realistic applications of data.	Want to know the challenges and future opportunities that may be suggested by data.
Rely on my own experience to illustrate and clarify my points.	Rely on my hunches and imagination to embellish my points.
Want others' suggestions to be straightforward, feasible, and practical.	Want others' suggestions to be novel, unusual, and challenging.
Be orderly and step-by-step in my approach to presentations.	Be roundabout in my approach to presentations.
Refer to specific examples in my discussions.	Refer to general concepts in my discussions.
Follow the agenda and its time frames in meetings.	Digress from the agenda when it gets in the way at meetings.
Use detailed descriptions frequently.	Use metaphors and analogies liberally.

People communicate using different kinds of information. The Sensor may be more practical and down-to-earth. The iNtuitive may be more global and imaginative.

Here is a vignette that illustrates the differences between the communication styles of a Sensor and an iNtuitive as they give directions. Which individual in the vignette seems more like you?

Giving Directions

An iNtuitive was giving directions to a mountain lookout to a Sensor who was visiting her city. The iNtuitive told the Sensor to drive east on Route 55 and turn north at the road immediately beyond the fountain landmark. After making that turn, the Sensor was told to continue on to the tree line, which the iNtuitive said was quite noticeable, and at that point, to turn west and follow the two-lane paved road to the lookout point.

The Sensor wrote down the iNtuitive's directions and proceeded on her trip to the lookout point. Even though the directions seemed somewhat vague, the iNtuitive had convinced her that it would be an easy trip. However, the Sensor found out differently, becoming lost on a dirt road in the middle of nowhere.

When she finally got back to her hotel, she called her iNtuitive friend. In recounting her experience, she realized how she had gotten lost. The iNtuitive had neglected to tell her that the fountain landmark spouted only five minutes after every hour. Because it was flush with the ground except when it was spouting, it was indistinguishable from the landscape if one did not drive by it at the right time. Secondly, the tree line that had appeared distinct from her hotel was not clear at all when she drove up close to it. Scraggly trees dotted the mountainside for hundreds of feet, not stopping abruptly at any one line. She realized that she had no idea where the tree line really was and therefore had missed the turn.

The Sensor told her iNtuitive friend that she would have preferred directions to the lookout point as follows: Drive five-tenths of a mile east on Route 55 and turn left, or north, on Mountain Road; continue on for twelve and a half miles. Because the road is unmarked, at the sign for Marge's Restaurant, where there are also three to five scraggly trees, turn left and continue on the two-lane paved, winding road for three miles until you reach the lookout point, which is clearly marked by a stone monument.

*   *   *

Now that you have read something about how Sensors and iNtuitives communicate, which preference seems to be more like you?

———— Sensing   ———— iNtuition

RELATIONSHIP STYLES

The Sensing and iNtuition preferences also apply to the way people are in relationships. Sensors tend to gather information that deals directly with their partners and their relationships. They learn the actual facts about their partners and see their partners fairly realistically. INtuitives pay attention abstractly and are prone to embellish and idealize or theorize about their partners, without giving much care to specifics. They are more likely to ignore reality, especially if it contradicts their ideal or theory of what a partner or a relationship is all about.

As you think about your relationships, read through the following statements, selecting the preference that better matches your relationship behavior.

I am more likely to relate like a Sensor and:

View my relationships realistically, even pessimistically.

Want explicit signs of commitment, such as formal announcements and engagement rings.

Seek predictability as vital to my relationships.

Listen and factor in friends' input about my partner's character.

Daydream, but know what is realistic in the relationship.

I am more likely to relate like an iNtuitive and:

View my relationships optimistically, even unrealistically.

Value subtle signs of commitment, such as special gifts and unique cards.

Value change as vital to my relationships.

Discount or ignore the input of friends about my partner's character.

Daydream about the "ideal relationship" and overlook reality.

Face facts directly when things go wrong.	Face difficulties as challenges for changing the relationship.
Have clear roles and expectations for the relationship.	Believe roles or expectations will always be negotiable.
Expect the couple's spoken plans to become realities.	Expect to continue to dream about what is possible for the couple.

Here is a vignette that illustrates the differences in the Sensing and iNtuition relationship styles. Which individual, the Sensor or the iNtuitive, seems more like you?

The Move

A Sensor and an iNtuitive couple living in Pennsylvania have both received job offers from a large company located in Arizona. They respond to the news and its potential effects on their relationship differently.

The iNtuitive is very optimistically considering the offer, seeing the new and exciting possibilities for each of them. She loves change and believes that this one in particular will strengthen their relationship and their careers. She knows that she and her partner are different from more traditional couples, and she knows that *she* can easily change jobs, friends, and habits. When she envisions the two of them living in Arizona, she sees them at the end of the work day riding horses into the Arizona sunset or sharing moments by their pool watching the desert sky and learning about the Western lifestyle. That both of them were offered jobs by the same company and are able to have this fantastic opportunity is considered a lucky break by the iNtuitive.

Her Sensing partner, on the other hand, has a realistic view of the move and all of its upheaval. He knows that the company offering the jobs has had financial difficulties. He is also aware that moving can be strenuous on a relationship. He is personally acquainted with several couples who broke up when they moved. Furthermore, he has just gotten settled comfortably into his current job, he has recently renovated their house, and Pennsylvania is his home. He has family members close by with whom he enjoys spending time. He is worried about the financial costs of the move and the stresses it will place on their relationship.

Hearing his wife's "daydreams" about the move only complicates the matter further. He knows that she is aware that he is allergic to most animals and does not like to ride horses. He is well aware that too much sun can lead to skin cancer, and he figures that the electric bill in Arizona will be higher because they will need to use more air conditioning. He values his roots and traditions, and he cannot see himself functioning well in that part of the country. While she is "thrilled" about the move, he is "very concerned" about it.

Now that you have read about the differences in relationship styles of Sensing and iNtuition, which preference seems more like you?

_____ Sensing   _____ iNtuition

WORK STYLES

The Sensing and iNtuition preferences are applicable to the work that people choose, the work setting that maximizes their strengths, and the kinds of workers with whom they feel most congenial and productive. Sensors generally choose a work setting that produces practical, useful products or services for people or organizations. They are likely to be where they are able to use their Sensing preference to work carefully with people, things, and data. They tend to prefer work settings that allow them to learn a skill and practice it to the point of mastery. INtuitives are likely to choose a work setting that produces new products or services. They like to be where they are able to use their iNtuition preference to meet future needs or to find new possibilities for people, things, and data. They tend to prefer work settings that allow them the opportunity to continually learn to do new things.

As you read through the following statements, choose the preference that better matches your preferred work style.

I am more likely to work like a Sensor and:

Use my previously acquired work experience.

Appreciate standard ways to solve problems and reach solutions.

Apply skills that are already developed, rather than take the time to learn new ones.

Distrust and ignore my inspirations.

Like things to be concrete and seldom make errors of fact.

Prefer work that has a practical aspect to it.

Want to understand how the details of my work make up a complete picture.

Prefer to continue with what is tried and true and make adjustments for fine tuning.

I am more likely to work like an iNtuitive and:

Do things differently than my previous work experience may dictate.

Use new and different ways to solve problems and reach solutions.

Enjoy learning new skills for the challenge and novelty involved.

Follow my inspirations regardless of the facts.

Like things to be generally stated and seldom worry about specific facts.

Prefer work that has an innovative aspect to it.

Want to see what is involved in the overall picture first and then fill in the details.

Prefer change, often with major readjustments, to continuing on with what is.

Here is a vignette to further illustrate the differences between Sensing and iNtuition. Which individual, the Sensor or the iNtuitive, seems more like you?

The New Computer System

A Sensor and an iNtuitive have been asked to gather some information before purchasing a new computer system for their office. Both have made lists of questions they want answered. The Sensor has determined his major concerns, and his list reflects them. He specifically wants answers to the following questions:

> What are the detailed needs of the office?

> How much productivity, in exact dollar amounts, has been lost to justify a major purchase? (Maybe the old system will do.)

> What are the training costs, in dollars and in time, that would be involved in getting everyone familiar with a new computer system?

> Who will do the training?

> Who specifically will manage the current work flow while a new system is installed? How will this be done?

> How easy will it be to do simple things like making address labels and billing notices on the new system?

> What happens when the computer system breaks down? Is there a system override?

> Is this system compatible with the equipment that already exists in the office?

> Is it compatible with other systems in other departments in the organization?

The Sensor's list contains nine detailed questions and is focused on obtaining hard data of a practical nature.

The iNtuitive's questions are different. He has a set of questions that he will ask in order to gather the necessary general and long-range information about the computer system.

First of all, he wants to know what is available on the market and how effective any given system will be ten years from now. Because the iNtuitive wants to have an integrated and unified system, he wants to find out how a given system can be linked and networked with the telecommunications and security systems the office now has. He wants information about the system's ability to report out various data to illustrate future trends and about the new challenges the office will face from working with a new system.

Whereas the Sensor wants answers to practical applications and needs, the iNtuitive has some general questions with a focus on the future implications and needs for the new computer system.

Now that you have read something about the work styles that relate to Sensing and iNtuition, which preference seems more like you?

_____ Sensing _____ iNtuition

CAREER INFORMATION

To perform well at work, individuals may need to use all of the eight preferences at the appropriate time and when required by the situation. Knowing this, people tend to select occupations that allow them to use the preferences that are most natural to them.

Sensing types frequently choose occupations that require more hands-on and direct experience dealing accurately with problems. Usually the jobs Sensors enjoy call for attending to and mastering detail. INtuitives frequently choose occupations that call for seeing relationships and patterns and dealing with them. Usually the jobs that iNtuitives enjoy call for attending to underlying meanings and anticipating future possibilities and needs.

While Sensors can and do enter all occupations, some are more appealing to them than others. According to available research,[1] some occupations (in alphabetical order) seem especially attractive to Sensors: accountant, bank manager, cleaning service worker, dentist, farmer, food service worker, law enforcement officer, mid-level manager, secretary, steelworker, and other occupations that allow for specific experience. These occupations are not meant to be an exhaustive list but serve to illustrate some areas that a Sensor might enjoy.

While iNtuitives can and do enter all occupations, some are

more appealing to them than others. According to available research,[2] some occupations (in alphabetical order) seem to be especially attractive to iNtuitives: artist, attorney, clergy, consultant, counselor, entertainer, journalist, psychologist, social scientist, writer, and other occupations that allow for generalization. These occupations are not meant to be an exhaustive list but serve to illustrate some areas that an iNtuitive might enjoy.

If your specific occupation or one that you are interested in is not listed here, think instead of its general characteristics and ask yourself how those fit the profiles we've drawn of Sensors and iNtuitives.

POPULATION STATISTICS

The Sensing and iNtuition preferences appear to be unevenly distributed. Current research on the United States population indicates that approximately 70 percent of the population prefers Sensing and the other 30 percent prefers iNtuition.[3]

IN A NUTSHELL

ATTENDING
(Perception)[4]

Sensing (S)	iNtuition (N)
The five senses	Sixth sense, hunches
What is real	What could be
Practical	Theoretical
Present orientation	Future possibilities
Facts	Insights
Using established skills	Learning new skills
Utility	Newness
Step-by-step	Leap around

MY PREFERENCE

Now that you have sorted through your preferences for Sensing and iNtuition as they relate to general characteristics, communication styles, relationship styles, and work styles, it is time to summarize what you have discovered so far. Indicate with a check mark the preference you have selected in each of the sections.

General Characteristics	———Sensing	———iNtuition
Communication Styles	———Sensing	———iNtuition
Relationship Styles	———Sensing	———iNtuition
Work Styles	———Sensing	———iNtuition

Overall, my preference seems to be for _____.
Write in "Sensing (S)" or "iNtuition (N). "

If your check marks do not clearly indicate a preference for Sensing or iNtuition and you are still undecided about your preference, keep track of what kinds of information you gather and what you attend to over the next few weeks. See whether you notice information that is perceived directly, via your senses, or whether you notice information that is perceived more indirectly, via your intuition. Additionally, you may wish to take the Myers-Briggs Type Indicator™ and have it interpreted by a qualified professional.

Chapter Three

THE THINKING AND FEELING PREFERENCES

This chapter focuses on the third set of personality preferences, Thinking (T) and Feeling (F). The Thinking and Feeling preferences have to do with how a person decides or reaches conclusions. Thinking is the preference that relates to deciding in a logical and objective way. To Thinkers (people who prefer Thinking), it is the logical reasons and consequences that are important in making a decision. Feeling is the preference that relates to deciding in a personal and values-oriented way. To Feelers (people who prefer Feeling), what is of value to them and to others is the key in making a decision. Both Thinking and Feeling are rational ways of making decisions and reaching conclusions. Both have specific meanings in the context of this book.

The Thinking preference works well for evaluating and deciding an impersonal issue. Often the conclusion is reached based on pros and cons or on truth and falsehood. The Feeling preference works well for evaluating and deciding on personal issues based on liking and disliking or agreeableness and disagreeableness.

While Thinking types have and use values and emotions to decide, these are used only to support their logical conclusions. While Feeling types use logic and reason to decide, these are used only to support their values-oriented conclusions. The Thinking and Feeling preferences can be thought of as two trains going down separate tracks yet both arriving at the same destination—a decision or a conclusion. Thinking types use an impersonal, objective ordering system in order to find a standard of truth. Feeling types tend to be concerned with finding what is of value or what is important to themselves and others.

Either Thinking or Feeling decisions can be flawed. Thinking decisions can be flawed when Thinkers use an irrelevant standard of truth; for example, during the Renaissance, scholars thought that the earth was the center of the universe and dismissed other theories as incorrect. Feeling decisions can be flawed when Feelers use a set of values that is self-centered or at odds with universal understanding. An example of this is the values conflict that existed over slavery. Some individuals did not view slaves as people.

GENERAL CHARACTERISTICS

To gain further understanding of the general characteristics of Thinking and Feeling, read through the following lists and select those statements that most apply to you.

I am more likely to act like a Thinker and:	**I am more likely to act like a Feeler and:**
Have truth as my objective.	Have harmony as my objective.
Decide more with my head.	Decide more with my heart.
Prefer on principle to question others' findings, believing their findings may be inaccurate.	Prefer to agree with others' findings, believing people are worth listening to.
See my encounters with people as having a purpose.	See my encounters with people as friendly and important in themselves.
Notice ineffective reasoning.	Notice when people need support.
Choose truthfulness over tactfulness.	Choose tactfulness over truthfulness.

Critique and point out the negatives, overlooking the positives.

Overlook people's negative points, stressing areas of agreement.

Focus my attention on universal principles.

Focus my attention on personal motives.

Deal with people firmly, as required.

Deal with people compassionately, as needed.

Expect the world to run on logical principles.

Expect the world to recognize individual differences.

What others might say when you've overused your Thinking:

"You're hardhearted!"

"You're so cold; quit acting like a computer!"

"Why can't you at least be more pleasant?"

"How can you be so heartless?"

"How could you say something so cruel?"

What others might say when you've overused your Feeling:

"You're a bleeding heart!"

"You're such a softy, a real people pleaser!"

"Why can't you be more logical?"

"Don't you ever use your head?"

"Quit taking it so personally!"

Here are two vignettes to further illustrate the differences between Thinking and Feeling. In each vignette, which individual seems more like you, the Thinker or the Feeler?

Truth Versus Tact

A mother was on her way out when her daughter, a Thinker, stopped her and said, "Mom, that outfit looks terrible on you!" Then her son, a Feeler, walked by and said, "Mom, that's a nice outfit, but don't you have something else to wear?" The mother stopped in her tracks, looked at her clothes, and decided that her children were right. She would look better if she changed her clothing.

Later, in reflecting about her children's comments, the mother realized that she took her Feeling son's comment—"Don't you have something else to wear" more easily than her Thinking daughter's critique—"That outfit looks terrible on you." The messages reflected the Thinking and Feeling personality preferences of her children. Her son, a Feeler, gave a more tactful comment meant to preserve his mother's feelings. Her daughter, a Thinker, was truthful and pointed out what was wrong. The Feeling son assumed his mother would get the message. The Thinking daughter assumed that her mother would not be upset by her comment, which was obviously made with her mother's benefit in mind.

The Rent Is Due

Two managers of an apartment complex noticed their different styles in dealing with late rent. One used a Thinking approach, the other a Feeling approach in relaying information about late rent to their tenants. The Thinking manager thought it was appropriate to write a brief note stating, "Your rent is late. Please pay immediately. Sincerely, your apartment manager."

The other manager, a Feeler, felt that such a brief and to-the-point note was too cold and might upset the tenants. To this manager's Feeling way of concluding, having happy tenants meant less turnover and therefore less wear and tear on the building. He preferred a different approach for the overdue rent. First, he would try to catch the renters and talk to them personally, addressing the overdue rent in addition to normal pleasantries. If this tactic did not get the desired rental check, only then would he write a note using the following phrasing: "I'm concerned about you, especially since we talked and I have not as yet received your rent. I hope all is well. Please let me know if there are any problems. Thank you, your apartment manager."

The first apartment manager, a Thinker, preferred his brief and business-like approach. He felt it important to enforce the rental agreement unless there were major reasons to do differently. The other apartment manager, a Feeler, wanted harmonious relationships with the tenants and therefore was inclined to give special considerations.

Now that you have read something about the general characteristics of Thinking and Feeling, which preference seems to be more like you?

_____Thinking   _____ Feeling

COMMUNICATION STYLES

The Thinking and Feeling preferences are revealed in the way people communicate with each other and the manner in which they decide. In general, Thinkers focus their communication on data and things that are based on principles. They are less interested in communicating about personal matters. In general, Feeling types focus their communication on people issues and the values that are important to them. They are less interested in impersonal discussions of data and things.

As you read through the following paired statements about the preferences, choose the one that better matches your communication style.

I am more likely to communicate like a Thinker and:

Prefer brief and concise communication.

Note the pros and cons of each alternative.

Show objectivity and readily critique ideas and people.

I am more likely to communicate like a Feeler and:

Prefer sociable, friendly, and even time-consuming communication.

Note how a given alternative has value and how it affects people.

Show appreciation and readily empathize with people and their ideas.

Convince others by cool, impersonal, logical reasoning.	Convince others with personally meaningful information enthusiastically delivered.
Present goals and objectives first.	Offer pleasantries and then present points of agreement.
Recognize people's feelings and emotions as data to consider, but without undue emphasis on them.	Recognize logical and objective arguments as data to consider, but without undue emphasis on them.
Focus my communication on tasks and impersonal occurrences.	Focus my communication on relationships, people, and personal happenings.
See others' flaws.	See others' positive points.

Here is a vignette that illustrates the differences between the communication styles of Thinking and Feeling in giving a presentation. Which individual in the vignette seems more like you?

Planning a Presentation

A Thinker and a Feeler are participants in a community education class entitled "Effective Presentations." Each class member has been asked to deliver a ten-minute speech to practice presentation skills. Both the Thinker and the Feeler have decided to speak on topics relating to community volunteerism.

The Thinker made his decision in the following way. As a board member of a United Way agency, he had given many presentations on the subject of community volunteerism. He knew it would not take him much time nor would he have to do much additional research to prepare this speech. He concluded that his presentation ought to give an objective view of volunteerism and ought to include enough information to support each point he would make. In order to create a more personal presentation, he would add some pieces of humor.

The Feeler decided on her topic using a different set of considerations. Her first concern was delivering a topic that would be of personal interest to the class participants. Because the class had a large number of community volunteers, she believed a topic relating to volunteerism would be of interest to them. She also wanted to make her presentation enjoyable and useful to her audience. She decided that her speech ought to include personal anecdotes and experiences to illustrate the value of volunteerism. She hoped that her audience would respond to her in a warm and friendly fashion. This would indicate that they not only liked what she was presenting but, as importantly, that they would like her as a person as well.

Now that you have read something about the communication styles of Thinking and Feeling, which preference seems to be more like you?

_____ Thinking   _____ Feeling

RELATIONSHIP STYLES

The Thinking and Feeling preferences also apply to the ways people behave in relationships. Thinkers tend to relate to others in a more impersonal and objective way. Feelers tend to relate to others in a more personal and emotional way.

As you read through the following statements, choose the preference that best matches your relationship behavior.

I am more likely to relate like a Thinker and:

Identify logical reasons for relationships.

Focus more realistically or critically on my partner.

Control my expressions of love.

I am more likely to relate like a Feeler and:

Identify my personal reasons for relationships.

Focus more positively or favorably on my partner.

Offer my expressions of love.

Show my caring more impersonally.	Show my caring through personalized words and actions.
Give improvement messages out of regard for my partner.	Find improvement messages unloving.
Separate out and possibly ignore the emotional aspects of messages.	Look for emotional meanings in seemingly straightforward messages.
Tolerate occasional queries as to my emotional state.	Appreciate frequent queries as to my emotional state.
Ignore the niceties that are helpful in my relationships.	Shy away from negatives that have a potential for undermining my relationships.

Here is a vignette that illustrates the differences in Thinking and Feeling relationship styles. Which individual, the Thinker or the Feeler, seems more like you?

Finding an Apartment

A couple, a Thinker and a Feeler, are trying to find an apartment. Each has come up with criteria to help them make the decision as to which apartment will suit them best. The criteria on each of their lists reflects their Thinking and Feeling decision-making preferences.

The Thinker's list includes factors such as the cost, length of the drive to work, the duration of the lease, and the distance to grocery stores and sporting events. He has made a thorough analysis of the available apartments and come up with the pros and cons of each.

The Feeler's list is grounded by her values for maintaining warm, close relationships with those about whom she cares. She is concerned about the distance to her parents' house in the country, the amount of time it takes to visit her best friend's home, and the wish of her partner to be close to sporting events.

Because they both have done their homework, the Thinker and Feeler are ready to come to a joint decision. Using his analysis, the Thinker has concluded that the Mayflower apartment complex is the best choice for them. On hearing her partner's choice, the Feeler becomes uncomfortable. She believes that the Mayflower is too far for regular visits with her parents; yet it is still close enough to her best friend and to sporting events. For the Feeler, it is important to please her partner and yet meet her parents' needs and her friend's desire for a short commute to visit her. She believes that a decision can be made that will please everyone if she can persuade her partner to look for a compromise location. Because the Thinker has factored into his decision the effect of an unhappy spouse on his life, he agrees to the compromise, and they find a different location that meets everyone's needs.

Now that you have read about the differences in the relationship styles of Thinking and Feeling, which preference seems more like you?

_____ Thinking   _____ Feeling

WORK STYLES

The Thinking and Feeling preferences are applicable to the jobs that people choose, the work settings that maximize their strengths, and the kinds of workers with whom they feel most congenial and productive. Thinkers are likely to choose a work setting that is more impersonal and governed by logic. Feelers tend to prefer a work setting that is personal, focusing on relationships between people and meeting people's personal needs. As you read through the following statements, choose the preference that better matches your preferred work style.

I am more likely to work like a Thinker and:

Orient myself toward the tasks.

I am more likely to work like a Feeler and:

Orient myself toward my relationships.

Like harmony, but can get along without it and still be effective at work.	Need harmony in order to work most effectively.
Use logic and analysis as a basis for my work.	Include others' opinions in addition to my personal values as a basis for my work.
Hurt people's feelings without being aware of it.	Pay attention to others' feelings and enjoy pleasing them even in unimportant things.
Decide impersonally and sometimes overlook others' wishes so I can get my work done.	Allow others' likes and dislikes to influence my decisions, sometimes taking precedence over getting my work done.
Manage and deal firmly with others.	Manage and relate sympathetically with others.
Readily offer criticisms or suggestions for improvement.	Avoid and dislike giving and receiving unpleasant feedback, even when well deserved.
Factor in principles and truths when making work-related decisions.	Factor in underlying values and human needs when making work-related decisions.

Here is a vignette to further illustrate the differences between Thinking and Feeling. Which individual, Thinker or Feeler, seems more like you?

Moving Offices

A Thinker and a Feeler are partners in a small organization that needs more floor space. Luckily for them, additional space has opened up in an adjacent building. Together, they decide to move their business into that space. Some differences, based on their Thinking and Feeling preferences, exist about how to proceed.

One difference has to do with when and how to announce

the move. The Thinking partner prefers to immediately send to each employee an announcement giving the reasons for the move. The Feeling partner wants to speak to each employee individually, discussing the move and its effects on him or her personally. The Feeler also hopes to solicit the employees' help with moving.

Another difference between the partners has to do with the placement of the employees in the new office space. The Thinker wants to reorganize the office along functional lines. She believes the current layout is inefficient because employees have to run from office to office and thereby waste valuable time.

The Feeler has a different perspective. She wants to keep the office layout as it is in order to maintain office friendships and to facilitate interaction among employees. She knows the current layout is not particularly efficient for two senior employees whose responsibilities are not that closely related. However, these two employees are special friends who enjoy discussing their work. The Feeling partner wants to accommodate them.

A third disagreement between the partners relates to an employee whose work has not been up to standard. The Thinking partner believes that the move offers an excellent opportunity to fire this employee and save the costs of moving him. The Feeler, however, sees the move as a way to offer this employee a "fresh start."

Now that you have read something about work styles that relate to Thinking and Feeling, which preference seems more like you?

_____ Thinking _____ Feeling

CAREER INFORMATION

To perform well at work, individuals may need to use all of the eight preferences at the appropriate time and when required by the situation. Knowing this, people tend to select occupations that allow them to use the preferences that are most natural to them.

Thinking types frequently choose occupations that encourage the use of logical and impersonal analysis. Feeling types frequently choose occupations that have a values basis and involve people relating personally.

While Thinkers can and do enter all occupations, some are more appealing to them than others. According to available research,[1] some occupations (in alphabetical order) seem to be especially attractive to Thinkers: attorney, auditor, bank officer, chemist, computer systems analyst, engineer, farmer, manager, police officer, systems researcher, and other occupations that allow them to be logical. These occupations are not meant to be an exhaustive list but serve to illustrate some areas that a Thinker might enjoy.

While Feelers can and do enter all occupations, some are more appealing to them than others. According to available research,[2] some occupations (in alphabetical order) seem to be especially attractive to Feelers: child care worker, clerical supervisor, clergy, counselor, dental hygienist, librarian, nurse, physical therapist, secretary, school teacher, and other occupations that reflect their values. These occupations are not meant to be an exhaustive list but serve to illustrate some areas that a Feeler might enjoy.

If your specific occupation or one that you are interested in is not listed here, think instead of its general characteristics and ask yourself how those fit with the profiles we've drawn of Thinkers and Feelers.

POPULATION STATISTICS

The Thinking and Feeling preferences appear to have a relationship to gender. In the United States population, more men—as many as two-thirds—tend to prefer the Thinking preference. More American women, as many as two-thirds, tend to prefer the Feeling preference.[3]

IN A NUTSHELL

DECIDING
(Judgment)[4]

Thinking (T). . . . . **Feeling (F)**

Head. . . . . Heart
Logical system . . . . Value system
Objective . . . . Subjective
Justice . . . . Mercy
Critique . . . . Compliment
Principles . . . . Harmony
Reason . . . . Empathy
Firm but fair . . . . Compassionate

MY PREFERENCE

Now that you have sorted through your preferences for Thinking and Feeling as they relate to general characteristics, communication styles, relationship styles, and work styles, it is time to summarize what you have discovered so far. Indicate with a check mark the preference you have selected in each of the sections.

General Characteristics ——————Thinking ——————Feeling
Communication Styles ——————Thinking ——————Feeling
Relationship Styles ——————Thinking ——————Feeling
Work Styles ——————Thinking ——————Feeling

Overall, my preference seems to be for _____.
Write in "Thinking (T)" or "Feeling (F)."

If your check marks do not clearly indicate a preference for Thinking or Feeling and if you are still undecided about this preference, keep track of your decisions over the next few weeks and notice whether they are made on a logical, impersonal basis (Thinking) or a values-oriented, personal basis (Feeling). In addition, you may wish to take the Myers-Briggs Type Indicator™ and have it interpreted by a qualified professional.

Chapter Four

THE JUDGMENT AND PERCEPTION PREFERENCES

This chapter focuses on the final set of personality preferences, Judgment and Perception. The Judgment and Perception preferences have to do with the lifestyle a person adopts. Judgment is the preference that relates to living in a planned and organized manner, with the ability to make decisions confidently. For Judgers (people who prefer Judgment), coming to a conclusion and making a decision are important. Perception is the preference that relates to living in a spontaneous and flexible way, with the ability to stay open for new information. For Perceptives (people who prefer Perception), staying open and allowing life to proceed in an impromptu way are important.

Judgment, in this framework, refers directly to the processes of Thinking and Feeling, which are both rational ways of making decisions and reaching conclusions. Perception, in this framework, refers to the Sensing and iNtuition preferences. These preferences are the different ways of attending and gathering information. With this in mind, it is necessary to remember that the gathering of information (the Perception process) is a more spontaneous process, whereas the making of a decision (the Judgment process) is a more planned process.

Judgers set a course of action and run their lives accordingly. They like to have matters settled and will make decisions based on their goals and final objectives. Judgers often characterize themselves as organized. Perceptive types like to adapt and move with the flow of life, and they prefer a tentative approach to it. They are able to let life happen. They enjoy gathering information and staying open to the potential life has in store. Perceptives often characterize themselves as flexible.

Judgment and Perception have specific meanings in the context of this book. Judgment does not mean that a person is judgmental, and Perception does not mean that a person is always able to perceive things accurately.

It is important in evaluating your preference for Judgment or Perception that you consider what you truly do prefer. With this preference, people often decide according to what they think they ought to do or are required to do, rather than with what they naturally prefer to do. It is the natural inclination that reveals the basic preference.

Either the Judgment or Perception lifestyle can have its problems. The Judgment lifestyle can be a problem when the Judger is too directly goal oriented and does not allow new information to be processed. For example, a Judger decided at an early age to be a physician in order to fulfill her parents' expectations. However, she hated science, did not get good grades, and was not accepted into medical school. Because she had her heart set on her goal, she was stuck and floundered, unable to redirect herself easily. The Perception lifestyle can have its problems as well. For example, a Perceptive did not set any career goals or directions for his life. Because of this, he did not focus his academic efforts, and he did not develop the necessary skills and abilities he needed for employment; it took him much time before he found work.

GENERAL CHARACTERISTICS

In order to further understand the general characteristics of Judgment and Perception, read through the following lists and select those characteristics that better apply to you.

I am more likely to act like a Judger and:

Prefer my life to be decisive, imposing my will upon it.

I am more likely to act like a Perceptive and:

Seek to adapt my life and experience what comes along.

Work for a settled life, with my plans in order.

Keep my life as flexible as possible so that nothing will be missed.

Prefer to reach conclusions.

Prefer to keep things open.

Use words such as "should" and "ought" liberally, on myself and others.

Use words such as "perhaps," "could be," and "maybe" in regard to myself and others.

Enjoy finishing things.

Enjoy starting things.

Desire to be right, to do the right thing.

Desire to have many experiences and miss nothing.

Regiment myself and be purposeful and exacting.

Be tolerant and adaptable.

What others might say when you've overused your Judging:

"You shoot from the hip!"

"Lighten up; you're too intense!"

"You sure can be rigid!"

"How could you decide before knowing all the facts?"

"Relax, what's your hurry?"

What others might say when you've overused your Perception:

"You're into analysis paralysis!"

"You ought to shape up!"

"You sure can be loosey-goosey!"

"You never make a decision!"

"You put everything off to the very last minute!"

Here are two vignettes to further illustrate the differences between Judgment and Perception. Which individual in each vignette seems more like you?

Paper Organization

Two partners, a Judger and a Perceptive, have managed the paper flow in their offices very differently. The Judger's office was very organized, with "a place for everything and everything in its place." At the start and end of each work day, his desk generally was "clean as a whistle," with no stray pieces of paper anywhere to be seen. Papers and materials were either filed, responded to, tossed, or in other ways managed.

The Perceptive's office looked quite different. It had piles of papers and materials relating to past and possible future work assignments scattered around the room. It was almost impossible to see his desktop because it was filled with mounds of paper. The Perceptive did not like to throw anything away because he was never sure when he might need it.

When the Judger would visit the Perceptive's office, he would shake his head with dismay. He did not understand how the Perceptive could get anything done with all the papers scattered everywhere. He felt that the Perceptive ought to make greater use of his bookshelves and filing cabinets, and he even proposed this to his Perceptive partner, but to no avail.

On the other hand, the Perceptive partner worried about the quickness and correctness of the Judger's decisions. He thought that his Judging partner was overorganized and that his paper-management style was too encompassing. He suspected that his Judging partner sometimes tossed out information that might be valuable to them in the future. He even proposed, but to no avail, that his partner adopt a "wait for a week and see" approach before deciding on his paperwork.

Both partners had their paper-management system. The Judger believed that a "cluttered desk indicated a cluttered mind" and operated accordingly. The Perceptive truly believed that "an empty desk was a symbol of an empty mind" and practiced otherwise.

Transitions

Two individuals have been laid off from their jobs and are at a transition point in their lives. Both have received three months' severance pay. Because the Judgment and Perception preferences reflect lifestyle, the Judger and the Perceptive regard the transition differently.

The Judger feels that he needs to get things structured and into some sort of scheduled routine during the three months. He feels uncomfortable with this transition period since he likes his life to be organized and settled. The idea of having free time without any major focus makes him anxious. He quickly decides to seek a new job as soon as possible.

In order to communicate with friends and former colleagues, he sets up a meeting schedule to enlist their help in finding him a new position. He methodically organizes his "pitch" for each person so that he is sure to cover all the major points he needs to make. In order for him to gain the type of work he wants, he believes that he needs to take a very direct approach. His communications with the people on his schedule are to the point: Can they help him find job openings?

The Perceptive individual welcomes this transition point as a time for reassessment before putting himself back into a structured nine-to-five work situation. He looks at this time as an opportunity for him to do career exploration. Without following any preconceived structure, he starts to collect the necessary information. He enjoys his open and unscheduled days. This paid, three-month break is valuable because he can gather new information about himself and his career without needing to commit to anything before he thinks he is ready.

The Perceptive communicates with people he encounters in the course of his day. He makes general conversation about work with them, and he welcomes the opportunity to hear about their careers. He has not established a time frame for finding a new job, and he frankly prefers it that way. He believes that "something will turn up" (it always does!) if he keeps himself open to the possibilities.

Now that you have read something about the general characteristics of Judgment and Perception, which lifestyle is more like the one you lead?

———— Judgment   ———— Perception

COMMUNICATION STYLE

The Judgment and Perception preferences are revealed in the way people communicate with each other. In general, Judgers communicate using a decisive, forceful, and straightforward style. How they and others "ought to" and "should" behave figures into their conclusions about life, and those words are sometimes found in their conversations as well. Because they are results-oriented people, they need an outcome for their communications.

In general, Perceptives communicate using a spontaneous, situational, and roundabout style. How they and others "may" or "could be" figures into their information gathering, and sometimes these words are found in their conversations. Because they are spontaneous and flexible people, they focus on the process of communication.

As you read through the following statements about the preferences, choose the one that better matches your communication style.

I am more likely to communicate like a Judger and:	I am more likely to communicate like a Perceptive and:
Discuss schedules and timetables and set realistic deadlines.	Dislike schedules and feel constrained by too many deadlines.
Dislike surprises and want advance warnings.	Like surprises and enjoy adapting to last minute changes.
Expect others to move their thoughts to conclusions.	Expect that others may not reach a conclusion.
Fix positions and decisions, stating them clearly.	Regard positions as tentative and subject to change.
Orient communications toward results and achievements.	Orient communications toward options and contingencies.

Talk with purpose and direction.	Talk about flexibility and change.
Focus my discussions on the content.	Focus my discussions on the process.
Dislike side discussions in meetings.	Not mind getting sidetracked in meetings.

Here is a vignette that illustrates the difference between the communication styles of Judgment and Perception. Which individual in the vignette, the Judger or the Perceptive, seems more like you?

On Ordering from the Menu

Two co-workers went out to lunch. Since they were at a steak house, the Judger knew exactly what she would order. Obviously, it would be steak. She looked quickly through the menu only to confirm that she had made the right choice. She did not take much time to decide when the waitress asked for orders. "I'll have the T-bone steak, medium rare," she said.

It was different, however, for the Perceptive. After the Judger ordered, he asked the waitress several questions. He wanted to know what the best choice on the menu was and what the restaurant served most frequently. He glanced at several nearby tables to see what the other diners were eating. Only after knowing what his colleague ordered, getting the waitress' recommendation, and seeing the actual food on other diners' plates did the Perceptive have enough information to make his decision. He selected veal cutlet. After placing his order, however, he changed his mind and told the waitress that he would have the steak, medium rare.

Now that you have read something about the communication styles of Judgment and Perception, which preference seems to be more like you?

_____ Judgment   _____ Perception

RELATIONSHIP STYLES

The Judgment and Perception preferences also apply to the ways people behave in relationships. Judgers, when they are certain of their feelings, tend to commit to a relationship and focus their energy on obtaining the partner's commitment as well. Perceptives may make some commitment to the relationship, but may do so more reluctantly, believing that in deciding they may have cut off some of their options. Judgers tend to see a commitment to a relationship as being established and final. Perceptives tend to see a commitment to a relationship as an open and changing thing that needs to be continually reevaluated.

As you read through the following statements, choose the preference that better matches your relationship behavior.

I am more likely to relate like a Judger and:	I am more likely to relate like a Perceptive and:
Feel bound to doing the activities on the social calendar.	Feel less committed to the activities on the social calendar.
Seek to do the right thing for my partner and assume that a right thing exists.	Make no assumptions about what is the right thing and go with the flow of the relationship.
Want designated time periods to work on relationship issues.	Deal with relationship issues as they arise.
Easily decide on the status of my relationships.	Agonize over deciding on the status of my relationships.
Postpone the playful aspects in my relationships until all my work is done.	Seek opportunities to combine work and play.
Regard working together as building my relationships.	Regard work as an infringement on my relationships.
Respect and feel comfortable with traditional forms in my relationships.	Feel hemmed in and restricted by traditional forms in my relationships.

| Like the security and stability of a committed relationship. | Like introducing change and new dynamics into my relationships. |

Here is a vignette that illustrates the differences in the Judgment and Perception relationship styles. Which individual, the Judger or the Perceptive, seems more like you?

The Perfect Vacation

A Judger and a Perceptive are planning a vacation. Each wants to make the trip especially enjoyable for the other. Their approaches to the perfect vacation reflect their Judgment and Perception preferences.

The Judger enjoys the planning process and deciding where they ought to go. After she makes a decision on a destination, she diligently checks to find transportation and hotels that are pleasant yet inexpensive. Once her husband agrees on their destination, she will make the necessary reservations in advance. In addition, she generally tries to find cultural events that are happening in the vacation area and will make reservations for these as well. Although she wants to plan most of the vacation, she does allow some space in the schedule for free time and shopping. By making the arrangements in advance, the Judger believes that she is doing loving things for her husband. He will be able to relax knowing that things will go smoothly and that everything will be taken care of.

The Perceptive also envisions the perfect vacation for his wife. Because he believes that she could use some rest and freedom from her schedule, he plans a way this can occur. He loves the element of surprise and believes that his partner would enjoy a surprise as well. He particularly does not want to plan or overschedule their vacation time. Having two weeks with nothing on their agenda will be a perfect vacation for both of them. With a flexible and spontaneous schedule they will be able to get up late if they feel like it, take a detour to a small town if it looks interesting, or catch the local events if they look promising. Any advance planning, other than booking their flight, will not be necessary; in fact too much planning could result in overkill by not allowing them to have a truly relaxed vacation. By planning in this fashion, he feels that he is showing his love and care for his overscheduled wife.

When the couple begins to discuss their plans, it is immediately obvious that they have two different vacations in mind. They need to resolve their very different dreams and do the following things. In order to meet the Judger's need for structure, they decide where to go and then plan the first and last two days of the trip. They keep the rest of their time open for exploration, as desired. With their hotel and transportation reservations confirmed in advance, the Judger can relax and enjoy herself. And because a large block of vacation time is left open for flexibility and spontaneity, the Perceptive can also relax. Together they are able to plan their perfect vacation.

Now that you have read about the differences in relationship styles of Judgment and Perception, which preference seems more like you?

_____ Judgment   _____ Perception

WORK STYLES

The Judgment and Perception preferences relate to the work that people choose, the setting that maximizes their strengths, and the kinds of workers with whom they feel most congenial and productive. Judgers are likely to choose a work setting that is structured and organized, with plans in place. Judgers like settings in which decisions get made. Perceptives tend to prefer a work setting that is spontaneous, flexible, and open to change. Perceptives like gathering information as a part of their work. As you read through the following statements, choose the preference that better matches your preferred work style.

I am more likely to work like a Judger and:	I am more likely to work like a Perceptive and:
Do my best when I can plan my work and work my plan.	Do my best when I can deal with needs as they arise.
Enjoy getting things settled and finished.	Enjoy keeping things open for last-minute changes.
Like checking items off my "to do" list.	Ignore my "to do" list even if I make one.
Overlook new things that need to be done in order to complete my current job.	Postpone my current tasks to meet momentary needs.
Narrow down the possibilities and be satisfied once I reach a decision.	Resist being tied down to a decision in order to gather more information.
Decide quickly and seek closure.	Put off decisions to seek options.
Seek structure in scheduling myself and others.	Resist structure and favor changing circumstances.
Prefer to regulate and control my work and that of others.	Prefer to free up my work and that of others.

Here is a vignette to further illustrate the differences between Judgment and Perception. Which individual, the Judger or the Perceptive, seems more like you?

Organizing the Project

Two colleagues, a Judger and a Perceptive, are assigned to a highly complex project. At their first meeting, the Judger comes with a plan. She wants to organize the project by determining who will do what parts of it, what the time lines will be, how they will obtain the necessary approvals, and what their final deadline will be. She wants to produce an outline for the project at this meeting so that both of them can start efficiently and increase the odds that they will accomplish their respective tasks on time.

The Perceptive comes to their first meeting with some thoughts; however, she has no particular plan in mind. She believes that at first it is necessary to start on the project and deal with things as they arise. This will give them a sense of what will be required. In her mind, it is important to see what turns up in the initial project exploration. She knows that the project approvals will come without much work on their part, so there will be little need to worry about them, that the deadline will be shifted or at least will have a built-in grace period, and that the outline can be developed as they write. In her opinion, there is no need to lock into a plan too early.

The Judger finds it essential to have several drafts completed within the first month of the project. She knows that, in working on the drafts, they will uncover holes in their plan. These holes will reveal where further research will need to be done.

The Perceptive also believes that several drafts will be necessary, but prefers to wait before committing anything to paper until the research is finished. She thinks the information search will take about two months before writing can begin. Because they have such different approaches to their project, the Judger and the Perceptive have to compromise.

During the first two months, the Judger will write the first draft, and the Perceptive will do the anticipated research. They agree that some individual and joint advance assignments are appropriate. The Judger offers to make a time line of the steps to meet their due date. After this is done, the Perceptive will look over the draft to be sure that there is necessary flexibility to it. Together they work out a plan to meet their individual working styles.

Now that you have read something about the work styles that relate to Judgment and Perception, which preference seems more like you?

———— Judgment   ———— Perception

CAREER INFORMATION

To perform well at work, individuals may need to use all of the eight preferences at the appropriate time and when required by the situation. Knowing this, people tend to select occupations that allow them to use the preferences that are most natural to them.

Judgers frequently choose occupations that have requirements for organization and closure. Perceptives frequently choose occupations in which they can define their own schedules, be flexible, and remain open to new information.

While Judgers can and do enter all occupations, some are more appealing to them than others. According to available research,[1] some occupations (in alphabetical order) seem to be more attractive to Judgers: accountant, administrator, bank officer, dentist, elementary school teacher, guard, judge, manager, nurse, police supervisor, and other occupations that allow for closure. These occupations are not meant to be an exhaustive list but serve to illustrate some areas that a Judger might enjoy.

While Perceptives can and do enter all occupations, some are more appealing to them than others. According to available research,[2] some occupations (in alphabetical order) seem to be more attractive to Perceptives: artist, carpenter, counselor, editor, entertainer, journalist, laborer, researcher, surveyor, waiter and waitress, and other occupations that allow for flexibility. These occupations are not meant to be an exhaustive list but serve to illustrate some areas that a Perceptive might enjoy.

If your specific occupation or one that you are interested in is not listed here, think instead of its general characteristics and ask yourself how those fit the profiles we've drawn of Judgers and Perceptives.

POPULATION STATISTICS

Current research data indicates that in the United States population, there are more Judgers than Perceptives. Approximately 55 to 60 percent of the population appears to prefer

Judgment, with 40 to 45 percent of the population appearing to prefer Perception.[3]

IN A NUTSHELL

LIVING
(Orientation to the Outside World)[4]

Judgment (J) . . . . **Perception (P)**

Planned . . . . Spontaneous
Regulate . . . . Flow
Control . . . . Adapt
Settled . . . . Tentative
Run one's life . . . . Let life happen
Set goals . . . . Gather information
Decisive . . . . Open
Organized . . . . Flexible

MY PREFERENCE

Now that you have sorted through your preferences for Judgment and Perception as they relate to general characteristics, communication styles, relationship styles, and work styles, it is time to summarize what you have discovered so far. Indicate with a check mark the preference you have selected in each of the sections.

General Characteristics ———Judgment ———Perception
Communication Styles ———Judgment ———Perception
Relationship Styles ———Judgment ———Perception
Work Styles ———Judgment ———Perception

Overall my preference seems to be for _____.
Write in "Judgment (J)" or "Perception (P)."

If your check marks do not indicate a clear preference for Judgment or Perception and you are still undecided about this preference, keep track of your work habits and reflect on your lifestyle over the next few weeks to determine whether you prefer a more organized and structured existence (Judgment) or a more spontaneous and flexible existence (Perception). Additionally, you may wish to take the Myers-Briggs Type Indicator™ and have it interpreted by a qualified professional.

Part Two

THE
TYPES

Introduction

Now that you have read about the preferences, we invite you to explore your LIFEType. The four preferences combine and produce an effect in which the impact of one preference builds upon and augments the impact of the others.

Sixteen types result when the four preferences are combined into a single type:

Extraversion (E) or Introversion (I) plus
Sensing (S) or iNtuition (N) plus
Thinking (T) or Feeling (F) plus
Judgment (J) or Perception (P)

For example, if you selected Extraversion, iNtuition, Feeling, and Perception, your type is ENFP. If you selected Introversion, Sensing, Thinking, and Judging, your type is ISTJ. If you are uncertain about your type, compare several possible type descriptions to help you determine which LIFEType more accurately describes you.

My preference is ———— ———— ———— ———— .

Each of the sixteen type chapters has descriptions about:

Living—what you might expect during your lifetime, childhood through retirement.

Learning—how you are most effective as a learner.

Laboring—what you prefer in a work setting, how you like to organize, and what occupations may be attractive to you.

Leading—how you prefer to take charge.

Leisure—how you like to relax and play.

Loving—how you behave in intimate relationships.

Losing Out—how you might overuse your strengths and what strategies are available to help you through difficult times.

In a Nutshell—how each type describes itself.

The chapters on the sixteen types include examples drawn from our experience with each of the types. In addition, they have been verified by several individuals of that type.

Each type is unique and different in its LIFEType. Some types are more straightforward than others, some are more fun loving, some are more complex, some are more serious, and some are warmer than other types. However, you may notice that several of the type descriptions are similar. This is because some of the types have several preferences in common. For example, the ESTJ type is similar to the ISTJ type because they share three of the four preferences, Sensing (S), Thinking (T), and Judging (J). When there is overlap in the descriptions, it is because there is overlap in the preferences that affect how those types actually behave.

Now on to your LIFEType.

Chapter Five

ISTJ

ISTJs Chose the Following Preferences:

Extraversion . . . . ENERGIZING . . . . **Introversion**
Sensing . . . . ATTENDING . . . . iNtuition
Thinking . . . . DECIDING . . . . Feeling
Judgment . . . . LIVING . . . . Perception

In general, ISTJs are systematic, painstaking, thorough, and hardworking. They get the job done and complete it on schedule. They are serious and sincere in whatever they do. They work well within a structure, follow the hierarchy, and are particularly strong and careful in keeping track of facts and details. They are cautious, generally seeking to maintain the status quo. They are at their best getting things to the right place at the right time. They honor their commitments.

LIVING

ISTJ children are serious, dutiful, and reserved. They like a great deal of order and structure. In new situations or with new people, they are quite cautious and perhaps even uncomfortable. They prefer familiar friends to new ones and select friends carefully. When they know what is expected, they act more at ease with others.

ISTJ children are keen observers who tend to focus on what is at odds or at variance with the standard way of doing things. If a piece of furniture has been moved in the house, the ISTJ child notes it and sets out to determine why.

ISTJs tend to enjoy traditional childhood activities such as learning to bake, cook, and repair broken things. When they feel comfortable, they also enjoy group activities such as scouting, with "doing their duty and serving their country" fitting their world view of what is right. ISTJ children like to be read to and appreciate hearing the story read with vocal intensity or tonal inflections. They enjoy the sounds of the stories and the pictures that accompany them. ISTJs particularly like stories in which good triumphs over the forces of evil. Horatio Alger–type stories, in which individuals achieve success in life through hard work and application, are particularly appealing.

ISTJ children, perhaps more than others, enjoy having a schedule to follow and, even as kids, show a propensity for getting work-related responsibilities out of the way before they play. Two sisters were put in charge of cleaning their home. The ISTJ sister thought it was important to follow a schedule and commit to a time frame for the accomplishment of the house-cleaning tasks. By approximately 11:00 A.M. every Saturday, she would have her tasks completed. Her sister's style of dusting, vacuuming, listening to music, talking on the telephone, and taking time out for short trips to see friends was a different way of "getting the job done." The ISTJ wondered why her sister would not want to finish her tasks directly so that the afternoon would be free for playing.

ISTJ teenagers are down-to-earth types who seek to do the appropriate thing at the appropriate time. If dating and dancing and being involved with parties are traditional at their school, ISTJs will participate in those activities. If they date, they tend to single out one person and date steadily. ISTJs may be chosen to lead school activities. For example, an ISTJ was selected as captain of the football team because he was so dutiful in participating in practice and executing the coach's instructions. ISTJs are often good role models for their teams and classmates.

ISTJs believe that one should earn one's keep. Even as children, they may request chores that help the family. ISTJ teenagers, similar to other dutiful types, often have part-time jobs. The money they earn tends to be used for the important practical things in their lives, such as clothing, gasoline for cars, or, even more importantly, saving for college or other future needs. ISTJs do not like to ask their parents for money.

As young adults, ISTJs begin their career training early and find it hard to understand people who start an education but do not complete it. They believe that dropping out is irresponsible. They complete what they start, representing traditional values and norms and pushing themselves to find early employment. They may choose large and stable organizations in which they hope to find security and an opportunity to prove their worth. It is not the size that is important, rather that large companies tend to have long track records that imply stability. They are particularly realistic about their skills and needs, and prefer to learn the basics before risking something beyond their capabilities.

Slow and steady on an unambiguous course is the way ISTJs prefer to navigate through life. As a result, they may select undergraduate programs in college that lead directly to employment. Some ISTJs choose liberal arts because of traditional values, particularly when a connection can be made to eventual employment. An ISTJ social studies education major graduated and immediately began to teach junior high school history classes. In conscientiously doing her job, she learned how to work well with her students and observed what textbooks and assignments were most useful to them. As a result of her careful notation of what best met the students' needs, she was selected to be on a district-wide committee to purchase textbooks. She used her attention to detail and thoroughness to keep the committee focused on finding the most appropriate textbooks at the lowest prices. Her management skills in combination with her teaching ability led to her appointment as the chair of the district's social studies department. Although this assignment meant more work and additional responsibilities with little extra pay, the ISTJ saw it as the "right thing to do." Her curriculum was noted for its teaching of the basics.

ISTJs have a need to "do right" with what they've been given, safeguarding traditions of the family and of the community. They often will take on extra personal responsibilities in order to maintain what they believe is important. An ISTJ with a busy professional life was active on weekends in his church and became trained to lead the prayer services. Even though he was, by nature, uncomfortable speaking in front of large groups, especially in a personal way such as prayer, he did what was necessary for his church by relying on established liturgies and prayer books.

Because ISTJs are stable, persistent, and thorough in their work, they are often rewarded by their organizations with positions of responsibility. If an organization needs to provide a reliable and consistent service or product, the ISTJ is often selected to manage it. They pay attention to precise requirements, strict schedules, and tight budgets, and quietly meet their deadlines, by filling in themselves if there are problems.

Because ISTJs often seek work in stable organizations and then dutifully put in their time, they are usually eligible for retirement benefits. ISTJs may stay with a job or company they do not particularly like because they tend to regard financial well-being as very important and are willing to do without things, including emotional gratification, so that they can provide for their retirement. They worry particularly about being dependent on others for their needs and work hard to avoid that state.

Because ISTJs have worked long and hard in both their professional and their family lives and most likely have earned their keep, they need to relax and allow others to shoulder family and community responsibilities in retirement. In making this transition, they are then able to enjoy their retirement by moving into a leisure mode. Developing hobbies and relationships beyond their previous work helps them adjust to the changes in their lives. For many ISTJs, however, retirement means only moving from paid to unpaid responsibilities.

LEARNING

ISTJs learn best and apply themselves most carefully in subject areas that are practical and useful. They are diligent and persevering in their studies. As learners, ISTJs tend to need materials, directions, and teachers to be precise and accurate if they are to trust the information that is presented. They prefer concrete and useful applications and will tolerate theory only if it leads to these ends.

An ISTJ teacher wanted to make learning to use a computer as easy as possible for his students. This goal meant developing a guide that would have step-by-step, straightforward, and clear directions for each operational step. He took pride in his drawings that illustrated the exact keys to push to make specific things happen. In constructing the manual, he remembered how he had learned to use the computer. Everything was organized in a common-sense fashion, with the potential possibilities for error reduced to a minimum. ISTJs look at learning as a step-by-step building process in which one relies on past experiences to move ahead.

ISTJs want learning materials to be correct in every detail and readily applicable. A trainer in an industrial organization was delivering a course on supervision. The workbook for participants was filled with good ideas for supervisors. But because the material contained typographical errors, several ISTJ participants expressed concern with the program. Specific errors might indicate more general errors, and the ISTJs wanted to be assured that this was not the case. When details are inaccurate, ISTJs may be sidetracked and miss the larger conceptual framework.

ISTJs like learning activities that allow them time to reflect and to think. If the material is too easy or appears to be too enjoyable, the ISTJ may be skeptical of its merit. Because of their practical bent, they believe that work is work and play is play. Therefore, their preferred learning environment is task oriented, starts and stops on time, and has clear and precise assignments.

LABORING

At work, ISTJs get things done on a timely basis. They honor deadlines, and they believe in thoroughness. A half-finished job is not a job well done. When ISTJs give you their word that a project will be completed at a certain time, they will do whatever is necessary to make sure it is. They manage according to established procedures and schedules, and are uncomfortable with those who do not do the same. ISTJs put duty before pleasure. As long as they can fulfill their responsibilities, they feel useful and thereby satisfied. Their work does not have to be fun, but it has to count toward something productive. ISTJs believe that vacations are something that one takes only when work has been accomplished; thus, at times they do not take vacations even when they could and should. One personnel manager commented that it is rare to find ISTJs who take all of their allotted vacation days.

Work Setting

ISTJs prefer work settings that contain hard-working people who are focused on facts, details, and results. They want structure, order, and some privacy for concentration without interruptions. They like tangible products and concrete accomplishments. They want to be secure and to be rewarded for their solid accomplishments at a steady pace. Because ISTJs believe that the tangible results of their work and their paychecks can be reward enough, they do not seek much attention for themselves, nor do they give much recognition to others, except for contributions clearly above and beyond the call of duty.

Organizing Style

ISTJs pride themselves on their organization, yet often think it is still not quite good enough. They usually have a great deal of factual information to deal with, and they take pains to properly label and file it. They put emphasis on cross-referencing and easy retrievals. One ISTJ reported that when his father died, his mother invited him to look through the family papers. He spent eight full days organizing family materials, carefully cataloging each important document as well as family photos and other mementos. He has become the family archivist; now when his mother or other family members need to find an important paper, they call him. He can visualize the office and his filing system, and can tell people exactly where to look.

A hands-on approach is important to ISTJs, because they make use of the actual or the visual memory of the concrete data in their hands. They may not feel comfortable delegating to others since they do not feel fully on top of things without a thorough immersion in the data. ISTJs will put a high degree of effort into a project when it makes sense for them to do so, and their drive for completion keeps them going in a thorough and careful way when others would give up.

Occupations

To perform well at work, individuals may need to use all of the eight preferences at the appropriate time and when required by the situation. Knowing this, people tend to select occupations that allow them to use the preferences that are most natural to them.

ISTJs prefer occupations that require thoroughness, accuracy, perseverance, and follow-through. They would rather work in situations in which they can see concrete, tangible results.

While ISTJs can and do enter all occupations, some are more appealing to them than others. According to available research,[1] some occupations (in alphabetical order) seem to be especially attractive to ISTJs: accountant, auditor, dentist, electrician, first-line supervisor, math teacher, mechanical engineer, police supervisor, steelworker, technician, and other occupations that allow for a thorough handling of facts. These occupations are not meant to be an exhaustive list but serve to illustrate some areas that an ISTJ might enjoy. If your specific occupation or one that you are interested in is not listed here, think instead of its general characteristics and ask yourself how those fit with your type.

LEADING

While not directly seeking leadership positions, ISTJs are often placed in such roles. They build a reputation for reliable, stable, and consistent performance that causes others to select them to lead. As leaders, ISTJs use their past experience and their factual knowledge in their decision making. They focus on the immediate, the practical, and the tangible. They respect traditional, hierarchical approaches and seek to reward those who get the job done by following the rules and standard operating procedures. In their view, rewards should go to outstanding contributors who do not violate the rules while completing their work.

ISTJs are more task oriented than relationship oriented in their style. Since results speak louder than words, they may not verbally acknowledge the contributions of those they lead. They often pattern themselves after those who have led them, especially if that style produced results they liked. Seeing others use different styles that work may cause the ISTJ to loosen up. When there is no pattern or model for ISTJs, they are likely to lead by setting a standard and expecting others to do their duty. ISTJs know and carefully follow company policies and procedures. If a budget review is to be held at a certain time, it will be held then unless a higher priority supersedes it.

An ISTJ directed a voluntary meal delivery program for the elderly. Because the program's clients were totally dependent on her service for their daily meals, the ISTJ organized procedures so that the service would be reliable at all times. In her area, weather could be so severe as to disrupt the normal delivery schedules for the meals. In order to prevent that occurrence, the ISTJ thoroughly organized her staff, her contingency plans, and her delivery options. In one case, cold weather and freezing rains prevented telephone communication and caused the closing of some delivery routes. Because the ISTJ had so thoroughly worked through her responsibilities, she was able to contact volunteers by CB radio and set up a "command post" in her home. She then plotted new routes so that the volunteers could deliver the meals. During this long period of program coordination, to take a breather from her tasks would have been unthinkable because she realized how much the elderly relied on the service. By paying attention to the precise requirements, the strict mealtime schedules, and the weather conditions, the ISTJ was able to maintain uninterrupted service.

LEISURE

Leisure for ISTJs must be earned. Leisure-time activities usually take place after work is accomplished. If they engage in leisure before their work is done, it is usually because of the circumstances in which they find themselves. For example, an ISTJ with a fun-loving spouse might engage in more playful activities out of duty to that spouse. ISTJ parents may attend their children's sporting events because they are specifically asked to be there.

For ISTJs, leisure needs to have a purpose and a result, and a beginning and an end. If a canoeing trip is planned, it is usually to go to a particular place, not just to be on the river and enjoy the scenery. Sociability with peers, mates, or children may also be sufficient reason to take recreation breaks. Out of duty, ISTJs may entertain and invite others into their homes. They are likely to make a habit of traditional get-togethers year after year, since they enjoy the security of customary things.

ISTJs like to schedule their leisure time. In planning to have her sister as a guest, one ISTJ arranged the three-day visit to run like clockwork. In advance of the trip, she phoned museums, theaters, and other cultural institutions to check on the times they were open and the activities they were offering. Once she had this information, she made a schedule that equaled that of any official sight-seeing tour group. Another ISTJ was accused of putting his garden on a strict schedule. He wanted to know exactly when the beets would be up and the lettuce ready to eat. Thorough planning of all details is important to ISTJs, both in their work and in their leisure.

ISTJs enjoy spending time alone and need to be aware of their potential to become isolated from others. For example, they may become absorbed in watching television because it allows them time to reflect and yet appear to be doing something. This time may also be an opportunity for them to be physically present with their family, though in some cases somewhere else mentally.

LOVING

For the ISTJ, love means commitment, steadiness, and consistency. ISTJs expect themselves and their mates to be responsible, practical, and dependable. When in a relationship, they behave appropriately for what the situation or their role demands. For example, if the relationship is in the courting stage, the ISTJ will exhibit courting behaviors, such as giving boxes of candy, red roses, traditional cards, and presents. These are worthwhile and important traditions to uphold and observe because they give direct evidence of commitment.

When ISTJs give their word and are ready to settle down, they follow through. Because they are dutiful, they expect their partners to behave in a similar fashion. When their partners do not, the ISTJs may accept this fact and make exceptions but still feel uncomfortable internally.

ISTJs offer their partners stability and security. They do sensible things for the relationship, such as paying the bills and making household repairs. With their practical outlook, they often do not see the need to glamorize much in their lives. An ISTJ wife had a housecoat that was warm, durable, and of a practical dark color. She wore it for many years because she could see no reason not to. At the request of her spouse, she attended a seminar on couples communication and learned that clothing could be a communication device. She decided to update her navy housecoat to a more enticing style and color. The new garment was not quite what others might call alluring, but it represented her effort to appear more attractive to her spouse.

ISTJs may stay in poor relationships out of their sense of duty, even when it is to their benefit to leave. They prefer the certainty of the current relationship to any future unknowns. When feeling scorned, ISTJs may not let their partners or others know it. Because they focus internally and because the facts all support the conclusion that the relationship is over, ISTJs may feel it redundant to express to their partners or others what is going on. When it seems clear to the partners that the relationship really is over, ending it is the practical thing to do. However, when a decision to part is not so clear to ISTJs, they may continue to rehash the past rather than look to the future and other relationships.

LOSING OUT

Each type has the potential to overuse or abuse its preferences. This is likely to happen when individuals are under great stress or pressure. At such times, they may act in ways that are unlike their usual style. The following paragraphs describe some of these experiences, as well as some strategies that ISTJs can use to get back on track.

For ISTJs, one way of losing out has to do with the overuse of their ability to immerse themselves in detail. They may become rigid in their ways and be thought of as inflexible, interpreting the letter of the law and not reckoning with the spirit behind it. Rather than attend to the overall meaning suggested by the details, ISTJs can become detail bound, overwhelming others with minute details and ignoring the larger issues.

To demonstrate how well her department was counseling people, one ISTJ had her staff count the number of people they helped each day. The quality of their work was ignored. The staff became unhappy because the focus was on the numbers, not on their actual work. As a strategy, ISTJs need to focus on the overall objective and not become distracted by facts and details. ISTJs may want to ask themselves questions such as: What am I trying to accomplish? What other alternatives might get me there?

ISTJs may overlook interpersonal niceties, such as complimenting people, in favor of getting the job done. Rather than making direct personal comments to show others they care about them, they may keep their compliments inside. Some ISTJs rely too heavily on written forms of communication. By concentrating on praising others more often and doing what is necessary to show both personal and professional interest in them, ISTJs gain added benefits for their projects and tasks. ISTJs might want to meet more frequently with their colleagues, both formally and informally, to gain important and practical information about what is important to them.

Another way ISTJs may lose out is through overlooking the long-range implications in favor of day-to-day realities. ISTJs may be helped by the realization that the world is changing and that, in order to retain what they value, it is necessary to antic- ipate how they want to change. Without a clear-cut, step-by- step method of approaching the future, ISTJs find it difficult to construct a vision. They may rely too much on the standard way and ignore the innovation. While they readily focus on what will not work, they may overlook subsequent changes in people and the environment that could make a new way possible. An ISTJ knew that her current job was not rewarding but could not see how a different job in the future could provide anything better. Through career counseling, the ISTJ identified her skills, as well as other careers in which she could use those skills.

ISTJs can draw upon their ability to see the details and to move forward in a step-by-step way. They should not allow themselves to concentrate on what is not working right now, but rather push themselves to focus on at least three possibilities and options that have a potential for working out. They need to avoid getting stuck in a rut and seeing the future in doom- and-gloom terms.

Some ISTJs may lose out by not recognizing their emotions and the values that they represent. Knowing this would advance their own self-understanding and their understanding of others. They may be seen as insensitive. Values clarification may help them recognize their own feelings and those of others. By dealing directly with their feelings, ISTJs will find that they are less likely to explode. They will also find that others enjoy working with them more when they show more human sensitivity.

When ISTJs are back on track, they are using their strengths of recognizing the pertinent facts and applying experience to problems that need current attention. They can be tireless in following through to do their duty.

IN A NUTSHELL

Hallmarks:[2]

Factual
Thorough
Systematic
Dependable
Steadfast
Practical
Organized
Realistic
Duty bound
Sensible
Painstaking
Reliable

Acronym:[3]

I Save Things Judiciously

Chapter Six

ISTP

ISTPs Chose the Following Preferences:

Extraversion . . . . ENERGIZING . . . . **Introversion**
Sensing . . . . ATTENDING. . . . . iNtuition
Thinking . . . . DECIDING . . . . Feeling
Judgment . . . . LIVING . . . . **Perception**

ISTPs are realists who apply expediency and reasoning as they manage and adapt to situations. They are aware of what is going on in the environment and are able to respond quickly to the actual facts, making sure the odds of success are in their favor. They do not like to be tied down and will feel hamstrung when they must operate within tight structures and schedules. They are able to anticipate immediate, practical needs in situations and to present a logical, straightforward plan for meeting those needs. They are at their best in situations that require immediate attention.

LIVING

ISTP children want life to be logical, flexible, and action oriented. While they like hands-on activities, they also may want to stand aside and observe what is taking place. They are especially observant of what makes things tick and may take apart a toy to see its inner workings. ISTP children are curious and are great gatherers of data and detail. They rarely forget what they have noticed about places and things. ISTPs observe their parents in order to find out if and in what ways their parents vary their actual behavior from what they say. ISTPs monitor the differences between what people say and what people do. They are aware of flaws and try to correct them.

ISTP children become very absorbed in their hobbies. The grandmother of an ISTP gave him a train set for his birthday. He looked carefully at each train car and included many of its details in a thank-you note to her. This train set started an interest in trains that he continued throughout his adult life. He collected trains, train memorabilia, train schedules, and train design specifications. When one of his friends needed to know about shipping materials from Milwaukee to Omaha, for example, the ISTP could tell him the company, the route, the types of train cars, their dimensions, and the products that were shipped via rail between the two cities on this route. This thorough recall of practical, numerical, and logical information is characteristic of ISTPs.

ISTP teenagers may have several close friends but generally are not social butterflies. They relate to others by sharing detailed information about one of their interests or sharing in physical activities that involve a measure of risk. They like sports in which they can challenge themselves and master specific techniques and strategies. Bowling, skiing, wrestling, soccer, flight training, and wind surfing are activities that often interest ISTPs, because these sports involve a measure of risk and strategy.

One ISTP teenager became very involved in wrestling. He knew the exact limits and tolerances of his body. He was also able to remember the "Achilles heel" of his opponents, their records, their teams' statistics, and their usual conduct in matches. While he was not as physically strong as others in his weight class, he was still able to win most of his matches because he used his attention to detail to make the most of his wrestling skills in outmaneuvering them.

ISTPs are willing to take charge of their lives and develop their interests but see little need to do the same for others. ISTP teens often select part-time jobs that allow them to indulge their interests or hobbies. The ISTP who enjoyed trains worked in a hobby shop in which he was able to learn more about them and to purchase models at a reduced cost. It was not so much that he needed to work as it was that he wanted to be in an environment in which he could get more information about trains and interact with other train buffs.

As young adults, ISTPs tend to follow a path of least resistance when thinking about their careers. "I don't like planning ahead," said one ISTP, "because things don't turn out like the plan. I relax my brain while everyone else is busy using theirs to plan." ISTPs are efficient types who find the quickest and most expedient way to get what they need. For example, a part-time job as a teenager may lead to a full-time job as an adult.

ISTPs are pragmatists and gamblers who play each hand as it is dealt. As a result, they are able to take advantage of opportunities as they arise. An ISTP who was raised in Japan learned to speak Japanese. With her ability to recall specific details, she also was able to write Japanese characters. She enjoyed managing money and playing the stock market, which she saw as a game involving strategy and opportunism. She combined her love of stock market management and her knowledge of Japanese into a career as a market analyst for a large bank in Japan. While it did not seem as if she had a plan to start with, she allowed her interests to direct her toward career opportunities as they arose.

In adult life, ISTPs are fairly laid back and mellow. They do not impose much structure on themselves or others. Because they retain and use detail for logical ends, they are often recognized by their employers as people who do well with the careful and precise understanding of factual data. They are at ease handling interruptions in their work, and, in some cases, they become energized by the challenge of overcoming an unforeseen obstacle.

An ISTP was attending a conference in a large city. While he was walking with a colleague to one of the sessions, his companion stumbled, fell, and fractured her arm. While still in the parking lot, the ISTP calmed her down, hailed a cab, and kept her in good spirits on the way to the hospital. He felt pleased that he had helped her on a moment's notice.

Mature ISTPs want a measure of flexibility and spontaneity in their work. They are able to combine work and play, often making games of the numbers and details that they manage. However, they become restless if they do not find adequate use of their interests in their work or hobbies. Because of an ability to remember numbers and recall detail, one ISTP rose through the ranks in the accounting department of her company and became its controller at the fairly young age of thirty-three. When her work life began to restrict her life in general and her cooking hobby specifically, she became restless. At this point in her career, even though things were going extremely well, she thought that she needed a change. She left the controller's job to practice her hobby full-time by starting her own cooking school. She had always enjoyed cooking, collecting recipes and kitchen utensils, and observing the many techniques of food preparation. She used her financial background to develop the business side of the cooking school, and it became a great success. Equally important to her, however, was that she now was able to make her own rules and to live her life as she saw fit.

Most ISTPs, when questioned about their careers, reveal that they would love to have more time and income to pursue their interests full-time. One ISTP said that she would love to go to school because there was so much there of interest to her. Another ISTP particularly enjoyed fishing, hunting, and collecting sports cars. He pursued all of these avidly, and would arrange his work schedule to allow him to do these things with his friends.

Because retirement may allow ISTPs to further pursue their work as well as leisure interests unhampered by time demands, it is a very desirable state for them. If their work is interesting, they may resist retirement because their work is a key element in their lives. When their work does not provide them with enough enjoyment and challenge, they may try to arrange things so that they can retire early and thus obtain more time to enjoy their leisure pursuits.

One retired ISTP school teacher loved detailed sewing, tailoring, and upholstering. She was intensely focused on her sewing and often needed to be reminded by her family that it was time to eat or do some other activity. Her absorption was so complete that at times she was aware of little else. She found her retirement very fulfilling because she could lose herself in her interests.

LEARNING

ISTPs learn best when they can observe first-hand in a one-to-one situation. They are particularly fond of subjects that have a logical basis; mastering certain rules or principles allows them to efficiently work with the subject matter. They like individual projects that require them to solve problems systematically.

ISTPs prefer to learn alone, at their own rate and in their own time frame. Because they are able to assimilate a great amount of detail in areas that interest them, they usually do well in those areas. ISTPs earn their best grades when it is necessary to accurately report facts and data. They are impatient with theoretical subjects and like their learning to be directed toward concrete and practical outcomes.

An ISTP student commented that, in a language-arts class, she rebelled at an assignment to write a poem about a computer as something that was alive. "A computer is a computer and no more," she stated. Looking at inanimate things and describing them as living seemed ridiculous. She further told her teacher that she could see no benefit in imagining things to be something other than what they actually were.

Teachers are not particularly important to ISTPs in the overall scheme, unless they can show ISTPs how to do things more easily. When the teacher obstructs or gets in the way of something ISTPs want to learn, they may ignore or go around the teacher. They like classes in which they can practice close observation, followed by hands-on activities that focus on the technical properties or functions of things. They want assignments in which they can explore their interests in depth.

The formal or traditional school setting is not as important to ISTPs as is the opportunity to increase their own practical knowledge. Nontraditional programs or approaches often attract ISTPs, especially when they can learn about things that they see as vital and central to their interests. An ISTP learned mathematics by playing card games and chess. Because he wanted to understand the plays and moves to win more games, he took his mathematics lessons very seriously. What was important to him was not the subject itself but how he could apply his understanding to being more effective in card games and chess. At one time, he was playing fifteen chess and eight checkers games by mail with people across the country. During this period, his involvement in his mathematics lessons was very high, and his math grades were excellent. He was motivated to learn the necessary theories, but only for a specific outcome, that of winning his games.

LABORING

At work, ISTPs contribute their realistic and logical way of meeting situational requirements. They can see the easiest and most expedient route to completing a task, and they do not waste their effort on unnecessary things. They often act as trouble shooters, rising to meet the needs of the occasion. In many organizations, they get things done in spite of the rules, not because of them. Since many ISTPs have a natural bent in technical areas, they may often function as "walking encyclopedias" of technical information. One ISTP said that his colleagues comment on his knowledge of American banks. He knows the names, locations, strengths, and sizes of hundreds of American banks. He keeps track of all information on the United States financial system and markets for his brokerage firm. ISTPs know the standards, specifications, and requirements of their work; they use this information in a calm manner, even during a crisis. At such times, they have a settling effect on others, because they know so much practical information and use it to "save the day."

Work Setting

ISTPs prefer a work setting that is project oriented and unconstrained by rules. They want a chance to be active, independent problem solvers. They do not like routine but want the opportunity to be somewhat inventive in meeting current needs.

Organizing Style

The ISTP organizing style is based on expediency and quick application of information. They often organize their hobbies or collections and make a game of finding the best way to arrange things such as their rock collections, their spice cabinets, or their antique automobile magazines. In the rest of their lives, their approach to organization is largely incidental.

One ISTP farmer had several acres of old farm equipment. Thus he had all the parts he needed ready to repair any farm equipment he was currently using. He knew exactly where each piece of machinery was, what other machines it fit, and how each piece could be installed. He could not, however, find a single thing in his kitchen. Another ISTP had an attic full of things that she collected at various garage sales and flea markets. Whenever a family member needed a particular item, she delighted in going to her attic and finding it. ISTPs may not have a system of organization that is discernible to others, but through the use of their memory for detail, they can usually locate what they need at the time.

Occupations

To perform well at work, individuals may need to use all of the eight preferences at the appropriate time and when required by the situation. Knowing this, people tend to select occupations that allow them to use the preferences that are most natural to them.

ISTPs prefer flexibility and impersonal dealings with others. Because they often have a technical orientation, they prefer to work in an environment that produces a practical product. They pay attention to the organization's hierarchy only to the point of learning how to bypass or go around it if it stands in their way. ISTPs may have mastered the details of the organization (how everything fits together) but may rebel if it is too rigid.

While ISTPs can and do enter all occupations, some are more appealing to them than others. According to available research,[1] some occupations (in alphabetical order) seem to be especially attractive to ISTPs: carpenter, construction worker, dental hygienist, electrical engineer, farmer, mechanic, military personnel, probation officer, steel worker, transportation operative, and other occupations that allow them to use their ability to act expediently. These occupations are not meant to be an exhaustive list but serve to illustrate some areas that an ISTP might enjoy. If your specific occupation or one that you are interested in is not listed here, think instead of its general characteristics and ask yourself how those fit with your type.

LEADING

The ISTP leadership style is one of leading through action, by setting an example. They respond quickly when trouble is at hand. They operate logically from their internal ruling principles. They give their staff the necessary information to do their jobs, allowing them to complete their work in their own fashion. ISTPs hold to an egalitarian approach in the midst of hierarchy and authority. They prefer to be managed loosely and with minimal supervision, and they manage others in a similar fashion.

An ISTP was an engineering manager in a manufacturing company. He gained the loyalty of his staff because he treated them fairly and used his humor to help them through the rough spots. When asked to review the pertinent facts and details about his unit, he would give his presentation in a relaxed style. He knew each of his staff members individually, and he would invite them to sporting events such as baseball games and wrestling matches. By contrast, he was rather remote from people in other departments, and, when he related to them, it was only about work. He generally let small lapses in performance go but held people accountable when they were not producing effectively. He allowed for individual ways of handling assignments and did not impose his will upon others, but framed the work in such a way that he would get the expected results on time.

LEISURE

The opportunity to pursue their interests is very important to ISTPs. They will do what it takes to have the time and money to accommodate their leisure-time pursuits. ISTP leisure activities often have a physical and risk-taking aspect to them. ISTPs get deeply involved in their activities, adding new ones when boredom sets in, finding that one interest may lead to another. Often interests begun in childhood, such as stamp collecting, cooking, and chess, are maintained throughout their lifetimes.

ISTPs love to have the latest and finest equipment for whatever their hobby or interest is. For example, if ISTPs are into tennis, they enjoy having the very best tennis shoes, racket, and tennis balls so that they can achieve the most efficient and effective results.

While they can and do enjoy themselves in solitary activities, ISTPs may also like being involved with their children and with others who share their interests. They may, for example, encourage their children in sports, collections, hobbies, and mechanical activities. An ISTP, whose first car was a 1963 Triumph, located a badly damaged one and worked with his son and daughter to repair and rebuild it so that they could experience the same fun of refurbishing a car that he had enjoyed more than twenty-five years earlier.

ISTPs retain detail accurately and often use their spare time to learn more facts. One ISTP stated that, instead of playing the game Trivial Pursuit, he preferred to read the answers on the cards, just to gain the knowledge that was available. In her spare time, another ISTP was often observed reading encyclopedias. ISTPs often enjoy spectator sports in which they can participate by observing and keeping track of the statistics of the game. They are likely to know players' names, numbers, and averages, as well as the team's history and records.

LOVING

For the ISTP, love means being responsive yet realistic. ISTPs seek partners who either are willing to allow them to have their necessary freedom (especially for their hobbies and interests) or who will participate in these activities with them. They may introduce their partners to their interests if they are ones that they want to share. When this is the case, they will acquaint their loved one with all the facts and details of their interest. One ISTP, who grew up in Italy, loved Italian cooking. She shared her detailed knowledge of European customs concerning food and cuisine with her husband. They frequented Italian restaurants, visited Italian grocery stores where she pointed out all the pastas, cheeses, and unusual sausages, and cooked Italian dishes together.

When falling in love, ISTPs are very attentive to small things that might be enjoyed by their partners, surprising them with those particular gifts. They would rather show their feelings through their actions than verbalize them. They are not likely to discuss their feelings about their relationships with their partners (and almost never with others) because they believe that the experiences that they have had together will speak for their feelings. Feelings are discussed only when necessary.

When scorned, ISTPs are not likely to share their hurt feelings with the external world. If the couple still has some interests in common, ISTPs may maintain the relationship with the loved one, but on a different plane. They do not give up easily on their relationships, however, unless the weight of the factual evidence convinces them to do so. When the relationship is actually over, they are usually not vindictive. They see the end of the relationship as a concrete fact about which it does little good to worry. They can therefore move on to new experiences.

LOSING OUT

Each type has the potential to overuse or abuse its preferences. This is likely to happen when individuals are under great stress or pressure. At these times, they may act in ways that are unlike their usual style. The following paragraphs describe some of the ways ISTPs may lose out, in addition to some strategies that they can use to get back on track.

One way of losing out for the ISTP has to do with looking for the easiest route by taking shortcuts and slacking off in their efforts. One ISTP, in her desire to have more free time, did her work in the most expedient way and cut corners. She did not document her shortcuts to her manager, and her work was often incomplete. She appeared indifferent and unmotivated. When work was complete, it was usually the part of the work that she enjoyed. Her haphazard style got her in trouble, and she was put on probation.

A strategy for ISTPs is to develop a step-by-step plan, put in the effort to accomplish the plan, stay on plan by developing perseverance, and make sure that others are aware of their efforts.

ISTPs may lose out when they keep important things to themselves and fail to let others know what is going on inside of them. When they do share with others, they may unintentionally point out only the faults and problems that they see in others, not the good things. As a result, others may see them as insensitive and uncaring. As a strategy, ISTPs may need to be more open in their relationships with others, even when this feels unnecessary to them. Others need to know where they (and the ISTP) stand.

Because ISTPs are oriented toward collecting new facts and details, they may sometimes feel overwhelmed by all of this information. They may resist decision making in order to keep their options open. In this process, they may appear indecisive and undirected, especially to those who are waiting for the ISTP's decision.

An ISTP bought a floundering word processing company. He became so involved in the day-to-day problems and data gathering that he did not pay much attention to the long-range needs of the business, nor did he develop or communicate priorities to his staff. Subsequently, his staff felt a lack of direction, and the company continued floundering. What he and other ISTPs need to do in these situations is to develop priorities, set both short- and long-range goals, and communicate those to others.

The final way ISTPs lose out is that they may move on to new tasks before their previous efforts bear fruit. One ISTP opted to take a job offer during the last semester before his college graduation. The offer looked so tantalizing at the time. Several years later, the ISTP realized that he had shortchanged himself by not completing his degree; most advancement in his company was based on formal education. As strategies, ISTPs may need to develop perseverance and the ability to stay with tasks, projects, or programs until they have completed them.

When ISTPs are back on track, they are using their strengths of problem analysis, trouble shooting, and responding quickly to meet the needs of the occasion. They can be tireless in the pursuit of expedient problem solving.

IN A NUTSHELL

Hallmarks:[2]

Logical
Expedient
Practical
Realistic
Factual
Analytical
Applied
Independent
Adventurous
Spontaneous
Adaptable
Self-determined

Acronym:[3]

I See The Problem

Chapter Seven

ESTP

ESTPs Chose the Following Preferences:

Extraversion . . . . ENERGIZING . . . . Introversion
Sensing . . . . ATTENDING . . . . iNtuition
Thinking . . . . DECIDING . . . . Feeling
Judgment . . . . LIVING . . . . **Perception**

In general, ESTPs are action oriented, pragmatic, outgoing, and realistic people. In situations that require resourcefulness, they use their quickness and flexibility to find the most efficient route to accomplishing whatever needs to be done. They are lively, entertaining, and fun. They like to be where the action is and participate fully in what is happening. Characteristically, they are direct with their comments and mince no words. They are at their best in situations that require an orientation to the present and a direct, no-nonsense, pragmatic approach.

LIVING

ESTP children are rambunctious, energetic, and freedom-loving individuals. They do what they want to do when they want to do it. ESTP children like life to be action packed and fun. They stir things up when they find life too boring. They do not like to sit still and are often involved in energy-intensive sports and other activities with their many friends. At an early age, they combine a high-energy approach with a laid-back, accepting style with people and things that interest them. They seem unfazed by whatever comes along and prefer life to hold a challenge or two.

ESTP children enjoy lively activities in which they can use their motor and observation skills to respond quickly to the moment. One ESTP would complete his paper route as quickly as he could so he could play baseball or hockey. ESTPs often enjoy physical contact sports, practicing enthusiastically in order to gain the necessary skills to have fun. Another ESTP said her mother was constantly admonishing her to slow down and reduce her involvement in so many after-school activities.

ESTP children experience and do things in order to learn about life. They are particularly inquisitive about inanimate things. They like having nice toys, games, and equipment, and take care of these material possessions willingly.

School is important to ESTPs as a place to meet their friends and to be involved in activities, and is less important to them as an educational or academic experience. An ESTP teenager said her academic life was an "activity," parts of which she enjoyed (her friends and clubs) and parts of which she did not enjoy (the classes with lots of theory). As she stated, "I was a B student. I knew I could be an A student if I wanted to, but other things were more interesting to me." ESTPs can exasperate their parents and teachers, who appreciate their abilities and want them to apply themselves so as to excel academically. However, ESTPs have different needs and wants. Pleasing themselves is their aim, not necessarily achieving top grades for others. Generally, they want to do things their own way and in their own time, and they are rather direct in telling others what is on their minds.

As teenagers, ESTPs continue to be action oriented. They are likely to be on sports teams or involved in other after-school activities. If they have a part-time job, they use the money to purchase or save for the things they want, such as sporting equipment, clothes, stereos, cars, and college education. A part-time job may give them regular, consistent, and immediate feedback about themselves in the form of paychecks. Work also means doing things and being active rather than just reading about others doing things. Part-time work may allow ESTPs to gain access to an activity or facility through which they can pursue one of their interests. One ESTP worked in a health center, where he had the use of the facilities and fitness devices.

Another ESTP was working part-time parking cars at a yacht club. One evening, at the request of the club's bartender, he drove home a patron who had had a bit too much to drink. On the way, the patron asked the ESTP what he thought about him. The ESTP proceeded to give a barrage of blunt yet truthful comments. The patron turned to him and said, "I have many people on my payroll who will kiss my ———, but no one will tell me what they really think. You did, and I want to reward that. I will pay for the rest of your college education." The astounded ESTP became the designee of an exclusive scholarship fund, established solely for him, to pay his college expenses. In this instance, the ESTP's characteristic straightforwardness literally paid off.

As young adults, ESTPs tend to fall into their careers. If they are mechanically oriented, they may find a career in mechanics; if their friends are going to college, they are likely to go to college; if their friends are joining the armed forces, the ESTP may go along as well. One ESTP found a job in banking through a personal contact with a friend's father. Although he liked numbers, he had not considered banking; however, because a job was offered to him, he took it and has remained in banking ever since.

ESTPs look forward to their independence and are likely to leave home as soon as they can afford to. Being pragmatic types, however, they may find that home, if less restrictions can be negotiated, is a practical and good place to be, because it is cheaper and allows them more money for other important things.

In adult life, ESTPs often focus on work, where they can directly or vicariously experience high risk and high reward. These risks may be physical, intellectual, personal, or financial. ESTPs are likely to look for loopholes, special niches, or other unusual opportunities for finding high rewards for the investment of their time. They are willing to play by the rules but only to the point of using the rules to help them be or do what they want. They particularly like to learn all the "angles" and gather all the "inside information" on how to approach their work and get ahead.

For example, one ESTP inherited a family shoe store. It was quite lucrative, but after several years the ESTP was bored with "fitting people's feet into fancy shoes." He knew that the stock market was a place where one could take some risks and gain financially. Before making a change, and at the urging of his spouse, he gathered some hard factual data. In his data gathering, he figured out the most efficient course of action for becoming hired by the finest brokerage house in the city. Knowing that in his city the commodities market was particularly volatile, he decided to focus there. He had heard that people who managed to meet the challenges in this market were often handsomely rewarded. The market's rapid pace matched his own action orientation, and he was happy with his job change.

ESTPs often fill their lives with many activities besides work. They are busy primarily with their families and with friends when they have time. One ESTP managed his son's hockey team and thoroughly enjoyed taking care of all the arrangements. He became excited watching the team develop. As soon as games were over, he would avidly discuss the plays with his son and the other parents. He enjoyed this opportunity to participate in his son's activities.

If and when life becomes too routine for ESTPs, they find ways to jazz it up, either through their own actions or those of others. They may take unusual trips or add to their lives some excitement such as hang gliding, mountain climbing, white-water rafting, or big-game hunting—activities that call for quick and effective handling of unpredictable, difficult, and often tense situations.

ESTPs like a life filled with zest. One ESTP, participating in a church seminar with his family, was asked to draw a coat of arms that would symbolize his family. The coat of arms that he drew was literally a coat made completely of arms, a very literal view of the assignment. In explaining his drawing, he said that each arm represented the fun activities the family had together.

ESTPs may choose to retire early so that they can have more time for activities that they consider fun. They enjoy being around others in pursuit of a good time. While they may be members of organized groups, they seldom do the organizing or structuring themselves. They are not necessarily joiners and do not need reinforcement from the group. Therefore they can flow in and out of organizations with ease. ESTPs usually take pleasure in their grandchildren because they can indulge in such fun things as trips to the zoo, sports outings, and play. Children love their spontaneity and ability to improvise games on the spot.

LEARNING

ESTPs learn best in situations in which the subject matter applies directly to one of their interests, where the expectations are realistic, and where the explanations are clear. They like observation and hands-on experience, and have little tolerance for theory and material that could be, but that is not currently, useful. They may apply themselves to their studies if there is an immediate payoff for doing so. Teachers' comments that knowing certain ideas or theories "will someday pay off" leave most ESTPs cold. ESTPs are restless when required to sit for any length of time; they like active learning. Often this high-energy, high-activity orientation is misunderstood by their teachers as hyperactive behavior. It is just that the ESTPs want few constraints put on them. ESTPs prefer teachers who are entertaining and make learning active and fun. One ESTP commented that he hated assignments that were written on the board with the expectation that he was simply to do them. To sit at his desk was too constraining. One of the ESTP's main strengths is using the five senses to notice what is happening, to find any flaws and inaccuracies that may exist, and to act quickly on them.

ESTPs like learning activities such as field trips, hands-on experiments, and applications-oriented tasks. However, when learning requires much attention to long-range planning, theories, or concepts, they find themselves bored. One ESTP adult learner was very interested in how people behaved in relationships. Her business was running a dating service, and to learn more about the people who were part of it, she enrolled in a course on human behavior. Unknown to her, the class included a great deal of theory, with not much of it relevant to her needs. Throughout the course, she constantly wanted more specifics and challenged her teacher, who spoke in generalities. Because the course contained long lectures and little active learning, the ESTP found herself taking numerous breaks to keep her interest up. Additionally, she made jokes about the class terminology because this helped her to remember the terms. She brought an air of levity to those who were seriously involved in their study. Without her, the class most likely would have been fairly dry and academic. With her in the class, it was more fun and much more specifically focused. The more academic types were forced to think about how their theories worked in reality. While her behavior could have been seen as disruptive by those who prefer a more structured and staid atmosphere, the class enjoyed her liveliness and her pragmatic approach.

LABORING

At work, ESTPs contribute a straightforward attitude that calls on people to make things happen quickly. They keep things lively and are willing to take personal and organizational risks. They enjoy crises and like to dive right in and skillfully negotiate through them. Because ESTPs notice and remember factual information, they often contribute a realistic assessment of what is actually happening. When given assignments, they do them the most efficient way, which allows them time to take on something else or to play.

Work Setting

ESTPs prefer a work setting that contains lively, results-oriented people who use first-hand experience to solve problems in a practical way. In order for ESTPs to be most productive, their work environments need to allow time for flexibility. They enjoy technical problems for which they can use their powers of observation, a real strength of ESTPs. They do their best in organizations that are nonbureaucratic and responsive to the needs of the moment.

Organizing Style

ESTPs' organizing style is expedient and related directly to the operational needs of the moment. They organize as they go along, and they may improvise as needed. Because they value a quick response, ESTPs operate under the organizational principle that it is easier to beg for forgiveness after committing the act than to ask for permission in advance (even though ESTPs would hardly beg for forgiveness). The parts of their work environment or homes that are well-organized tend to relate to their interests. One ESTP teacher was exceedingly well organized, with all her papers in files and notebooks. She needed to be organized and was. Other parts of the environment or life of ESTPs may be disorganized. However, when they use something regularly, they know where to find it.

The ESTPs' final product, event, paper, or other accomplishment may be excellent, but it belies the ESTP process. ESTPs tend to leave a trail of papers, piles of resources, and messy files and closets, but usually their work is well put together in the end. One ESTP said, "I hate a clean desk. My desk is workable and is organized and categorized as needed."

An ESTP small business owner had just built a new company headquarters. He was very proud of his office, particularly its furnishings, which were functionally designed to allow him to run his affairs smoothly. His handsome office contained a formal mahogany desk that symbolized his top position in the organization. The contents of one drawer, however, would lead others to think that a handyman owned the desk because it was filled with such things as drills, hammers, screwdrivers, and other tools for emergency repairs. Although he had a staff whose job it was to take care of such things, he could not give up his love of being able to fix things on the spot. Expedient response guides ESTPs, even if it is not within their formal job descriptions. They organize whatever they deem important; however, they can put off to eternity organizing or fixing things that do not matter to them.

Occupations

To perform well at work, individuals may need to use all of the eight preferences at the appropriate time and when required by the situation. Knowing this, people tend to select occupations that allow them to use the preferences that are most natural to them.

ESTPs prefer occupations that allow flash and dash, ones in which they can respond dramatically with speed to the present needs. If they choose an occupation in which this is not the case, they bring these characteristics to their work. They do not like to be constrained in their activities and generally seek work that gives them a great deal of latitude.

While ESTPs can and do enter all occupations, some are more appealing to them than others. According to available research,[1] some occupations (in alphabetical order) seem to be especially attractive to ESTPs: auditor, carpenter, craft worker, farmer, laborer, marketeer, law enforcement officer, sales representative, service worker, transportation operative, and other occupations that allow ESTPs to use their action-oriented sense of expediency. These occupations are not meant to be an exhaustive list but serve to illustrate some areas that an ESTP might enjoy. If your specific occupation or one that you are interested in is not listed here, think instead of its general characteristics and ask yourself how those fit with your type.

LEADING

The ESTP leadership style is one that takes charge readily, especially in crises. ESTPs have a direct and assertive style, and they move ahead without necessarily paying attention to all of the rules. They find the immediate cause of problems and seek immediate solutions. They can react to any given situation, expedite it, and make it work. They hear different sides of the problem, make decisions, and keep things moving. One ESTP executive stated that he hated to be in a meeting with people who were looking at twenty theoretical possibilities to solve a manufacturing problem. His response was, "Let's just fix it and get on with it." Because ESTPs are outgoing and talkative, they are able to persuade others to their point of view. They are "doers" who decide crisply and impersonally, based on the facts. They plunge right in to do what needs to be done.

An ESTP was put in charge of a department in her organization. Deciding that her people needed to "enjoy their work," she initiated a weekly staff meeting at a neighborhood bar. Generally, she did not have an agenda for the meeting, preferring to have people talk about what had happened and where they saw or solved problems. Periodically, she would get comments from her manager, who was concerned that she did not carefully plan ahead. However, the ESTP would point with pride to the results she was able to obtain using her more flexible approach. Her staff generally had the necessary information and resources to accomplish the task, and when they could not, the ESTP would jump in. Her staff members enjoyed her style, and she was known throughout the larger organization for her responsive leadership approach.

LEISURE

ESTPs love leisure, and they do all they can to maximize their leisure time. They are usually involved in activities, particularly sporting ones, either as players or as spectators. As spectators, they are quite lively, jumping up and yelling. They may enjoy out-of-doors, risk-taking activities. For example, ESTPs who like to canoe generally do not like the run-of-the-mill variety of canoe trips. Their ideas of canoeing may feature physical challenge and daring-do, such as a run through wild rapids where few others would venture to go or a gentler river trip with gourmet meals and skinny dipping. The former prefer more active leisure, and the latter might be called "lazy leisure" ESTPs.

ESTPs often collect tangible things related to their hobbies. One ESTP was especially fond of sports cars. While he could afford only one classic sports car, he had parts and pieces to four similar cars in his garage. He enjoyed the process of collecting various bumpers, seats, and steering wheels, and fully anticipated that with these parts, he would someday assemble another car or two. He spent a great deal of his free time going to classic car events, where he liked exchanging stories and car parts with the other car buffs.

ESTPs enjoy spending time in active pursuits, not necessarily needing others but not minding if they are there either. They like to be associated with individuals who have taken physical risks, even if they choose not to do so themselves. One ESTP said he got along best with people who "lived on the edge." It is not common to find an ESTP who participates in or enjoys solitary activities such as journal writing. One ESTP enjoyed reading mystery novels because she could vicariously enjoy the thrills and challenges. She further explained that her recreational reading could not require too much thinking. It had to be fast paced and escapist, and had to allow her to stop and start her reading with ease.

LOVING

For the ESTP, love means finding someone to have fun with, sharing life's ups and avoiding life's downs. When an ESTP sees an intended partner as one with whom many exciting experiences can be shared, the ESTP will use persuasiveness and his or her outward, fun-loving orientation to impress and win the chosen partner. The ESTP may view this as a challenge and may use whatever expedient means are available. ESTPs enjoy falling in love but do so quite practically by finding common ground with their loved one. This companionship aspect, in which activities can be jointly pursued, is important to them. A couple, both ESTPs, liked construction and home repair projects that yielded tangible results.

Generally, ESTPs can be fairly straightforward about the more sensual side of love, regarding it as a major part of life's enjoyment. They may like parties, ribald stories, and entertainment that has an earthy undertone, seeing these activities as a part of life not to be taken too seriously. For ESTPs in relationships, too much daily routine can feel confining and boring. When this happens, they are likely to "liven" things up by surprising their partners with a second honeymoon, a large or extravagant gift, or some other tangible expression of their love.

When scorned, ESTPs may wallow in their grief for some time, then decide that such behavior is impractical and therefore cut their losses and move on. ESTPs usually approach the breakup of a relationship with a fairly straightforward and realistic orientation. After they have dealt with the emotional part, it is as if fate has taken its course. It is as though they might say, "The relationship is over. Life dealt me a blow, and it's time to move on."

LOSING OUT

Each type has the potential to overuse or abuse its preferences. This is likely to happen when individuals are under great stress or pressure. At these times, they may act in ways that are unlike their usual styles. The following paragraphs describe some of the ways ESTPs may lose out, in addition to some strategies that they can use to get back on track.

For the ESTP, one way of losing out has to do with their overreliance on improvisation, which invites emergency-like complications. "I work better under pressure" is the reason given. One ESTP prided herself on being a "doer." She loved the "fire-fighting" aspect of her job. She would deliberately overload her schedule the day before a major business trip. The day of departure would find her scurrying about asking her staff to do "rush" jobs so that she could have her desk cleared before leaving. This pattern caused much stress to her office staff but seemed to energize her. When an appointment with a major client had to be cancelled because of her style, she was asked to change her ways. As a strategy, ESTPs may need to look beyond the quick fix and plan ahead, considering the wider ramifications of their improvisational activities.

Another way ESTPs may lose out is when they sacrifice follow-through in their efforts to meet the problems of the moment. They may have taken on too much to do and not realize it until they feel overloaded. They may need to develop a plan of action and consider the follow-through and necessary perseverance that will allow them to gain a sense of accomplishment. They do not have to be busy all the time to be worthwhile.

Additionally, ESTPs may lose out if they focus on specific material possessions to the point of ignoring other things in life, including the people around them. One ESTP had difficulty accepting the professionalism of her colleagues when they wore blue jeans to work. She was always well dressed and liked to spend her money on clothes. As a strategy, ESTPs may need to look beyond material pleasures to more enduring interpersonal ones and to accept that other people value different things than they do.

Another way ESTPs lose out is when they appear too direct, blunt, and uncaring of the needs of others. This may happen particularly when they are responding quickly to the moment. In their fun-loving and down-to-earth orientation, they may overlook customary social niceties that others may expect. Because ESTPs are observant of people and pick up cues from the rest of the environment, they can anticipate the needs of others when it serves their purpose to do so.

An ESTP found a business meeting particularly boring and dry. He felt that the participants needed something to wake them up and get their energy focused. In his briefcase he carried several slides with crude drawings and representations of the company's products. He decided, after a break, to momentarily take charge of the meeting and show his slides. His business colleagues, who treated their product with more respect, were shocked and offended to see the crude caricatures he had made of the products. The ESTP, however, roared in laughter as he put up each slide. He did note, however, that the silence in the room became more intense as he went along, and he decided he had better quit and get back to the task.

A strategy for ESTPs would be to factor in the feelings of others and the effect of their actions on them. They may need to curb their assertiveness, directness, love of fun, and high energy in order to not overwhelm others. Because ESTPs almost deliberately work on being outrageous, they may not be easily accepted by others. They need to carefully pick the situations in which their being outrageous is appreciated.

When ESTPs are back on track, they are using their strengths of responding to the moment, action orientation, and directness of approach. They can be tireless in the pursuit of adventure.

IN A NUTSHELL

Hallmarks:[2]

Activity oriented
Adaptable
Fun loving
Versatile
Energetic
Alert
Spontaneous
Pragmatic
Easygoing
Persuasive
Outgoing
Quick

Acronym:[3]

Everyone **S**eems **T**oo **P**roper

Chapter Eight

ESTJ

ESTJs Chose the Following Preferences:

Extraversion . . . . ENERGIZING . . . . Introversion
Sensing . . . . ATTENDING . . . . iNtuition
Thinking . . . . DECIDING . . . . Feeling
Judgment . . . . LIVING . . . . Perception

In general, ESTJs are doers who roll up their sleeves, dig in, and proceed directly to get the job done. They use logic and analysis as guiding principles for their lives. They are quick to decide and set a plan of action. They marshall resources in an organized fashion, implement, and follow through. They like closure. They focus directly on tasks to accomplish and are able to anticipate the steps needed to complete an assignment. In doing so, they see what might go wrong and take the necessary preventive action. They monitor events continually and make sure that commitments, both their own and those of others, are honored and the job gets done. They are at their best in situations that have some structure to them and involve activity, not contemplation, and in which an end product is desired.

LIVING

ESTJ children want life to be logical, practical, organized, and fair. They are often responsible, reliable, and obedient—if the rules make sense. They may be upset by a change in rules or routine, particularly if the rationale for the change is not given. They like others to be clear about their decisions. ESTJs learn early on how to use set formulas to make their own firm decisions.

ESTJ children like results-oriented activities and are often busy in some type of sporting or organized group, such as scouts. For example, one fourth-grade ESTJ child was quite involved with her Girl Scout troop. Like a typical, planning ESTJ, she set aside a half hour each evening, after her homework was done, and diligently applied herself to the task of earning her badges. Because of her sustained efforts, she was able to earn many badges; however, her reasoning was challenged by a friend who had earned an equal number of badges without adhering to a similar nightly routine. For the ESTJ, the deliberate follow-through is what makes accomplishments possible. ESTJs are perplexed at how others with a "haphazard" style get things done at all.

ESTJ children want to learn how to do things correctly and may take lessons that help accomplish this. For example, in taking figure-skating lessons, the ESTJ child usually likes the various tests that are a part of this sport. Here too they are able to measure their accomplishments. Learning and play activities are not left up to chance; they are planned, and that planning brings comfort.

The ESTJ teenager may value the traditional things that teenagers do, such as team sports, band, and class offices. If playing soccer is the tradition of the school, the ESTJ teenager is likely to play soccer. ESTJs enjoy being involved with their peers and choose friends with whom they share their activities, but it is less probable that they share many secrets with others. They may join organizations if they see a purpose for them. With their ability to organize and get things going, they often assume leadership roles.

ESTJs begin early to assume responsibility for themselves. They believe it is necessary to "earn their keep" and as teenagers they often have part-time jobs. These jobs usually are for specific purposes, such as saving money for college or buying useful things such as cars or clothes.

As young adults, ESTJs focus on their goals, both personal and professional. They build on education and career goals set earlier in life and do all that they can to make these goals become reality. They seem to have less confusion or difficulty than some types in choosing a career or selecting a mate because they like focusing and making decisions.

During the Vietnam War, an ESTJ joined up to "do his duty." When he was released from the service, he enrolled in a two-year accounting program. "I don't see why I need French or English literature and all those other courses. I'll never use them," he said. After getting his Associate of Arts degree, he secured an accounting job near his home and married his high school sweetheart. It all seemed relatively straightforward and according to plan.

His life continues on the same track today, "I don't see the need to change jobs. I've been promoted. I like it here. The kids are happy," he responded when he was urged to accept a job offer elsewhere. "It just doesn't make sense to change, especially when things are going just fine." Typically, ESTJs make their decisions based on practical and realistic criteria, and are unlikely to chance something that seems uncertain, frivolous, or risky.

In adult life, ESTJs are likely to take seriously their roles— such as parent, employer, employee, or church member—and to be committed to them and the responsibilities they represent. They are able to compartmentalize their lives and recognize discrete areas of responsibility, such as parenting, working, and playing. ESTJs often gain the respect of others because of their dependability, follow-through, and task completion. They may be pillars of the family, community, church, or business world.

Because ESTJs usually have long tenure with their organizations, their financial needs in retirement may be taken care of; however, their new free-time needs to be planned carefully. They are the people for whom the statement exists, "If you are what you do, what are you when you don't?" Unless they have retirement activities and personal relationships already in place and have developed their personality to include flexibility and spontaneity, the transition to retirement may be difficult.

One retired ESTJ kept her life full this way: "Well, on Monday, I visit with my neighbor, Clara, who is recovering from a stroke. On Tuesday, I go to the Senior Citizens' Center and spend the day there. Wednesday, I ride the Senior Citizens' van to town with three friends. On Thursday, I watch my grandchild in the morning, and in the afternoon, I go to the grocery store. On Friday, I go shopping at the Tri-City Mall with three friends. Weekends . . . well, weekends, they are the hardest. During that time, I remember my husband and many of the things we did together. I sure do miss him. However, to pass the time, I watch the football or baseball games on TV just like we used to. These keep me busy, and, besides, not much else is going on." In her response, she reflects the scheduled and planned activity orientation of the ESTJ.

LEARNING

ESTJs learn best in structured situations in which the objectives are clearly established. They like schedules or agendas so that they can plan ahead. It is important for them to know the time frames, the course content, the requirements, and when papers or projects are due. It is not sufficient to know that a short paper is a class requirement. The ESTJ wants to know things like an appropriate topic or two, the number of pages, and the due date. ESTJs like plenty of advance notice and dislike changes in class schedules. However, when the teacher's authority is established, these changes may be tolerated. Their idea of a good teacher is one who is consistent, fair, and applications oriented.

ESTJs may be good students when they put in the necessary time and effort. There needs to be a direct payoff to them. One of their main strengths is their ability to follow through and meet deadlines.

ESTJs like learning activities such as field trips, experiments, and anything that gets them actively involved in the learning process. Because of their realistic bent, they may get so caught up in activities that they may not see what concept the activity represents.

As learners, ESTJs can get stuck if they concentrate only on the facts without putting them together into some kind of coherent whole. An example of this is a high school student in history class who, on a written test, was asked to define the reasons for revolution. She regurgitated the various reasons she had memorized when she had studied the Russian revolution and was pleased with her ability to recall so much about that historic situation. She was unhappy, however, when her teacher gave her a C because she had not seen how the Chinese revolution had differed and therefore missed the overview. "You did not put your facts together conceptually," was the teacher's written comment.

LABORING

When an organization wants a job done—on time, according to schedule, with strict specifications—ESTJs can deliver. They contribute their logical and orderly way of evaluating and monitoring programs. They are direct and decisive, especially when they see a flaw. They are especially adept at organizing the steps and the resources needed to get the job done. They follow through with a thoroughness focused on the actual, practical facts of the situation.

Work Setting

ESTJs prefer a work setting that is task-oriented, structured, organized, and filled with other hard-working people. They want stability, predictability, and efficiency. Only those who meet their goals in a timely fashion should be rewarded. Surprises and changes in the schedule are tolerated only as long as they make sense and the general schedule is still adhered to.

Organizing Style

The ESTJs' organizing style is to set a goal and to make plans around it so that they can clearly note when the job is done. Initially, they tune in to the requirements of their plan in minute detail, figuring out the appropriate categories and systems to handle the requirements. When things are in order, ESTJs act.

ESTJs are fond of "to do" lists because checking off the items demonstrates accomplishment. The setting of priorities is natural to ESTJs, and they do so rather dispassionately without being caught up in the emotional meanings of things.

Efficiency is important to ESTJs. For example, an ESTJ father has children to watch and errands to run. Before starting on his errands, he makes a list of what needs to be done and where he needs to go, and plots the most efficient route to get there. He is not likely to waiver from his plans even in the face of his children's requests for a stop at the ice cream store since that stop is not on his list and there is no time to spare. It is important to ESTJs to make every move count. They will do so even when others are trying to sidetrack them.

Occupations

To perform well at work, individuals may need to use all of the eight preferences at the appropriate time and when required by the situation. Knowing this, people tend to select occupations that allow them to use the preferences that are most natural to them.

ESTJs prefer occupations that require an organized, logical, and practical bent that incorporates an effective use of time and resources. They pay attention to the organization's hierarchy, and use policies and procedures to help them to move the tasks along. They like making decisions and dealing with concrete, specific facts.

While ESTJs can and do enter all occupations, some are more appealing to them than others. According to available research,[1] some occupations (in alphabetical order) seem to be more attractive to ESTJs: government worker, insurance agent and underwriter, judge, manager, military personnel, nursing administrator, police officer, sales representative, supervisor, trade and technical teacher, and other occupations that allow ESTJs to see tasks accomplished. These occupations are not meant to be an exhaustive list but serve to illustrate some areas that an ESTJ might enjoy. If your specific occupation or one that you are interested in is not listed here, think instead of its general characteristics and ask yourself how those fit with your type.

LEADING

The ESTJ leadership style is the one on which many American businesses are based. Whenever situations require a leader, ESTJs take charge quickly and give advice directly, whether solicited or not. When situations are off track, ESTJs want to know what happened, why it happened, and how it is going to be fixed. ESTJs' opinions of what ought to be done are based on their past experiences. They are more task than relationship oriented and can appear to others as tough, driven, or heartless. They are quick, crisp, and direct in getting at the core of the situation, and while they invite input from others, they expect them to adhere to the ESTJ's final decision.

An ESTJ was put in charge of merging a newly acquired hospital into his organization. The merger required that the new facility change its services from those of a hospital to those of a nursing home. His end goal was to operate at a profit within two years, but until the merger was fully completed, the system would operate at a loss. Since he had two years to meet his goal, he thought of all the necessary steps, such as merging the facilities' benefits programs, and recorded everything on a master schedule. The master schedule detailed the steps in a logical order. Each step had due dates noted and written on the calendar. For example, steps were established to determine the final staffing needs for the nursing home. He first noted the average number of beds that would be filled in a given time period in that facility, the number of staff required to service those needs, and an estimate of the likely staff attrition during this same time period. He would monitor these steps and make an analysis to logically decide if he needed to lay off or hire people. He also factored in how to keep employee morale high during this two-year time frame and scheduled special employee involvement programs to accomplish this end. He felt that he was in his element during this time because he was able to take charge of the many details and the structure of the merger.

LEISURE

ESTJs put work before pleasure and generally keep these activities separate. Leisure time occurs only after work is completed and must be earned or oriented toward some goal, such as enhancing good family relationships or maintaining health. ESTJs do not spontaneously go for walks; the walk must have a purpose, for example, exercising to lose weight or talking with a family member. If a business trip occurs in a vacation spot, the ESTJ may be efficient and combine the two purposes. Time for fun is often seen as a reward for accomplishing a given task.

ESTJs like active leisure pursuits or observing action-oriented events such as sports. They enjoy involving their families with them in some type of organized group activity such as scouting. ESTJ men often enjoy traditional male pursuits, such as hunting, fishing, camping, and golf. ESTJ women often choose leisure that has several purposes. ESTJ mothers involved in child rearing usually engage in activities that their children enjoy. In building relationships with their spouses or significant others, ESTJ women may be involved in the same activities as their spouses.

LOVING

For ESTJs, love means stability and steadfastness. However, when they first fall in love, they are much more likely to be spontaneous and open to the moment. They typically enjoy active pursuits, such as going to parties and sporting events, and taking walks together. ESTJs give and expect security and loyalty in relationships. When commitments are broken, ESTJs become upset because they hold others to the same standards of steadfastness to which they hold themselves.

Because ESTJs are logical, they expect logically that relationships will have ups and downs. They firmly believe that with a proper foundation, their relationships will survive expected down times. Because they expect this, they may ignore helping their partner or examining their relationship during those down times. In some cases, this inaction can be detrimental to their relationship, and in some cases, not.

A woman, married forty years to an ESTJ husband, described an incident early in their marriage. She was having a hard time accepting the death of a family member and wondered about talking this over with a psychologist. Her ESTJ husband focused on the practical financial needs of the family, not immediately on her personal needs. Without thinking, he suggested that she wait until they paid for the new porch. When he realized what he had said, he knew he had sounded uncaring. He apologized and encouraged her to get the kind of help she wanted. Somehow they would manage to pay for it all.

ESTJs, when scorned, may not quickly acknowledge their feelings of hurt. They are, however, supersensitive to being rejected, but they may not readily share that hurt with others. They continue to go about their tasks acting as if nothing had happened when, in fact, much has changed.

An ESTJ college student had been dating one young man since junior high school. One day, he made an "off the cuff" statement to her: "I don't think we should see each other any more." The statement was taken literally by the ESTJ to mean that the relationship was over. Instead of discussing her needs and true feelings, and how deeply hurt she felt, the ESTJ accepted his statement as an absolute truth with no alternatives. She worked out her hurt by continuing with her studies and did not see her friend again.

Only years later, in a chance encounter with him, did she learn that his "off the cuff" remark was meant to test her commitment and to provoke a loving response. In her ESTJ style, she thought a final decision had been made and life needed to be gotten on with, regardless of how she felt.

LOSING OUT

Each type has the potential to overuse or abuse its preferences. This is likely to happen when individuals are under great stress or pressure. At these times, they may act in ways that are unlike their usual style. The following paragraphs describe some of the ways ESTJs may lose out, in addition to some strategies that they can use to get back on track.

One way of losing out for ESTJs has to do with their directness in getting the job done. They tend to decide too quickly and to form opinions of how things ought to be done. When things vary or change, the original "ought to be" may not fit the new situation. ESTJs may hold consistently to their original plan and stand firm against what they consider to be impertinent or irrelevant new information. The result of this is that they can be "boxed into corners" and miss reaching their goals.

As a strategy, ESTJs need to remember that a decision can be changed and perhaps should be changed. Sometimes a change in the ESTJ's plans, based on new information, may allow him or her to get the job done more readily. ESTJs also may need to "bite their tongues," ask others for advice, listen to it, and stop themselves from giving their own directions and decisions right away.

Another way ESTJs may lose out is when they do not see the need for change. They hold to their view and become quite rigid and unyielding in favor of upholding their principles. They may need to prod themselves to look at the benefits of change, determining if their plans are still workable in that context. They need to avoid being stuck in ruts because "that's the way we've always done it." ESTJs will discover that changes in plans can be positive and may even be better than their original way.

ESTJs may lose out when they overlook the niceties in working with others. They may drive themselves and others hard, forgetting to say the necessary "pleases" and "thank yous." They may need to make a special effort to show appreciation to others and also to encourage others to be involved in the accomplishment.

Another way ESTJs lose out is when they get emotional. Being so conscientious, reliable, and task-oriented, ESTJs may not be consciously aware of their needs or those of others. When they ignore their feelings, a seemingly inconsequential incident may set off an emotional explosion.

An ESTJ mother was focused on the task of having dinner

ready by six. Her small children were playing in the kitchen and demanding her attention. When one of the children asked her for a snack, she exploded in anger, which, on later analysis, she recognized as out of line for such a simple request. ESTJs may find it helpful in such situations to use the proverbial method of counting to ten. In addition, they might remind themselves of what is important (a six o'clock dinner may not be) and rebuild control in a step-by-step fashion.

Because ESTJs rely heavily on logic, they may overlook their own and others' feelings and values. An ESTJ college student had managed to earn enough credits to graduate a semester early. Because this saved him time and also saved his parents' money, it seemed the logical thing to do. He decided to graduate in the middle of his school year, not factoring in that he would miss his graduation ceremony and a whole semester of fun with his friends. He also forgot that his parents had wanted to attend his graduation ceremony and share in his accomplishment.

In retrospect, he realized this was the wrong decision to have made. He had not seen the value of those activities nor appreciated the relationships he was leaving. He did not anticipate that his family would want the opportunity to experience the pride, joy, and association that comes from the graduation ceremony.

When they are back on track, ESTJs are using their strengths of structuring things in a logical way, using critical analysis to find the right way to proceed, and standing firm on principles. They can be tireless in getting the job done.

IN A NUTSHELL

Hallmarks:[2]

Logical
Decisive
Systematic
Objective
Efficient

Direct
Practical
Organized
Impersonal
Responsible
Structured
Conscientious

Acronym:[3]

Execution Saves The Job

Chapter Nine

ISFJ

ISFJs Chose the Following Preferences:

Extraversion . . . . ENERGIZING . . . . **Introversion**
Sensing . . . . ATTENDING . . . . iNtuition
Thinking . . . . DECIDING . . . . **Feeling**
Judgment . . . . LIVING . . . . Perception

In general, ISFJs are sympathetic, loyal, considerate, and conscientious. They will go to any amount of trouble, when it makes sense to them, to help those in need. ISFJs operate most comfortably in situations where the rules are well defined and where traditions are to be upheld. They focus on providing practical help and services for others and for the organizations they serve. They are often self-effacing in getting the job done, and they are willing to make necessary sacrifices, especially for their families. They are at their best quietly providing assistance and making sure things are in proper order.

LIVING

ISFJ children are conscientious, diligent, and rarely a behavior problem to their parents or teachers. They like to know what is expected, and then they will dutifully and quietly follow through. In some respects, ISFJs behave like "perfect children" because they try to please their parents, teachers, and those in authority. They work to meet others' requirements if they are in keeping with the ISFJs' value system, even if this involves a sacrifice on their part. One ISFJ recalls with pride a perfect attendance record from kindergarten through twelfth grade. Because her mother held to the same value, she went to school even when she felt somewhat ill.

Security and routine are very important to ISFJ children. For some ISFJs, this means knowing exactly who is going to be there after school to take charge or who will be invited to play games with them. This need for security and order also applies in school. ISFJ children like to know exactly what they are supposed to do in school and like to feel certain that they have the skills before being called upon. ISFJs need gentle nudging to move beyond their comfort level. One ISFJ child was in a special reading class, in part because she did not let her teachers know that she could read. Only after standardized testing did those involved realize that the ISFJ was doing work far below her ability, according to the tests. When analyzing the situation, her parents and teacher determined that she was very comfortable in the lower reading group because she felt certain about what was going on; she had one-to-one instruction with lots of warm attention, and she was not distracted by misbehaving students. ISFJ children often want to practice their skills individually before showing them to others. This is especially true if they will be evaluated on these skills, because they want to be sure they know what they are doing before they demonstrate their skills to the world.

ISFJs may worry a lot about any number of things. This is apparent even in young children. One ISFJ would come home after school crying because she was worried that she would not be able to do all her school work. While there was ample time in school to complete the work, it was only on Fridays, when all her work was done, that she was able to breathe a sigh of relief.

ISFJ children are particularly introspective in the face of adversity. Because of their inward focus, it simply does not occur to them to share their problems with others. One ISFJ student was despondent over his school work. His mother noticed his despondency and decided, on her own, to talk to her son's teacher. She found out that her son was given extra assignments and asked his teacher why this was the case. His teacher responded that she had noticed that the boy wanted to be kept busy and seemed willing to do more. It was only later, when the mother talked with her son, that she discovered he felt extremely overworked but could not bring himself to tell the teacher. He felt a need to please his teacher, whom he admired and whose judgment he valued. His conflict resulted because he trusted his teacher's evaluation of his ability, in the process discounting his own feelings. He wanted to maintain the special relationship he felt with his teacher.

ISFJs usually have a few close friends whom they are likely to keep as close friends for a lifetime. They often belong to at least one social group. They avoid center stage and contribute willingly in quiet, practical, behind-the-scenes ways.

When comfortable, ISFJs can radiate their feelings and thoughtful values outward to others. They are often accepted for their kindness and quiet friendliness. They typically select a few special friends and nurture these friendships over long periods of time.

ISFJs shy away from disharmony and try to maintain cooperation at all costs. They may be more cautious and conservative than many of their peers. One ISFJ teen, facing peer pressure to drink alcohol, could not simply say "no thanks" and face being ostracized, even though he had a strong value about abstinence. Instead, he told his friends he was allergic to alcohol and would break into hives with a mere swallow of it. He avoided drinking, remained true to his values of not drinking, and maintained his place in his group. ISFJs can often come up with good excuses for what they do.

As young adults, ISFJs set goals with a variety of time frames, ranging from daily goals to long-range ones. If ISFJs have goals of summer vacation trips, they begin to save their money months in advance, gather accurate information on costs, and make lists of what to take. Few details are left unattended to. Because their focus is on the actual and the real, they know their plans can change. They accept this as "life," even though they would prefer to have things work out. They try to have things in order each day so they will not have to worry too much about tomorrow.

In their careers, ISFJs are often likely to take what comes along; for example, they may accept the first job offer, rather than continue to look for something else and remain in a state of flux. Once in a job, they generally try to make the most of it, since the known is preferable to the unknown. If the ISFJ is not in a job that provides intrinsic satisfaction, he or she feels uncomfortable yet may be slow in looking for anything else. ISFJs are loyal employees who diligently work at whatever tasks are given to them.

One ISFJ was assigned a position as a trainer for career development, even though she had no previous experience in that field. During her first year, she became physically ill before each class because she was uncomfortable in front of a group of people and because she wanted to be sure the information she was presenting was correct. In spite of this, she carried through. After five years, she is still in this job; she now feels confident that she can answer almost every question asked of her. She feels good about helping others with their careers.

ISFJs are likely to have done some retirement planning. Since they tend to save money throughout their lives, they often have the financial resources to live comfortably in retirement. In their retirement days, ISFJs focus directly on their families and carry on family traditions and histories. The ISFJ delights in encouraging grandchildren and other family members in projects that continue the family's customs and heritage.

Following a forty-year marriage and a career as a homemaker and mother, an ISFJ widow volunteered at a local senior citizens' center. The options at the senior center were many—card playing, dancing, arts and crafts projects—but the ISFJ chose to sit at the front desk, greeting visitors and answering questions about the various programs. She also met with prospective members and encouraged them to join the center. While others filled their retirement with leisure activities, this ISFJ enjoyed serving others in a somewhat structured yet personal way.

LEARNING

ISFJs tend to be good students, because they diligently follow through in their work to please their teachers. One aspect of pleasing their teachers is wanting to know their teachers' basic requirements so that they can meet them to the letter of the law. While some ISFJs may procrastinate about getting their tasks accomplished, they rarely put things off to the point of turning the projects in late unless something major intervenes. ISFJs like having assignments that are clear and that tangibly demonstrate that they have worked hard. They are not likely to feel comfortable with an independent study project, because independent study leaves them too much on their own without a set of definite procedures. While it is possible for ISFJs to stay up all night attempting to finish an assignment, this does not occur often. One ISFJ worked all night to type her boyfriend's paper because he really needed her help.

ISFJs learn best by doing. They like to be involved in their work, perhaps having a work sheet to follow along as the teacher speaks. They may feel comfortable in group activities as long as they are working with a cooperative and task-focused group. An ISFJ kept asking a friend to tell the teacher that some other students in the group were not being nice. The ISFJ did not want to tell the teacher directly, but she wanted something to be done about those who were misbehaving.

ISFJs learn well from lectures that are well organized, not too fast paced, and properly sequenced. Lectures that activate their senses or connect to sensory impressions are very rich for ISFJs. The history teacher who makes past events come alive with detail and facts will be appreciated. ISFJs do not like the debates and "arguing for the sake of arguing" that other types might find instructive and even enjoyable. They find arguing to be nonproductive and even uncomfortable. If differing viewpoints are to be discussed, they prefer to do so only with those they trust. One ISFJ remembers as her most disliked learning experience a required reading assignment filled with page after page of debate and discussion on the theory of the meaning of life. The assignment did not make sense to her because she viewed life as uncomplicated and straightforward.

ISFJs like clear conclusions to their learning. They want to know the right answer. They may need to accept that situations do not always have one answer and learn to feel comfortable with that.

LABORING

At work, ISFJs contribute loyal, sympathetic, consistent, and considerate service to others. They are known for their kindness and for their willingness to go to any length to help those in need. They take the practical needs of people into account when they do their work, and their strong follow-through skills allow them to carry out organizational goals. They do at least what is expected of them and oftentimes more, without attracting attention to themselves. They are painstaking and responsible with detail and routine, and feel it is important to have the right things in the right places at the right times.

Work Setting

ISFJs prefer an occupational setting that is attentive both to peoples' needs and to getting the job done. They like peers who are as conscientious, precise, and accurate as they are. They feel most comfortable if the organization provides security and if their work is clearly structured with practical service-oriented outcomes. They are calm, quiet, and efficient in their work habits. They prefer a work space that allows for privacy since they like to concentrate deeply on their work and avoid interruptions. Because interruptions make it difficult for ISFJs to recover their train of thought, they need to plan time alone in order to be most productive.

Organizing Style

ISFJs like to have everything organized in a manner that they have decided is appropriate. They cannot work when things are out of order. Everything has its place, both at work and at home. Their offices and their homes may contain special knickknacks and mementos that have personal meaning to them. Usually these knickknacks are put in a special and definite spot. One ISFJ said she allowed herself to have "junk shelves" for those things that could not be quickly placed in the right spot. She was comfortable with the disorder of these shelves because they were a place to store things that did not fit into neat categories and because they were only in one small area of her office.

When things are in disarray, ISFJs like to reorganize them immediately and often cannot leave their work until order is restored. They become distracted by disarray, finding that before a project is started, everything must be in its place. One ISFJ found it nearly impossible to get work started on the days when his desk was cluttered and messy. When he did not have time to straighten his desk, he would find an empty desk to use down the hall in order not to be distracted by the clutter. ISFJs enjoy ordering and structuring the small things of life; they may overorganize. One ISFJ had all of her sales receipts filed for individual stores by month. She was surprised to read a book on home files management that suggested the use of broad categories such as "Receipts—19———."

ISFJs tend to organize around their values. They will often set their priorities in terms of the people who are most important to them, usually putting their family's and then their boss's or their organization's needs first. ISFJs do what is required to serve their key values. One ISFJ had a value that "cleanliness was next to godliness" and spent her weekends carefully cleaning her home. After repeated urgings from her spouse to have some fun, she agreed to spend Sunday afternoons relaxing with him.

Occupations

To perform well at work, individuals may need to use all of the eight preferences at the appropriate time and when required by the situation. Knowing this, people tend to select occupations that allow them to use the preferences that are most natural to them.

ISFJs are attracted to occupations that require dedication to others, service, attentiveness to details, and thoroughness. They would rather work with things that they can see—the tangibles that result in something worthwhile for people.

While ISFJs can and do enter all occupations, some are more appealing to them than others. According to available research,[1] some occupations (in alphabetical order) seem to be especially attractive to ISFJs: bookkeeper, clerical supervisor, curator, family practice physician, health service worker, librarian, medical technologist, nurse, preschool and elementary teacher, typist, and other occupations that allow ISFJs to provide practical and helpful service to others. These occupations are not meant to be an exhaustive list but serve to illustrate some areas that an ISFJ might enjoy. If your specific occupation or one that you are interested in is not listed here, think instead of its general characteristics and ask yourself how those fit with your type.

LEADING

ISFJs may be selected for positions of leadership based on their conscientiousness, follow-through, dependability, and mastery of previous assignments. While they may be hesitant to accept leadership positions at first and, in fact, do not outwardly seek leadership positions, they will step in when asked because of their sense of duty and responsibility. They expect compliance with organizational needs, structure, and hierarchy, and tend not to ask others to do things that they themselves would not do.

They keep track of the details and focus their knowledge to achieve practical results.

As leaders, ISFJs are more relationship than task oriented, although they are dissatisfied with themselves and others if work is not completed on time. The values and needs of their followers are important to them. As leaders, they are sensitive to each individual's needs. One ISFJ, commenting on her leadership style, said that she was always placed in leadership positions but that she was never at ease in such roles, feeling that it was not her true style. However, she realized that she was a responsible leader. She led others by finding out "where they were at, not by commanding them." She encouraged others to do their work as they liked to do it, rather than demand that they do things her way. ISFJs desire harmony with their followers and work consistently to attain and then maintain it.

LEISURE

ISFJs get involved in leisure activities only after their work is done. Because ISFJs generally see so much work to do, they put off their leisure and relaxation. If they incorporate their own need to relax or to exercise as one of their duties on their "to do" list, they may then rest.

ISFJs tend not to be the center of attention, and often appear serious. Others may enjoy "making the ISFJ come alive," and feel very rewarded by a wide smile and special laugh. One ISFJ said his friends kept trying to get him inebriated so he would then "cut loose." ISFJs can be fun-loving, but only when they are comfortable and when it is the acceptable thing to do in the group to which they belong.

When time allows, ISFJs particularly enjoy the pleasures of finding and maintaining attractive things for themselves and their families. They pay attention to the practical needs of their homes and their offices. For example, many ISFJ women like to be well attired. They are willing to spend their available time searching for the right colors and styles. They find the right items at the best prices and feel good when they stay within their budget.

ISFJs also enjoy "feathering their nests" and like to keep those close to them as well as their houses and offices neat and tidy. They may collect small mementos that they enjoy having around. They take photographs of important events in their lives, for example, and when they have time, carefully label and place those photos in albums. An ISFJ male was the proud owner of a completely outfitted van that contained all of the comforts of home. He took great pride in sharing and maintaining his home on wheels, where he could play poker or entertain a few friends.

LOVING

For the ISFJ, love means security and commitment. Again, like other types, ISFJs tend to fall hard when they fall in love. Because they place a high value on marriage and family, they seek out a partner and feel unfulfilled without one. Marriage and family give ISFJs appropriate outlets for their love. In addition, they provide opportunities for them to meet their need to be of service to others. Because they are willing to give so much, they tend to expect the same sort of response from their mates and may be disappointed when their partners do not comply. However, they are realistic enough to know that they may not get exactly what they want and sometimes must accept their fate quietly.

ISFJs tend to stay in relationships that may not be in their best interests. Because ISFJs are responsible and dutiful, unless they are careful, their partners may take advantage of them. ISFJs are likely to stay in such relationships, because their values of commitment and stability are more important than their individual needs and wants. They may be taken for granted by the very people for whom they care and do so much.

In love, ISFJs tend to epitomize people who radiate warmth and good feeling. While ISFJs may not verbalize deep love or the underlying sense of security and commitment that they feel, their contented facial expressions and demeanors illustrate their inner thoughts. The ISFJ will do whatever is necessary to maintain this state. When the spouse or family of the ISFJ does not meet his or her expectations, the opposite facial expression or demeanor may occur. They are unlikely to talk with others about their disappointments.

When ISFJs are scorned, they are likely to be disappointed, angry, and bitter. However, they keep their feelings inside and often focus on themselves. After her spouse had left her to marry another, one ISFJ commented, "It wouldn't mean anything if I let the anger out." Even though she was in pain, she held back her feelings and tears, responding to a strong need to appear composed and stoic to others.

LOSING OUT

Each type has the potential to overuse or abuse its preferences. This is likely to happen when individuals are under great stress or pressure. At these times, they may act in ways that are unlike their usual style. The following paragraphs describe some of the ways ISFJs may lose out, in addition to some strategies that they can use to get back on track.

For the ISFJ, one way of losing out has to do with paying too much attention to what actually is and neglecting to look beyond the facts to find implications. They may often see the present so clearly that they cannot see any different possibilities for the future. Thus they may get stuck in ruts and not see a way out. Using their past experience as a basis on which to judge their future, they focus on past negative experiences and face the future with uncertainty and fear. When there is a noise in the car or when an appliance breaks down, for example, ISFJs may imagine the worst possible cause. When they look for meanings and relationships suggested by the facts, they tend to see what is missing, rather than what is possible or a potential opportunity. Additionally, because the future is filled with the unknown and past experience may not fully apply, ISFJs may see the future more pessimistically than necessary.

One ISFJ was caught in the present when she became widowed at an earlier age than her friends. She could not look beyond the fact of losing her husband to the other facts that she still had her health, four grown sons, and several very close friends. She continued to feel sorry for herself and did not seek new interests or develop the relationships she already had. She worried about the future and did not attempt to make it better.

As a strategy, ISFJs need to focus on the practical and the real and to know that this focus can guide them well in the future. They are well advised to look for at least three possibilities in their current situation that have the potential for working out. Because ISFJs are dependable, reliable, and conscientious, they usually are able to find a niche for their services in almost any situation. This fact can serve as a comfort to them.

ISFJs may be inflexible and unable to relax and take what comes. They want to plan excessively. They want things to go a certain way, becoming upset if they do not turn out to be right or on schedule. For example, they may get to the airport several hours in advance to avoid the worry of missing the flight, but instead replace that worry with another, such as potential bad weather delaying the flight or having their luggage misplaced. As a strategy, they may find that something as simple as a worry stone to rub may help them regain their orientation by giving them something specific to do. They can thus be freed up to look more broadly at all the facts and to be more flexible in their approach.

ISFJs may feel undervalued as a result of their quiet, self-effacing style. They may not be seen as sufficiently tough-minded when presenting their views to others. One ISFJ manager contributed quietly behind the scenes. Because he did not promote himself or his contributions, others in his organization did not accurately assess his contributions. Not until the ISFJ had a family emergency that kept him away from work for more than two weeks did the people in the office realize his worth to their organization. Whereas things had run effectively and smoothly when he was there, without him many records and facts were misplaced. Most in the office were anxious for his early return. ISFJs tend to undervalue their role and accomplishments because they see themselves as "merely doing their duty." Strategies to help in these situations may include the need to develop more assertiveness in speaking out for their own needs, in talking about their own accomplishments (even if this feels like boasting), and in remaining open to other ways of doing things.

When ISFJs are back on track, they are using their strengths of accurately focusing on reality and being practical, with a penchant for remembering details and facts. They can be tireless in the pursuit of providing service.

IN A NUTSHELL

Hallmarks:[2]

Detailed
Traditional
Patient
Organized
Devoted
Responsible
Conscientious
Loyal
Practical
Service minded
Meticulous
Protective

Acronym:[3]

I Serve Family Joyfully

Chapter Ten

ISFP

ISFPs Chose the Following Preferences:

Extraversion	ENERGIZING	**Introversion**
Sensing	ATTENDING	iNtuition
Thinking	DECIDING	**Feeling**
Judgment	LIVING	**Perception**

In general, ISFPs are gentle and compassionate, open and flexible. They are considerate of others and do not force their views and opinions on them. They often focus on meeting others' needs, especially those who are less fortunate. Having a quiet, modest, self-effacing style, ISFPs avoid disagreements and seek harmony with people as well as with nature. They enjoy life's precious moments and often add a touch of beauty to the environments where they spend their time. They are at their best ensuring others' well-being.

LIVING

ISFP children are pleasant, quiet, and kind. Their talents may be easy to overlook because they shun the spotlight and do not have a strong need to demonstrate their strengths to others. They may be particularly drawn to people, animals, and plants who need the gentle care that ISFPs provide. One ISFP was walking to the grocery store with his mother when he noticed a dog tied to a lamppost. He walked over to the strange dog and immediately developed a rapport with it. He petted the dog, who responded to him in a very friendly manner. His mother asked him about the dog as they were walking away, since normally she would not have allowed her son to approach and pet a strange dog. The boy replied that he had sensed the dog would be friendly and that he thought to himself as he walked to the dog, "Isn't it lucky that dog knows me." His thoughts and the quick rapport with the animal made him feel secure, even with a strange dog.

ISFP children generally relate well with others and tend to have friends because they are easy to like. They are interested in others' feelings and notice particularly when disharmony exists. It is quite difficult for ISFPs to see their friends in conflict with one another. When this occurs, they will try to help ease the disagreements by playing the role of peacemaker.

ISFP children notice and attend to the delights of the senses. Often they will make special gifts for people whom they particularly like. These gifts are usually unique and original, with much attention paid to color, line, texture, and form. One young ISFP developed a beautiful plant terrarium for her father's office. She lovingly gathered wild plants from a wooded area near her home and combed through pet supply stores to find the right container for the terrarium. She gave it to her father with a complete list of directions for keeping the plants nourished and alive. It was her quiet way of sharing with her father her love and respect for living things.

ISFPs are often very conscious of the internal sensations in their bodies. They tend to be aware of what their body will and will not do. One ISFP took up figure skating because he so enjoyed the process of making intricate designs on the ice. He could predict with great accuracy how he would complete his figures. He loved the feeling of his body in motion to the music, and appreciated the grace and freedom that skating allowed.

As teenagers, ISFPs may "blend into the woodwork" because they are quiet and unassuming. They are oriented toward deeply felt personal values, and they may find themselves on the outside of social groups if the groups do not share the same values. One ISFP grew up and was "best friends" with several girls. In junior high school, her values were tested when they took to stealing small items from the local discount store. She made a very conscious and painful decision to sever her friendships and leave her group. This breakup was particularly difficult because, in her school, every student belonged to a particular social group. Because she left her group, she was without friends. Finally, as a senior, she took direct and assertive action and "broke" into a new group. Leaving a group that was at odds with her values was one of the experiences she says she will always remember and one that makes her feel good, in spite of the difficulty it caused her at the time.

In adult life, ISFPs work quietly, often behind the scenes, helping individuals meet their goals and dreams. They like a life of action and interaction, and often choose careers that allow them to exercise their ability to see the needs of the moment and respond quickly. Generally they have little desire to impress others or to impose their will. However, they can be gently and persistently persuasive if they believe some action is in another's best interest. One ISFP manager believed the effective handling of incoming phone calls was extremely important to her employer's business. Several operators in the office were somewhat indifferent with customers on the telephone, and the ISFP felt this needed correction. She did not directly confront the lackadaisical operators as a group; instead, she talked with each one individually to help them understand how important it was to their business to be kind and considerate to their customers.

ISFPs enjoy their friends and their families, and spend time nurturing their relationships. Many ISFPs, if given their "druthers," would prefer part-time to full-time work so they could be with those people who are important to them. They bring an air of spontaneity and easy acceptance to all they meet and are rarely quickly judgmental. Only when people do something grossly out of line, such as violating the rights of others—especially the less fortunate or less powerful—will the anger of ISFPs surface. They will then stand firmly against the infraction to support the victim.

One ISFP talked about her work helping women in the transition from married to single and self-supporting status. She herself had been divorced and had needed to find employment;

she had learned lots of practical things that she could now share with others like her. She particularly liked, as she called it, "hitting the basics"—those things that allowed women to get jobs directly by using their past experience. "Too many people recommend further schooling to women who can't afford it and have little time to pursue it," said the ISFP. "I teach women solid things, like word processing, so they can get a job. I believe their experience as homemakers has worth to them and others. The example of my life makes an impression and has even turned others' lives around. All these things make me feel good about my work."

In retirement, ISFPs often find that they are loved, admired, and cherished by the people who know them well. Retirement for ISFPs is a welcome time to enjoy the fruits of their careful relationship building. ISFPs are often the kind of grandparents who are able to tolerate their grandchildren's behavior while additionally giving gentle nudges toward behavior improvement. Their spontaneity and the joy that they take from simple things such as walking, reading, sunbathing, and gardening makes them particularly delightful to have around. Their ease in accepting life as it is and enjoying the little things life has to offer is compelling to those who take the simple yet pleasant things in life for granted.

LEARNING

ISFPs learn best through hands-on experience. They may not be as interested in traditional academic subjects as some other types. They prefer application and practicality rather than studying the theoretical and only potentially useful. Making drawings, constructing miniature models, or using other direct representations to master the subject matter are appealing activities for them. They dislike structure and institutional settings that take away their spontaneity and freedom. Because they want their learning to be relevant to what is going on in their world, they have less tolerance for and patience with conceptual and abstract learning.

ISFPs enjoy learning subjects that relate to helping and knowing about people. Some ISFPs enjoy art, computer, and history classes if those classes are taught with an applied, sensible, humanistic approach, and if the learning objectives relate directly to their everyday lives. ISFPs do not have a strong desire to study things that may be "ultimately good for them," preferring instead more pragmatic and straightforward education.

ISFPs may be easily overlooked in the classroom unless the teacher has recognized their special ways of learning and their unique contributions. Encouragement helps to draw out ISFPs. Giving them an opportunity to use their sharp perception in an uncomplicated and direct approach to what they need to learn and master is very helpful. For example, when ISFPs have an art assignment to draw an animal, they would first enjoy looking at books full of animal illustrations. Even better for them would be a visit to see the animal in its natural habitat, where they could capture the spirit of the animal as it actually is. They could then use these experiences as a basis for their art work and probably would draw the animal as close to real life as possible.

When the learning is relevant to their experiences and needs, the exercises are applicable to real life, the teacher is caring, and the learning community allows for freedom and spontaneity, ISFPs enjoy being in school. When the environment is rigid and highly structured, with theoretical materials in use, ISFPs find themselves resisting the educational process.

LABORING

At work, ISFPs contribute by attending to the practical facts relating to the needs of people and all living things in their environments. They can infuse a particular kind of joy into their work and bring people and tasks together by virtue of their cooperative nature. Because they pay attention to the humanistic aspects of the organization, they act in ways that ensure others' well-being. People enjoy ISFPs because they bring understanding yet adaptability to the realities of their work.

Work Setting

ISFPs prefer a work setting that is egalitarian and contains cooperative people quietly enjoying what they do. They particularly like courteous co-workers who are flexible and compatible. They are people oriented and yet seek a quiet space for themselves that they often decorate to meet their aesthetic needs. By personalizing their work environments, they make them particularly pleasant places to be. One ISFP decorated the interior of her work truck with pictures of her pets.

Organizing Style

ISFPs organize according to their personal and humanistic values. They are willing to incorporate the needs of others in their plans. While not usually organized by nature, when they do have to organize something, they bring order in artistic ways.

An ISFP went into partnership with another consultant. Her partner's office seemed disorganized, with books and papers scattered all over. When her partner asked her for some practical organizing help, the ISFP remembered a color-coded system for managing the office's books and papers that was used in her former place of employment. With her partner's help, she developed a list of clients and general topical areas, and coded these to specific colors. To help others in the office be more consistent in their sorting and filing, a colored dot was put on each book and paper, according to the new code. Everyone in the office made use of the system, and the books and papers were quickly arranged by color. It was very easy for people who used the materials to know exactly where to find things because all the files, the file cabinets, the books, and the book shelves were matched by color.

Occupations

To perform well at work, individuals may need to use all of the eight preferences at the appropriate time and when required by the situation. Knowing this, people tend to select occupations that allow them to use the preferences that are most natural to them.

ISFPs enjoy occupations that allow them to be flexible and adaptable and to meet the here-and-now needs of others. They enjoy responding to the moment and choose work where they can offer practical, specific help in times of difficulty.

While ISFPs can and do enter all occupations, some are more appealing to them than others. According to available research,[1] some occupations (in alphabetical order) seem to be especially attractive to ISFPs: bookkeeper, carpenter, personal service worker, clerical supervisor and secretary, dental and medical staffers, food service worker, nurse, mechanic, physical therapist, X-ray technician, and other occupations that allow them to provide gentle help to all living things. These occupations are not meant to be an exhaustive list but serve to illustrate some areas that an ISFP might enjoy. If your specific occupation or one that you are interested in is not listed here, think instead of its general characteristics and ask yourself how those fit with your type.

LEADING

The ISFP leadership style is one that involves personal loyalty as a means of motivating others. ISFPs prefer an egalitarian and cooperative team approach and are more apt to lead others by praise and encouragement than by criticism. They persuade others by gently tapping into others' good intentions. When in emergency and crisis situations, they particularly rise to meet those challenges, adapting and dealing with what is needed at that moment. ISFPs generally do not seek direct leadership roles unless the situation or others demand that they do.

An ISFP was in charge of the communications department for a large company. This department handled the mail room, the messenger service, and delivery vans. The ISFP had a close-knit staff who met together regularly to coordinate their efforts to more effectively meet problems as they arose. He prided himself on his department's prompt reactions to changing circumstances.

He was always attempting to reduce the amount of time needed to send messages within his company. His leadership style was characterized as cooperative, friendly, and service oriented, especially in times of emergencies, such as when the computers "went down."

LEISURE

ISFPs like leisure, seek it out, and savor it. Enjoying life right now is valued by them. They may admonish those important to them (their children, spouses, or employers) to "stop and smell the roses," to take necessary rejuvenating breaks. ISFPs enjoy doing fun things for people who matter to them. Often this includes surprising others with tickets or trips to amusing activities. While they enjoy being with people, it is not essential that their leisure involve others. They also enjoy solitary pursuits such as painting, cooking, needlework, cross-country skiing, carpentry, home and car repair, and home maintenance and improvement projects.

ISFPs often have a unique, personal, and humorous approach that can make even difficult situations less tense and more fun. One ISFP was having a particularly hard time mastering a new computer and its word processing software. She enjoyed playing around with the machine and mastered most of its capabilities. At one point, however, despite her best efforts, the computer was not performing as she wanted it to. The fun she had been having changed to exasperation. She exclaimed, "This is more trouble than it's worth! I'm going to teach this computer a lesson!" She moved the computer from her desk, put it on her wheeled desk chair, found an extension cord, and rolled everything out on the lawn behind her house. When her surprised family and neighbors saw the computer outside, they asked her what was going on. She replied, "I just thought I'd come out here, enjoy the sun, and get really familiar with this computer!" From that point on, whenever she faced a computer problem, the people in her family would say, "It's time for you to go and sunbathe with the computer!"

ISFPs may enjoy community volunteer activities. One ISFP

belonged to an organization that sponsored meals for the less fortunate. She took it upon herself personally to organize the menus and find the most effective way to serve meals to meet cost, taste, and dietary requirements. She typed each week's menu and its recipes, oversaw all the food purchasing, paid the food bills, and, with great attention to detail, worked out the cost per serving of each of the menu items. The recipes that survived her practical scrutiny made their way into a recipe book that she wrote for the organization to sell and raise money. Not many people realized the depth or extent of her involvement because she did not make much fuss about her substantial commitment of time and energy. Her practical, service-oriented approach contributed directly to the organization's success.

ISFPs enjoy becoming involved with activities that appeal to their sensual side and combine this with as much spontaneity and impulse as possible. Because of this approach, they offer to themselves and others a sense of joy in most of the activities they undertake.

LOVING

For the ISFP, love means devotion, loyalty, care, humor, and consideration for the needs and wants of the loved one. When ISFPs first fall in love, they may feel consumed by it. They may become naive and focus entirely on the romance of it— "falling in love with love." Future worries are cast aside in favor of the present realities. ISFPs may ignore all else in order to experience their love life most fully. Doing this can leave them vulnerable to the whims of others.

Because being loved and cared for is important to ISFPs, they make sure that relationships are nourished so that they can continue to grow. When they are in love, they find a multitude of ways to show their affection and their appreciation for the other person. Often ISFPs will go so far as to rearrange their careers, start or stop working, move geographically, or make other changes to maintain their relationships.

The friends, family members, and even pets of the ISFPs' partners become important to them as well. ISFPs take it upon themselves to make their environments places where there is the potential to have a harmonious existence for all. An ISFP with no children of his own married a second time. He devoted himself fully to his new wife and her family. Because she liked warm weather, they relocated and found jobs in a warmer climate. When two of his wife's children were having problems with drugs, the ISFP enrolled in a parenting program in an effort to help the family in dealing specifically with this issue. He went to the classes and to subsequent family counseling sessions. His warmth, generosity, and care became the glue that held his new family together. Everyone in that family knew that the ISFP's priorities for their well-being were put over his own personal and career concerns. His unselfishness and true love for them pulled them through this difficult time.

In their desire to please others, some ISFPs may not be confident enough to speak up for themselves about what they need. If the relationship turns sour, the ISFP may believe that it was caused by something that they personally did. They may assume more of the blame than is necessary.

When ISFPs are scorned, they may retreat and repeatedly analyze the situation internally. When they do face reality and finally let go, they can become more assertive and self-directed in the resumption of their lives.

LOSING OUT

Each type has the potential to overuse or abuse its preferences. This is likely to happen when individuals are under great stress or pressure. At these times, they may act in ways that are unlike their usual style. The following paragraphs describe some of the ways ISFPs may lose out, in addition to some strategies that they can use to get back on track.

ISFPs may lose out when they neglect their own needs. Because they see others' needs so clearly and because they are heavily motivated toward meeting others' needs, they may overlook their own requirements.

One ISFP was told that her teenage daughter had a brain tumor and needed an operation. If successful, the operation could possibly eliminate the seizures her daughter was experiencing; however, if the operation were unsuccessful, her daughter might lose her sight or hearing, or even worse. During this time of extreme pressure, the ISFP overlooked her own needs and focused on keeping her daughter's and her family's spirits up. She relied on her faith that everything would work out and expressed this confident attitude to her husband and children. She surrounded herself with as many positive people as possible so that their outlook would influence her. She managed to work full-time during this period, with some exceptions for medical appointments.

When asked about her ability to withstand all this pressure, the ISFP said, "I put one foot in front of the other, and I don't look too far ahead. I take one day at a time." This ability to focus on the actual situation in a day-to-day fashion helped her. However, by giving high priority to everyone else's needs, she became extremely tired and came close to developing an ulcer. She realized that she needed to take a recuperative rest after the surgery was over and deemed a success.

As a strategy, ISFPs may need to learn how to respect their own needs more and to be assertive and direct with others in asking for their help and for time to take care of themselves.

ISFPs also lose out when they are afraid of conflict and mismanage it as a result. Sometimes they take personal responsibility for conflicts and issues that in actuality belong to others. They may become hurt and withdraw. As a strategy, they need to learn to give negative feedback in a timely manner. Confronting conflict directly may help them in the long run because the confrontation may "clear the air."

When ISFPs become too trusting and gullible, they may be taken in by people who have a strong need to control and take charge. They may need to develop a more skeptical and logical method for analyzing information and actions, rather than just accepting the views of others.

Finally ISFPs can lose out when they become self-critical, and do not appreciate their own accomplishments and contributions. Because ISFPs are gentle types and focus internally, much of their self-criticism is not apparent to the outside world. If it does get expressed outwardly, it is in a form that is anything but gentle, such as "Why did I do such a dumb thing!" A possible strategy for ISFPs would be to share their reflections and feelings with others so that their thoughts can be openly and realistically evaluated. Without outside scrutiny, these thoughts can become negative and destructive. Other people may be able to help ISFPs see that their concerns are ill founded or unusually harsh. Additionally, ISFPs may need to appreciate their own accomplishments more, even though this is likely to be difficult given their modesty.

When ISFPs are back on track, they are using their strengths of adaptability, gentleness, consideration, and concern about the needs of others. They can be tireless in the pursuit of gentle care for all living things.

IN A NUTSHELL

Hallmarks:[2]

Caring
Gentle
Modest
Adaptable
Sensitive
Observant
Cooperative
Loyal
Trusting
Spontaneous
Understanding
Harmonious

Acronym: [3]

I Seek Fun and Pleasure

Chapter Eleven

ESFP

ESFPs Chose the Following Preferences:

Extraversion . . . . ENERGIZING . . . . Introversion
Sensing . . . . ATTENDING . . . . iNtuition
Thinking . . . . DECIDING . . . . **Feeling**
Judgment . . . . LIVING . . . . **Perception**

In general, ESFPs are friendly, outgoing, fun loving, and naturally drawn to people. They are quite enthusiastic and exuberant, and are usually well liked by others. They are good at meeting people and helping them enjoy themselves. They are sympathetic toward people and generous with their time and money. They want to be where the action is, and they will often stir things up in their own special way. At their best, they are able to realistically meet human and situational needs in a fun and lively way.

LIVING

ESFP children are friendly, warm, active, and enthusiastic. One mother recalls her ESFP son, even at the age of three, as very giving and concerned about others. When he scraped his knee in a childhood game, for example, and she picked him up to comfort him, he instantly reciprocated by comforting her. When she patted him, he immediately started patting her. ESFPs need to give to others, and they use touch as one of the ways to show they care. They definitely like to make others happy, believing that "it is better to give than to receive." Being on the receiving end may make them feel self-conscious. They tend to be good at comforting others, regardless of whether others are in need.

ESFPs are aware of what is happening around them and notice much that escapes the eyes of others. Because they are tied into the present, particularly with people, they may sense what is happening with others before others know it. Additionally, they may notice what is going on in their environment and take delight in a spring flower, a bird's song, or a bright fabric, pointing these out in their enthusiastic way for others to enjoy. It is difficult to ignore ESFP children because they are so inclusive of others. Their style is winsome. One ESFP recalled that she had no problem in being shy with strangers; she talked to everyone. But this openness and trust of strangers worried her parents, who wanted her to be a bit more cautious.

ESFPs are popular and gregarious, and are often busy in social activities with others. As teenagers, they are likely to be instigators of activities with their friends. They are up and about, and it is difficult to catch them sitting still—ESFPs are "where the action is."

They tend to be bright and sunny in disposition and enjoy laughing at themselves and others. It is hard for ESFPs to be "down," mainly because of the excitement of each upcoming event. They are able to make fun of some of the more awkward teenage moments. One ESFP remembers being rather fun loving and doing crazy things. He said, "I'm lucky to be alive, but people around me kept saying what a nice well-mannered boy I was." If good fortune shines upon them, such as winning a contest, all who know the ESFP will likely join in the celebration.

ESFPs like to help other people and often join organizations that allow them to have fun while doing so. A young ESFP wanted to help alleviate people's suffering and bring some joy into their lives. She joined the candy stripers organization at a local hospital and was extremely well liked by the patients with whom she came into contact. During her frequent visits, she would ask many questions about them and would remember specific things to cheer them up. Often she would go to the trouble of making extra gifts to bring to her patients.

If ESFPs work in their teen years, their jobs are likely ones in which they can interact with people. They may work in gift shops, flower shops, and gasoline stations, where they can use their charm and friendliness. One ESFP was a particularly popular tennis instructor. He was always encouraging his students and made the game enjoyable for them, even in the frustrating moments of learning how to serve properly. He felt it was important to make his tennis lessons fun as well as instructional, so that his students would want to come back for more.

As adults, ESFPs lead what might look like "a charmed existence," even when things are not going well for them. They live with the idea that "the glass is half full" and seem to land on their feet, even when they are not sure how. They usually find a niche for themselves in any situation because of their spontaneity and flexibility. When they cannot find their spot (and this may have happened in school settings), they can be unhappy. Their social skills may attract the eye of a boss who then invites them to apply for a particular job. They tend to do well when "service with a smile" is important and when the needs of the customers are highly regarded. One ESFP was attracted to the restaurant business and began in high school to work as a waitress. She worked her way up to managing the restaurant because she was so attentive to the customers and the details of the business.

ESFPs bring a liveliness to the groups to which they belong. Life is meant to be enjoyed and is not taken too seriously. ESFPs contribute unique touches to social or work events. For example, one ESFP wrote a special, funny poem on his birthday, commemorating his friendships with everyone else in his office. Another ESFP sent his parents a humorous telegram on their fortieth wedding anniversary. He delighted in giving unusual gifts to others—his niece got musical socks for Christmas and his father received a musical tie. He found it a challenge to search out unique presents.

ESFPs often are able to interact with all ages, backgrounds, and types of people. Most individuals who connect with ESFPs feel that they are treated as equals by them, regardless of age or convention. A fifty-year-old ESFP charmed her young nieces by dealing with them as adults. She would help them apply nail polish, allow them to choose jewelry from her jewelry box, save her old hats and gloves for them, and talk to them in adult tones about being grown-up. She was always their favorite aunt.

ESFPs enjoy sharing their love of life with others, not just their mates and children. People around them benefit from this. When ESFPs are alone on business trips and when they have had enough time to themselves, they may seek out others. For example, one ESFP, when eating in a restaurant, engaged her waitress and busboy in easy conversation. She did not know either of them prior to this occasion, but her friendliness led to their gathering around her to participate in the talk. They left her only when they were forced to scurry away to handle their other duties.

In retirement, ESFPs continue their fun-filled, people-focused, activity-oriented life. They keep close friendships and continue to provide amusement to those who have been important to them in the past. They seem to maintain a "spark in their eye" and an optimism that is often contagious.

A retired ESFP who made shirts for more than fifty years in a factory was reminiscing with her sister about their days there. Her sister commented on the sweatshop atmosphere, the long hours, and the low pay. The ESFP had an entirely different perspective. For her, the factory was a place where she had friendships, where she had fun, where she knew what was expected of her, and where she could leave the work behind when she left. She was then free to spend her evenings as she saw fit—in dancing, going to movies, and other enjoyable activities.

ESFPs often look on the sunnier side of experiences, and this serves them well in retirement, not only as they reflect back about their past but also as they experience life's uncertainties. Their friends, having so enjoyed the ESFPs' spirit and zest, are willing to help out as they can.

LEARNING

ESFPs prefer learning through participating in groups where they can interact with others and do things, not just observe or listen about things. One ESFP stated that he learned best in chemistry when he could mix up elements, watch the reaction, and then learn the theoretical part. His learning was enhanced not by books but by hands-on activities. In his biology class, he did well because he could actually dissect the frog and learn its anatomy piece by piece.

Success in school has to do with teachers, and ESFPs want to get to know their teachers well. It is not that the teachers have to be nice, but they do need to care. One ESFP recalled, "My football coaches yelled at me a lot, but I knew they cared. Overall, the teacher makes the difference. In school, I never felt dumb, I performed for the teachers who cared and 'checked out' of the classes where teachers didn't care. In my sophomore year, my geometry teacher would give me extra help but would make me feel bad when I didn't understand theorem logic. By the end of the year, I had given up on the subject because of her cold indifference." ESFPs learn best when the teacher takes a personal interest in them and when the subject matter is focused on practical, helpful information.

ESFPs dislike and are upset by intellectual arguments and conflict. They need to experience the concept first before discussing it or receiving a didactically presented theory. Directions must be very concrete, simple, and accurate, with no tricks or nuances. The ESFP is plugged into the total environment. Atmosphere, attitudes, physical setting—all make a difference.

If the encouragement they receive for their social life is more than the encouragement they receive for their academic life, they may err on the side of being too social. They like fun in their learning activities and appreciate it in their teachers as well. Because ESFPs are present oriented and relationship oriented, they may not enjoy or feel that they have much to gain from standard academic subjects and teaching styles.

Most ESFPs learn actively and do not function as well when

they must read quietly by themselves about matters that are theoretical and, to them, esoteric. They find themselves easily drifting off while studying, and they are ultimately diverted by things more real to them.

One ESFP had a particularly difficult time in high school because the subject matter seemed remote from her day-to-day life, and she dropped out to get married. It was years later, when she was studying for her GED equivalency, that she discovered she could learn and that she enjoyed learning. She had felt out of place in high school because of her different orientation to learning. This realization that her preferred way of learning was not the way most classes were taught in high school, something she was unaware of at the time, caused her tears as she looked back. ESFPs may be at risk in traditional school settings.

LABORING

At work, ESFPs contribute their enthusiasm and cooperative spirit to the accomplishment of organizational tasks. They like action and excitement, and are able to link together people and resources. Because they accept and deal with people as they are, they are able to understand what is necessary in order to motivate them to get jobs done. They are upbeat and sociable, presenting a positive image of themselves and of the organization. Excitement and enthusiasm come from spirited accomplishments done together with others. More than one ESFP has been called the "goodwill ambassador" of an organization.

Work Setting

ESFPs prefer a work setting that is lively, action oriented, and harmonious. The atmosphere and overall attitude of the work setting means a great deal to them. They particularly enjoy adaptable people who are energetic, easygoing, and focused on the present realities. Because they notice what is around them, they like their work setting to be attractive. They will add their own personal touches to make it appealing to them. One ESFP, who enjoyed many happy family vacations on Cape Cod, had a jigsaw puzzle of the Cape Cod depth charts framed and hung on his office wall as a personal memento of those good times.

Organizing Style

ESFP organizing style is to factor in the needs of others and respond to their practical wishes and requirements. If something is not immediately useful or of intrinsic value, it may be quickly rejected by ESFPs. They notice what is going on with people and focus on these happenings intently. ESFPs are likely to adapt as the situation requires. While they may organize their personal possessions, they may leave other areas of their lives in disarray. If they have missed an appointment due to their disorganization, they feel terribly guilty about it and do all they can to make amends.

ESFPs want the results of their organizing efforts to be practical and to lead to greater harmony among people. An ESFP teacher related that she would organize her students into project groups based on who got along best with whom. She had a keen eye for the social relationships in the classroom and for those who made extra efforts to help people. She had a strong desire to see her students enjoy learning. When she digressed from her lesson plan, it was in an effort to make the class more meaningful to her students. This ESFP was particularly upset when there was conflict in the classroom. Learning materials and activities were arranged in such a way that conflict could be avoided. If an exercise had the wrong page number, she would correct it immediately so as not to distract her students or cause them to be confused.

Occupations

To perform well at work, individuals may need to use all of the eight preferences at the appropriate time and when required by the situation. Knowing this, people tend to select occupations

that allow them to use the preferences that are most natural to them.

ESFPs like occupations that allow them to be with people. Occupations must call for action and variety to be attractive to ESFPs. They want to be of direct and practical service to others and seek work that is self-fulfilling and rewarding. Being a resource to others is an important part of their work.

While ESFPs can and do enter all occupations, some are more appealing to them than others. According to available research,[1] some occupations (in alphabetical order) seem to be more attractive to ESFPs: childcare worker, clerical supervisor, coach, designer, factory supervisor, food service worker, receptionist, recreation worker, religious educator, respiratory therapist, and other occupations that allow them to be responsive to others. These occupations are not meant to be an exhaustive list but serve to illustrate some areas that an ESFP might enjoy. If your specific occupation or one that you are interested in is not listed here, think instead of its general characteristics and ask yourself how those fit with your type.

LEADING

The ESFP leadership style is one that promotes good will and team work. ESFPs are quickly adaptable and thus able to guide others in crisis situations, unless that crisis is one of disharmony among people. (In such a situation, they may get caught up with their emotions.) ESFPs are able to make things happen by focusing on immediate problems and using their ability to work with people. They are more relationship than task oriented but will work hard on the task part when the people part is going well.

An ESFP was in charge of an insurance sales force. He was very attentive and supportive of the salespeople on his staff as well as their customers. He noticed when their names appeared in the newspaper and would send them appropriate congratulatory notes. Additionally, he strongly but gently encouraged his staff to probe and find out what customers might need. He had regular meetings with his people at which he asked for their input. His style was inclusive and allowed for participative decisions on office policies. His sales force led in both policy renewals and in customer satisfaction surveys, because they provided such strong service to people. He was exceedingly well liked by everyone.

In describing his leadership style, one ESFP commented, "I see myself as a helmsman navigating a flat boat on the flow of the stream, going left and right to avoid rocks and to catch good fast water. I definitely like to make things happen! When in a meeting, discussing whether we should or shouldn't do something, I like to set down a strategy and have people react. The harder the group reacts, the more I let them control because then the group begins to take ownership. The action is monitored and promoted by me. I seek in myself and others a focus on quality and service, with continual improvement in the worth of the product."

LEISURE

ESFPs are quick to take leisure, give it a new twist, and create new enjoyment. They love being active, whether in craft projects, exercise classes, sporting events, or going out to dinners, parties, or movies with friends. Even watching TV is active for them because they get so involved with the characters. They enjoy card and board games as well as others in which activity and being with others are the appealing aspects. Often they are the instigators of fun pranks—April Fools' Day may be their special day.

ESFP reading tastes run toward what is useful or historical accounts about what happened, which they can use to make predictions for the future. They are more likely to read short things, such as newspaper and magazine articles, than long books. Whatever the case, they like to discuss their readings with others. Their minds randomly bounce new thoughts around, similar to the action of a cue ball around a billiard table.

ESFPs are fun to be with; they find enjoyment in most situations. Being out and about is more comfortable to them than sitting still with long periods of quiet. Because they are practical, realistic observers of what is, they appreciate the current situation and find fun in the moment. A posted sign in a parking lot that says "No Stopping" is likely to send them into gales of laughter as they imagine continually driving their car around in the lot in order to abide by the instruction.

Their friends are very important to them, and they are likely to let them know how much they care through small mementos, special poems, or cards. They regularly "reach out and touch someone." One ESFP puts a one-liner "quote of the week" on her office bulletin board. The quotations are usually clever comments that sum up life in the office for the previous week. Surprise parties—both giving and receiving them—appeal to ESFPs since they require flexibility, spontaneity, and just plain fun.

LOVING

For the ESFP, love means enjoyment of one another. ESFPs want to share values with the loved one. The way people are treated is usually one value they care about. They may move in and out of relationships quickly when the situation feels uncomfortable. They are not likely to take many interpersonal risks since they fear rejection themselves. They are warm and become more generous and outgoing in the face of approval. They can become quite hampered by disapproval.

An ESFP was very much in love with her partner. In her effusive, outgoing, generous style, she "flooded" her partner with verbal signs of affection and many gifts. They participated together in many social occasions. Her partner initially enjoyed being the center of this whirlwind of attention, but as it continued on, it took its toll. Sometimes ESFPs can overwhelm their partners with their outward display of love. One ESFP learned with time that her effusive gift giving was perceived by her mate as an obligation for him to match her style. It had never occurred to the ESFP that her husband felt challenged to keep up with her. She simply enjoyed giving.

Even when a relationship ends, ESFPs tend to be very respectful of the former partner. They do not want to call undue attention to the breakup and thus move on rather quickly, surrounding themselves with their valued friends.

LOSING OUT

Each type has the potential to overuse or abuse its preferences. This is likely to happen when individuals are under great stress or pressure. At these times, they may act in ways that are unlike their usual style. The following paragraphs describe some of the ways ESFPs may lose out, in addition to some strategies that they can use to get back on track.

One way ESFPs lose out is to spend too much time socializing and not enough time on the task at hand. They may talk on the telephone with their friends rather than concentrating on their work. One ESFP was both a successful business executive and a sailor. He enjoyed entertaining his clients, particularly taking them sailing. He purchased several boats, sailed regularly, and watched major races on cable television, even though it meant staying up until all hours watching races from halfway around the world. Eventually, his staff started to resent all the time and money he was spending on entertaining clients and sailing. They thought he was neglecting his work, and indeed he was. As a strategy, ESFPs may need to look at the wider picture, which includes more than good times, and to prioritize what is important and what needs to be done. Prioritizing can be stressful to ESFPs. They tend to take the first thing that comes along as most important, often delaying the completion of another project, although there is always good intention to do it all. That life can be enjoyed, even when it is not fun all the time, is an important concept for ESFPs to learn.

Another way ESFPs may lose out is when they are too much in the moment and move from one thing to the next without finishing what they have started. Developing planning skills, working on time management, and increasing their stick-to-itiveness helps them with this potential liability.

A third way ESFPs lose out is when they overemphasize subjective, personal data, look only on the good side of things, and fail to reflect and take note of the logical facts. In love relationships, for example, they want the moment to go on forever, when in reality it cannot. They need to build a firmer foundation beyond what is gained from their direct personal experience, paying attention, for example, to what can be learned from theories or books. They need to understand the pieces so that the whole can be seen. Then they are able to take the concept and move it into a practical application. Finally, consulting with others to see the implications of their current actions may help the ESFP.

A final way ESFPs may lose out has to do with being so action oriented and busy that they do not plan ahead. One ESFP was aware she would lose her job as a sales representative sometime within the next six months when her company was due to go out of business. Rather than beginning to plan ahead to start her job search, she simply waited. When she actually was laid off, she was at a loss for where to begin. She did not assertively seek assistance from others. She began to send her resume all over the state, without targeting what she wanted in her next job. This might have been avoided if she had planned ahead and asked others for help.

When ESFPs are back on track, they are using their strengths of noticing and enjoying what is, being realistic, and spontaneously adapting to help others. They can be tireless in the pursuit of fun.

IN A NUTSHELL

Hallmarks:[2]

> Enthusiastic
> Adaptable
> Playful
> Friendly
> Vivacious
> Sociable
> Talkative
> Cooperative

Easygoing
Tolerant
Outgoing
Pleasant

Acronym:[3]

Extra Special Friendly Person

Chapter Twelve

ESFJ

ESFJs Chose the Following Preferences:

Extraversion . . . . ENERGIZING . . . . Introversion
Sensing . . . . ATTENDING . . . . iNtuition
Thinking . . . . DECIDING . . . . **Feeling**
Judgment . . . . LIVING . . . . Perception

In general, ESFJs are helpful people who place a high value on harmony. Paying close attention to people's needs and wants, they work well with others to complete tasks in a timely and accurate way. ESFJs follow through on their commitments. They like closure and prefer structured, organized situations in which warmth and compassion are shown. They contribute to others by anticipating their day-to-day concerns and handling them with warmth and efficiency. ESFJs are at their best in organizing people to get a job done.

LIVING

ESFJ children want life to be uncomplicated, secure, harmonious, and structured. They are usually responsible, reliable, and cooperative. They thrive in situations in which there is consistency and personal attention. They enjoy the acceptance of others and will work hard to gain that acceptance. ESFJ children are concerned about doing the right things and pleasing their elders.

ESFJs follow the rules and tend to accept them as fair and reasonable. They admire people and teachers who are warm, friendly, and concerned. A nine-year-old ESFJ was mortified when his classmates broke a school rule by writing their names and his in chalk on their red brick schoolhouse. When his teacher continued to believe that he had written his own name on the walls, even though he said that he had not, he was very embarrassed and felt betrayed. To not be believed by someone he liked and admired was especially hard for him because it upset his belief that when one is well behaved and tells the truth, one will be rewarded. Sometimes when the rules or their enforcement are unreasonable, ESFJs may have trouble setting limits and not feeling guilty or betrayed by the system.

ESFJs are concerned about the feelings of others and like to help out when possible. An eleven-year-old ESFJ with a treasured doll collection watched a neighbor's house burn. She knew everything was lost in the fire, including the children's toys. In her compassion, she gave every one of her beautiful dolls to the two little neighbor girls. It didn't occur to her that this was a great sacrifice; it was just her way of doing something to help in a tragic situation.

ESFJs begin early to assume responsibility for the welfare of others. They believe it is necessary to give as well as to receive and will often volunteer their time and talents in service organizations such as the YWCA and hospital candy striper groups.

ESFJs radiate warmth and fellowship, and generally fit in well with their classmates. They value the traditional things that teenagers do and may be involved in various clubs and teams. Their friends often turn to them because of their "listening ear" and helpful nature. One ESFJ described herself as the peacemaker in her circle of friends. Whenever they had problems, they came to her. She was willing to listen, offer suggestions, and help smooth things over with the rest of the group.

As young adults, ESFJs focus on their relationships and values, which generally have to do with helping others and being with compatible people. They seem to have less difficulty than some other types in making friends and accepting their roles in life.

People play a significant part in every aspect of their lives. If friends decide on a particular college, for example, ESFJs may revise their own college plans in order to be with their friends.

Often the lives of ESFJs follow a traditional pattern. An ESFJ woman went to secretarial school because she knew that, with those skills, she would be able to find employment through which she could help others. In pursuing her studies, she met a young accountant, and they decided to marry. She continued to work and help her husband finish his degree. When his degree was completed and they had saved enough money, they bought a house and started a family. Until her children were of school age, she quit her work and assumed part-time employment. She felt a strong responsibility to personally meet her children's needs. While she was at home with her children, she was very involved in school, scouting, community, and church activities. ESFJs make their family responsibilities their utmost goal. They like tradition and stability and generally choose to do what is expected of them by others and society.

In adult life, ESFJs take their parent, spouse, employee, or community volunteer roles seriously and are committed to them. They are sensitive barometers to the needs of those around them, sometimes more attuned to others' needs than their own. They gain the respect of others because of their helpfulness, pleasantness, and ability to get things done. They carry out their commitments and are often in charge of events. With their high values for relationships, stability, and loyalty, they may have long tenure in their places of work. ESFJs may misread business relationships as friendships and be disappointed when changes occur and personal contacts are not maintained.

Mature ESFJs often structure both their work and personal lives so that they can meet the needs of others. One ESFJ wanted to teach her children the importance of giving to others. She helped them bake and attractively wrap several kinds of holiday cookies. The ESFJ, along with her children, delivered cookies to their immediate neighborhood. They did this year in and year out, and their neighborhood looked forward to the cookie delivery. The ESFJ felt good that she had started her children in such a beloved neighborhood tradition.

For ESFJs, retirement means continuing to nurture and maintain the relationships that are most important to them. They keep their lives full of activities with people. ESFJs are recognized for doing nice, thoughtful things for others, such as sending flowers and notes, and making follow-up telephone calls. They are likely to schedule regular lunches and leisure activities with their former colleagues from work. If they have grandchildren, they will fill their time by offering to babysit, often at a moment's notice, or by helping in any way that they can. One ESFJ particularly enjoyed going to garage sales. He continually brought back for his grandchildren toys that could not be found in stores. He would take great delight in finding antique toys at these sales. Another ESFJ had a regular bridge group that she attended faithfully. Her life was very full with her relationships with others. When she traveled, she became the social chairperson of the group, seeking out others and including them in the activities. Whatever she could do to make the trips more pleasant, she would do. It made her feel good that others appreciated her efforts.

LEARNING

ESFJs learn best in structured situations where they know what they can expect. They like to schedule their learning projects so that they can plan ahead to complete their lessons. They become uncomfortable with continuous interruptions and changes when they are trying to finish what they have started. Even more importantly, however, they want to like the person who teaches them. The teacher-student relationship is helpful to them in doing their best. When there is disharmony in the classroom, it interrupts their learning process. One ESFJ college student, when faced with choosing classes, would attend several the first week and attempt to find congenial professors. If she did not react positively to a professor, she would not select that class but would search until she found a professor that she liked. She decided on her major in the same manner, choosing a department that was academically rigorous but friendly.

Because ESFJs want to please others and themselves, they will participate willingly in school assignments and tasks. They place a high value on following through. When their work is criticized, even constructively, ESFJs may feel demoralized until they get it right and the teacher acknowledges this. Because they tend to personalize the feedback of their teachers, it is important for ESFJs to know teachers' expectations so that they can work to meet them.

Learning tends to be a personal experience for ESFJs. This attitude, combined with their ability to follow through and meet deadlines, results in a conscientious and effective student. ESFJs often enjoy studies about people and their well-being, and are usually less interested in theoretical and abstract subject matters. They need to thoroughly understand the practical applications of the subjects they study. The like to look at how pieces of information can be put together in a step-by-step manner. This process of seeing how the facts fit in an overall picture may take time and may cause some ESFJs to feel that they are learning more slowly than others.

ESFJs would rather directly experience a given topic or subject before they read about it. They like active learning activities such as field trips, experiments, group projects, and activities that get them personally involved with others. Because they value their friendships, ESFJs may neglect their studies in favor of pursuing these relationships. One ESFJ had to move off campus after his first semester as a freshman because he was so distracted by visiting with all the interesting people he met in his dorm.

LABORING

At work, ESFJs contribute their ability to cooperate with others and to complete tasks in a timely and accurate way. They respect rules and authority, and handle daily operations efficiently. They tend to be well informed and up-to-date on organizational actions that matter to people. ESFJs do what they can to make sure that personal relationships are running smoothly. Because they pay close attention to people's needs and wants, they are often involved in work activities that meet people's practical, day-to-day desires.

Work Setting

ESFJs prefer a work setting that contains conscientious, cooperative, values-oriented people who work at helping others. They want to be close to the action, working most effectively in settings that are friendly, sensitive to human needs, personal, and appreciative. ESFJs may not fit in well with departments that are highly bottom-line or production oriented. They tend to operate on actual facts and realities, liking things to be organized. Where possible, they make their workspace efficient, yet warm in tone.

Organizing Style

ESFJs want answers to questions such as: who, what, when, and where. They place a special emphasis on "who." They want information and structure because it enables them to quickly help others. They are often models of organization, with a "place for everything and everything in its place." Some ESFJs like the role of organizational "historian" because they remember facts as they relate to people. ESFJs enjoy providing useful data to those who need it. After being told that someone has lost some piece of information, ESFJs will generally be able to locate it.

ESFJs plan with the needs of others in mind. They are goal oriented and enjoy getting the job done. Their responsiveness, thoroughness, and reliability can be counted on. Even when they lack technical knowledge, this is easily forgiven by others because the ESFJ is so responsive and provides assistance in the depth that others may not offer. ESFJs prefer that expectations are made clear to them. When the priorities are not straight or are continually changing, ESFJs may feel uncomfortable until there are clear directions as to what they are required to do next.

An ESFJ office manager was particularly proud of the service-oriented, efficient office that she ran. She knew that freeing her boss from daily office matters gave him more time for sales calls. When he prepared to call on potential customers, the ESFJ provided him with background information and copies of previous proposals to similar customers. The telephones were answered promptly and courteously, and all information requests were handled in a personal and thorough fashion. Day-to-day operations such as typing and bookkeeping were delegated to the staff according to a master plan and schedule. Customer billing went out on time, and problems were managed in a firm, yet friendly fashion. Everything in the office was well organized; however, the office did not appear rigid because of the ESFJ's personable workstyle.

Occupations

To perform well at work, individuals may need to use all of the eight preferences at the appropriate time and when required by the situation. Knowing this, people tend to select occupations that allow them to use the preferences that are most natural to them.

ESFJs prefer occupations that allow them to provide direct and personal, yet practical, help to others. Occupations that call for organization and goal direction appeal to them. They are especially careful not to waste time or resources; to do so would go against their nature.

While ESFJs can and do enter all occupations, some are more appealing to them than others. According to available research,[1] some occupations (in alphabetical order) seem to be especially attractive to ESFJs: childcare worker, dental assistant, elementary school teacher, home economist, nurse, office manager, radiological technologist, receptionist and secretary, religious educator, speech pathologist, and other occupations that allow ESFJs to help others and serve their values directly. These occupations are not meant to be an exhaustive list but serve to illustrate some areas that an ESFJ might enjoy. If your specific occupation or one that you are interested in is not listed here, think instead of its general characteristics and ask yourself how those fit with your type.

LEADING

The ESFJ leadership style is one of leading through attention to personal values and the needs and wants of others. When a situation requires someone to take charge and no one does, the ESFJ will often volunteer. In taking charge, ESFJs will work to gain the goodwill and cooperation of others. ESFJs keep their people well informed and set a personal example of hard work and follow-through to uphold their own and their organization's commitments. They expect others to work as hard as they do. When others do not meet their standards, they often feel disappointed and coach them until things are made right; then all is forgiven. Sometimes ESFJs may hesitate to act as quickly as needed with performance issues, out of their concern to keep the relationship harmonious.

When ESFJs say, "I will try to do it," they really are saying, "I will do it." Organizational rules and regulations, when they are humanely derived and applied, are thought to be helpful in getting the job done.

ESFJs focus on the relationships, sometimes at the expense of the tasks. They usually appear to others as friendly, concerned, and warm. Often they are aware of what is happening between people and how that interaction may affect a particular situation.

An ESFJ was in charge of hiring for a significant new position in his team-oriented organization. He organized the selection process very carefully by personally writing standard interview questions, coordinating the interview schedule, and setting up a staff meeting for the final selection. This plan allowed for each staff person to work the process independently so as to not interfere with each other's opinions of the candidates. When all the candidates had been interviewed, the staff met together. The ESFJ encouraged all of the interviewers to share their true feelings about each candidate and to support those feelings with data. The meeting was long but pleasant, since the ESFJ kept things moving in a cordial way. The staff came to a joint conclusion on whom to hire and, furthermore, felt very good about their participation in the hiring process.

LEISURE

ESFJs believe that leisure is to be earned after work is completed. They prefer leisure activities that include others; however, many ESFJs find that after meeting others' needs throughout the week, they may seek to keep an evening open for themselves, for their own relaxation and recovery. Once they have met their needs for self-renewal, they seek out others with whom they enjoy discussing books and movies or exploring the values-oriented aspects of life, such as family and community needs.

ESFJs like leisure activities that are regularly scheduled. They plan social events for themselves and others. One ESFJ planned Tuesday night as movie night for herself and two other friends. While they kept Tuesday night scheduled, they generally did not plan which movie they would see. They saw the night together primarily as a time for fun and a time to be together and talk.

Social events for ESFJs include meals with their friends and colleagues from both home and work life. They may be in charge of the traditional family get-togethers such as Thanksgiving dinner. One ESFJ said she was the person in her family who was always responsible for buying birthday and anniversary gifts for her parents, as well as Mother's Day and Father's Day gifts. The purchase of the gifts included making the decisions as to what to get, collecting the money from her sisters, buying the gift and the card, and signing all the names on the card.

ESFJs prefer not to do things alone. They use their leisure time to keep in contact with others, sometimes even planning which friends to call on which evenings. Their leisure may also include community volunteerism.

LOVING

For the ESFJ, love means warmth and commitment. When ESFJs first fall in love, they show this warmth and concern for their partner in many tangible ways. They will send cards, notes, flowers, special gifts, and other mementos of their affection. If the partner casually mentions a desire for a specific thing, such as a sweater with a sailboat design, the ESFJ will try to find just that thing. Once committed in a relationship, ESFJs tend to stay with it even when there is inconvenience to them, and perhaps longer than may be healthy. They are able to bring out the best in their partners, even though it may mean putting their own needs second.

Because ESFJs are caring individuals, they expect to give and receive in their relationships. Because others may not be as thoughtful as the ESFJ, it is a possible source of disappointment to them if they expect the same awareness and caring on the part of the partner. Being practical and realistic, they may not always like effusive shows of affection and prefer moderation instead. ESFJs may be more loyal to the relationship or to the institution of marriage than to the person. ESFJs may take the end of the relationship as a personal failure.

ESFJs, when scorned, hurt all over and may need to take time to get over the relationship before pursuing a new one. They may too easily and incorrectly blame themselves for the unfavorable outcome and recall instances when perhaps they were not as giving as they might have been. However, ESFJs' standards for giving in a relationship are likely to be above those of some other types. At their worst when scorned, ESFJs can become spiteful and critical of the partner. Because ESFJs are keenly sensitive to others and are tuned in to emotional needs, they really know how to hurt a person in the rare instances when they choose to do so.

LOSING OUT

Each type has the potential to overuse or abuse its preferences. This is likely to happen when individuals are under great stress or pressure. At these times, they may act in ways that are unlike their usual style. The following paragraphs describe some of these experiences, as well as some strategies that ESFJs can use to get back on track.

One way ESFJs lose out is when they engage in too much harmonizing with the intention of smoothing over issues and differences. They tend to avoid conflict and sweep problems under the rug. Attempting to have others work cooperatively when problems actually exist may be less fruitful than actually allowing the conflict to surface. As a strategy, ESFJs need to learn how to manage conflict and appreciate that conflict can help people in relationships to understand each other better.

ESFJs may not always value their own priorities enough; as a result, they may put others' needs ahead of their own. ESFJs need to know that they can say no or negotiate. In many cases, they ought to do so without feeling that they hurt or disappoint others in the process. In fact, by saying no, ESFJs may find that others are challenged to rely on their own resources and may develop new skills. They need to remember that they can ask others to do for themselves.

However, when ESFJs are concerned about pleasing others, they may overlook their own needs. This can lead to taking on too much, both in terms of the tasks and responsibilities that are required. They thereby overload themselves trying to get everything done. One ESFJ was particularly busy at work trying to manage all his responsibilities, while taking care of two elderly parents. He did not have time for his own physical health and became ill himself. He was trying to meet his business responsibilities and the rigorous demands of his parents; as a result, he ended up putting his own health in jeopardy.

Sometimes it is difficult for ESFJs to give and receive corrective feedback. They may not tell others where they fall short thus depriving others of a chance to hear another point of view. Also, ESFJs may not ask for the appreciation and respect that they deserve and do not easily accept praise and nurturing from others. Developing assertiveness may help them. Learning not to be disappointed when others are not as sensitive as they are is important work for ESFJs.

ESFJs may also lose out when they assume they know what is best for others and state those opinions about what others ought to do. This can make them appear bossy and rigid, even emotional and irrational, to other people. When this happens, they may be hard to reason with and may back themselves into a corner and not see a face-saving way out. When they become overly domineering, they may destroy relationships that they have worked hard to build. One ESFJ father had strong ideas about his son's extracurricular activities. He wanted his son to do well in school. This meant, according to the ESFJ father, that his son should not stay out late at night. He set a ten o'clock curfew for his son and was quite rigid in enforcing it. In reality, the ten o'clock curfew was fairly restrictive because many school activities went beyond that time. But because the ESFJ father held to the value of early hours for students, he would not change his mind. Eventually, his son rebelled against the tight control and their relationship was damaged.

In situations like these, ESFJs need to accurately assess the facts—dispassionately and impersonally. They may need to see what a wise, impartial third party might say, listen to what others really need, and look beyond the immediate situation to the logical implications of their actions. ESFJs could think in terms of options, alternatives, and choices that others may find valid and then consider them.

ESFJs may lose out when they become caught up in the daily details and fail to see the overall larger picture. They may get into a rut because they overlook new ways to deal with situations and problems. Being traditionalists, they may need to step back to see if they are focusing on the standard ways and not looking for the novel, unusual, or global approach.

When ESFJs are back on track, they are using their strengths of harmonizing with others, creating warm, close, personal relationships, and meeting their immediate needs and those of others in responsible ways. They can be tireless in giving help to others.

IN A NUTSHELL

Hallmarks:[2]

Conscientious
Loyal
Sociable

Personable
Responsible
Harmonious
Cooperative
Tactful
Thorough
Responsive
Sympathetic
Traditional

Acronym:[3]

Extra Special Friendly Joiner

Chapter Thirteen

INFJ

INFJs Chose the Following Preferences:

Extraversion	ENERGIZING	**Introversion**
Sensing	ATTENDING	**iNtuition**
Thinking	DECIDING	**Feeling**
Judgment	LIVING	Perception

In general, INFJs are future oriented, and direct their insight and inspiration toward the understanding of themselves and thereby human nature. Their work mirrors their integrity, and it needs to reflect their inner ideals. Solitude and an opportunity to concentrate thoroughly on what counts most is important to them. INFJs prefer to quietly exert their influence. They have deeply felt compassion, and they desire harmony with others. INFJs understand the complexities existing within people and among them. They do not call a great deal of attention to themselves, preferring that their contributions speak for them. They are at their best concentrating on their ideas, ideals, and inspirations.

LIVING

INFJ children have two sides. They can be gregarious and very much involved in the world of people, as well as quiet, imaginative, and in their own world. One INFJ child described her favorite summer and how it reflected those two sides. She loved to go to the library and did so every other day, devouring two to three books between each trip. She also very much enjoyed her neighborhood friends and the adventures that they would have together. They collected bones and rocks that they found on a farm at the edge of town and painted them with white shoe polish. They then scattered the bones in her yard and played at being archaeologists on a dig.

INFJ children are gentle and often abhor violence, especially in their childhood games. An INFJ created his own swords, but he would not use them in games against other children because he was frightened by the potential of being too aggressive and of hurting them. It was the creativity involved in making the swords that intrigued him, not the actual use of them.

As teenagers, INFJs look for a small group of people who understand and appreciate them. Without this support, they can feel isolated from others. INFJs who do not find a supportive social group may find the teen years to be somewhat difficult for them because of peer pressure to be "popular" and activity oriented. They are not likely to enjoy large parties, but prefer intimate groups of close and long-standing friends. They may participate and even lead in such things as academic activities, yearbook, and newspaper, because these activities allow them to express outwardly their regard for others and enable them to exercise their creativity.

Many INFJs who have the opportunity gravitate toward higher education, where they often find their niche and "place in the sun." With their intellectual bent, they are led to endeavors that allow them to deal with theory and complexity. Professors often spot their intellectual inclination and encourage it. One INFJ stated, "I was often singled out as the student most likely to care about what my professors were saying." An INFJ engineering student with excellent grades was invited by his professor to be a research assistant. This led the INFJ into a new field, different from what he might have pursued. This new field, solar energy, fit with his ideal that effective heating could be obtained without necessarily depleting the Earth's natural resources. This also fit with his value of conservation, which focused on keeping the world as beautiful a place for future generations as it is today.

INFJs often settle early into a career choice and diligently apply themselves to the career's requirements. This same diligent pattern applies when selecting other important things in their lives, such as where to live, who to marry, and what activities are worthy of their dedication.

INFJs have an internal picture of how they would like their work to contribute to the general good. For example, an INFJ home economics teacher was particularly interested in family living. Her lifelong dream was to have her own day-care business. However, she was also very loyal to her teaching job because there, too, she was making life better for others. When she was laid off from her teaching job, she began to seriously look at her day-care dream. Things quickly fell into place, and she started her business with eight children. In three years time, the business had grown to forty children. She would not increase it further because that would result in a reduction of the personal relationships with parents, children, and staff. Her program was known for its gentle, compassionate, and innovative learning atmosphere and quickly became a model for other programs. Because of her involvement in her teaching, she did not activate her day-care-center dream until she was led into it by being laid off.

INFJs are committed more to their ideas than to any individual organization. One INFJ knew early on that her "mission" was writing. It took her many years to find a subject matter—home health care—that warranted her time and energy. When she did find one, she started her own newsletter relating to it.

If they are in an appropriate career area, INFJs may reap the rewards of their insight and hard work. Because of their future-focus, their people orientation, and their push toward task completion, they may rise to positions of responsibility.

INFJs tend to believe that if their ideas are sound, those ideas will carry them through their lives. As a result, retirement will take care of itself. They may vary in the amount of actual planning they have done for this stage of their lives. INFJs look forward to nurturing family relationships, to grandchildren, and to seeing the foundations that they have made for themselves flourish. They anticipate the time when they can engage in hobbies without interruptions and have peace and quiet for reflection. Retirement also gives them the opportunity to become further involved in interests that they have developed over their lifetimes. For example, INFJs who earlier pursued writing as a hobby will be able to indulge in it. INFJs who raised children can continue to enjoy those relationships, with ample time to devote to them.

LEARNING

INFJs have a strong love of learning, and they tend to do well academically. Their desire to please their teachers and elders, along with their natural inquisitiveness and ability to grasp concepts and relationships, produces a strong student work ethic. Through persistence, diligence, and conscientiousness, they complete their assignments on time. They are likely to enjoy research and will go to great lengths to find answers.

INFJs do well if material is presented to them as a vehicle by which to further their ideals. They particularly enjoy investigating the possibilities and meanings beyond the actual facts and realities. Reading holds a particular fascination for them because it allows them to have quiet reflection time and engages their imagination. They also like the written word (and rely on it more than the spoken word) since it is usually better structured and more coherent, with a ready-made framework.

INFJs write and communicate well because they want to formulate their ideas clearly. They seem almost obsessed in their desire to be clear. They place high regard on their reader and audience. INFJs seek to communicate their ideals to others. When their ideals need to be championed, they speak up in an enthusiastic and impassioned way. They may make a point of bringing their idealism into any and all conversations. Whether appropriate or not, off they go on their crusade.

As students, INFJs prefer learning from teachers whom they both like and admire, and who give them personal attention. INFJs are often "model" students. They are quiet and orderly, reflective and thoughtful, and sincerely want to please their teachers and learn the right thing. They learn best from others but want time to assimilate material by themselves.

INFJs will go beyond what has been presented and often mull material over in their minds. Occasionally they will discuss their ruminations with others in order to learn even more. They particularly like the more conceptual and theoretical classes; therefore, higher education is comfortable to them.

LABORING

INFJs tend to be devoted to what they believe in and seek work where their needs, values, and ideals can be deeply engaged. They move on the wave of their inspirations and are determined to see that their values are worked out in their lives. They will work toward their goals individually and, when needed, will put together a team of other highly dedicated people like themselves. They are personable with others, working with integrity and consistency, and they follow through on their commitments. INFJs, while concentrating on what is important to them, may ignore the political ramifications of their actions. They can be surprised by the necessity of being political and usually resent that aspect of organizational life. Being able to talk honestly and comfortably to people at work is much more important to them than "playing games."

Work Setting

INFJs prefer a quiet and organized work setting that allows them time and space for reflection, yet one in which it is possible to interact freely with others. Their offices may have a personal feel and be filled with mementos or photos involving persons or causes important to them. INFJs like to be around people who are strongly focused on making a difference to overall human well-being. They want opportunities to be creative.

Organizing Style

INFJs orient themselves toward their goals using a personal, values-based framework. They do not "advertise" their values and priorities because they believe in harmony and positive relationships. However, one would do well not to underestimate the amount of perseverance, energy, and time INFJs give to their priorities. What they do, they do with an almost religious intensity.

The INFJ external environment may be only partially organized. For example, INFJs may lose their glasses or misplace their car keys because they do not pay enough attention to organizing mundane, everyday things. Their internal environment, by contrast, is anything but haphazard. Their ideas need to fit into a coherent whole that has the pieces in place. Organization of the internal world takes precedence over organization of the external world. The external world will become organized if it is important to the INFJ's internal vision, if there is room for it, or if important people request it. One INFJ explained, "I feel the urge to dream up a plan, even if it cannot be put into action right then."

An INFJ worked for a research and development unit that had its own separate facility apart from the large organization. The facility was quiet and peaceful. People had space and time to think. The INFJ designed her office to fit her needs and included a couch where she could look out the window, catnap, or daydream. She also had a complete coffee service at her disposal so that she could be hospitable to people who might drop in. Once she had zeroed in on a project to pursue, she would spend hours quietly reflecting on all of its elements. She would seldom commit her ideas to paper. When she did, they were often just a few key words to help remind her of her thoughts. She had elaborate time lines in her mind but shared those with others only when required to do so. When she voiced her plans, they were clear and included the project's impact on the people involved.

Occupations

To perform well at work, individuals may need to use all of the eight preferences at the appropriate time and when required by the situation. Knowing this, people tend to select occupations

that allow them to use the preferences that are most natural to them.

INFJs prefer occupations that focus on the big picture, involve conceptual awareness, and lead to a better understanding of the spiritual, emotional, or future needs of people. They want their work to have impact and meaning and for it to bring them admiration and respect.

While INFJs can and do enter all occupations, some are more appealing to them than others. According to available research,[1] some occupations (in alphabetical order) seem to be especially attractive to INFJs: clergy, education consultant, English teacher, fine arts teacher, librarian, marketeer, psychiatrist, psychologist, scientist, social worker, and other occupations that allow INFJs an opportunity to make their own creative contribution. These occupations are not meant to be an exhaustive list, but serve to illustrate some areas an INFJ might enjoy. If your specific occupation or one that you are interested in is not listed here, think instead of its general characteristics and ask yourself how those fit with your type.

LEADING

INFJs lead through their quiet yet persistent and determined effort toward long-range goals for themselves, others, and their organizations. In working toward their vision, they win cooperation rather than demand it. INFJs work to make their insights real and are able to inspire others with their ideals. They use a low-key, soft, yet intense and determined course of action. When they do not directly lead others, they may still act as facilitators between people. In meetings, they focus on both people and new ideas. INFJs may lead by becoming champions for ideas or causes. After the birth of her own children, one INFJ psychologist became very interested in making the birthing process a psychologically healthy one. She began a very careful study by reading about the physical and psychological aspects of childbirth. She then assisted in home births. Out of her vision for well and happy mothers and children, she developed a series of workshops and support groups on the childbirth process.

When she hired staff to help her, she would give them several different tasks and then stand back for a couple of months to see where they could perform best. She would then make sure their next assignments were in areas where they would do well. She saw her role as one of "organizing the talents" of her people.

This INFJ has become known in the psychology of childbirth and continues to positively influence and affect the lives of others. This leadership resulted from her INFJ strengths: her vision, her intensive and extensive ability to study in depth, and her willingness to pioneer in a new area. Because she cared so much about her ideas, she was able to mobilize herself and others to follow through with action.

LEISURE

Leisure-time pursuits for INFJs are often solitary or involve the company of others who are particularly important to them. Sitting around with dear friends discussing feelings can be very special to INFJs. One INFJ who enjoyed building and carpentry work found it to be even more pleasant when he shared his work with the quiet company of an older, retired carpenter. They did separate, yet parallel, carpentry tasks, speaking to each other only as necessary. These times were particularly pleasurable because the INFJ was completing his dream home with someone who also appreciated and shared in his vision. Their feelings were deep, and their respective ideas were so well aligned that there was no need to talk out loud about them.

INFJs are likely to have friends of long standing rather than make many new acquaintances. They may meet with their friends fairly consistently to share what is happening in their lives. It is sometimes difficult for others to break into this circle. These deep friendships are important, even though INFJs may not share much directly about themselves. An INFJ woman saw a friend from college at their customary get-together to bake Christmas cookies. This occasion was special to them because they easily resumed their relationship. Other than their periodic telephone conversations, neither of them felt obligated to see each other on a more frequent basis to continue their friendship.

They knew they would always reserve that time for each other and would be able to readily share their feelings about their lives, their children, and their work.

LOVING

For INFJs, "still waters run deep." They tend to become attracted to someone special and prefer this one deep relationship over many superficial ones. The depth of involvement and feeling that the INFJ has toward loved ones is only partially communicated outward. At times, when alone, the INFJs become truly in touch with the depth of the love they have for their partner. They may not openly demonstrate or even verbalize their intense feelings. INFJs often have an ideal standard of what love is. They hold to their ideal and are disappointed when, inevitably, their relationship and/or their mate reveals flaws.

INFJs enjoy sharing activities like a regular "date," revisiting the place where they first met their mates, or doing other symbolic things that help to continue and confirm the existence of the bond that they feel for their partner.

INFJs want to give love and to be loved. They enter into relationships just to be cared for, even when the person is not right for them and they suspect it. However, when they meet that special person, they are quick to get into the relationship and make it a serious one. They will end their other relationships in order to pursue their loved one. They become very focused, intense, and direct in that pursuit.

INFJs, when scorned, take it personally and retreat inward. They may obsess about the relationship and their role in its failure. One INFJ explained, "People can do the most outrageous things, yet I blame myself for triggering their behavior or not recognizing it. I see myself as responsible for relationships. Other people can dismiss them—I'm not able to." INFJs may blame themselves and experience a period of mourning. If they do not marshall their resources, externalize their feelings, and take risks to move on, they may experience a long period of self-examination.

LOSING OUT

Each type has the potential to overuse or abuse its preferences. This is likely to happen when individuals are under great stress or pressure. At these times, they may act in ways that are unlike their usual style. The following paragraphs describe some of the ways INFJs may lose out, in addition to some strategies that they can use to get back on track.

One way INFJs lose out is when they become blinded by the idealism of their visions or focus only on their ideas. They hang on to those ideals, ignoring reality when it contradicts their views. Because of their persistent and single-minded belief in their vision, they stay with a commitment beyond what the facts would prudently seem to dictate and may not know when to cut their losses and move on. They may need to relax, be more open to the present realities, and stop fruitlessly searching for the ideal.

Another way INFJs lose out is when they do not behave assertively and feel reluctant to intrude on others with their ideas. As a result, they tend to keep many important things to themselves and find that they or their ideas are overlooked or underestimated. Others who might have been able to help them achieve their vision cannot because they were not included in the INFJs' thinking processes.

As a strategy, INFJs may need to develop assertiveness and political savvy to champion their ideals. They may need to involve others in the development and implementation of their visions.

INFJs may also lose out by not being forthright with criticism of others. They seem to believe, "If you can't say something nice, don't say anything at all." They hold their criticism inside longer than they should. When it becomes too much, they can blow up. As a strategy, INFJs need to realize that feedback can lead to self-correction. In presenting feedback to others, they can rely on their customary gentle style of focusing on the overall concept behind the behavior and encourage others to see for themselves where they fall short.

Another way INFJs lose out is when they zero in on unimportant or incorrect details or focus on a fact that is not relevant to the situation at hand. They may obsess, for example, over a hurtful comment or minor detail. One INFJ, in planning a large gathering for her close friends, wanted to have her home just perfect. She began cleaning obsessively. She even went so far as to refold everything in her linen closet. She knew full well that none of her friends would look in this closet and, even if they did, they would not think less of her. She was wasting her time obsessing on the mundane details rather than relaxing in preparation for the party. INFJs need to learn which details and routines are important and which are not.

When INFJs are back on track, they are using their visionary strengths, their creativity for finding new outlets for human expression, and their commitment to their values. They can be tireless in the pursuit of a vision for people.

IN A NUTSHELL

Hallmarks:[2]

Committed
Compassionate
Intense
Determined
Sensitive
Holistic
Loyal
Creative
Deep
Conceptual
Reserved
Idealistic

Acronym:[3]

Inner Nuances Foster Journeys

Chapter Fourteen

INFP

INFPs Chose the Following Preferences:

Extraversion . . . . ENERGIZING . . . . **Introversion**
Sensing . . . . ATTENDING . . . . **iNtuition**
Thinking . . . . DECIDING . . . . **Feeling**
Judgment . . . . LIVING . . . . **Perception**

In general, INFPs focus deeply on their values, and they devote their lives to pursuing the ideal. They often draw people together around a common purpose and work to find a place for each person within the group. They are creative, and they seek new ideas and possibilities. They quietly push for what is important to them, and they rarely give up. While they have a gentleness about them and a delightful sense of humor, they may be somewhat difficult to get to know and may be overlooked by others. They are at their best making their world more in line with their internal vision of perfection.

LIVING

INFP children often create their own fantasy world and live very much within it. They may daydream about what is important to them, and sometimes others wonder if they are in touch with reality. They often get lost in their thoughts and books, and may develop a special ability in communicating, such as writing.

They are somewhat reserved, especially in new situations, and they may not even like telling others their names, although they feel special when someone else unexpectedly remembers theirs. As a kindergartner, an INFP was called by his father's name, Don. His real name was John, but rather than speak up and possibly offend his teacher, he decided Don was close enough. It was two months into the school year, at the first parent-teacher conference, that the mistake was uncovered.

INFPs decide early on what is important to them, what is of value. They tend to rely on themselves for direction and are reticent to ask others for help. They would rather do things themselves, to make sure they are done properly. INFPs have found this to be both a strength and a curse. Depending only on themselves and being careful not to show mistakes to others is important. One INFP child was curious about the meaning of the D.C. in Washington, D.C. She was sure that everyone else knew and that she should know also. Having grown up in Brooklyn, she pondered a while and then decided D.C. meant "Da Capitol."

As teens, INFPs may have a bit of a rebellious streak. They may argue with those who hold different values than they do. They are also likely to have a small, close set of friends with whom they share good times. In the comfort of those close relationships, they can relax and are often quite entertaining, since they see the world in a different and special way. Their sense of humor is readily apparent. However, unless an INFP finds an appreciation for his or her uniqueness and personal values, he or she may feel like an odd person out. One INFP found a niche for himself in a group of "wild" teens. Their activities, such as soaping windows, were uncomfortable for him since they were not part of his value system. He discovered that, through being the "lookout," he could help his friends without being directly destructive to others.

When they set their minds on things, INFPs are not likely to give up easily, yet because of their outward gentleness, they do not show their determination. They may not take a direct path, but somehow they reach their dreams. One seventeen-year-old INFP has his heart set on buying a 1931 Model A Ford as his first car. (His choice already mirrored his unusual tastes, since his peers were more interested in Ford Mustangs.) After searching, he found a Model A for $650. His more practical father thought that the price of the car was too high—$600 was the top price he should pay. Without his father's knowledge, the INFP called the owner, suggesting that he pay him $50 in advance and the rest of the money upon purchase. The INFP took his father to meet with the owner, $600 was exchanged for the car, and all were pleased. The INFP was delighted because he got the car without creating a direct family ruckus. INFPs try to get what they want but will strive to have others feel good about it.

As young adults, INFPs may have some difficulty finding the ideal career and the ideal mate, in part because of that very word "ideal." They have a vision in mind of what they want, yet reality may not follow suit. They may make several starts and stops in their career until they find a comfortable place for themselves. One INFP drifted from one job to another; at the age of 33, she was teaching skiing. Her students kept marveling about her teaching skills, a profession she had never even considered. She went back to college for a teaching degree and then to graduate school, specializing in small group work. Eventually she became interested in the concept of quality circles because they helped people feel good about themselves and their work. (Quality circles are made up of people at all levels in an organization; their purpose is to improve the product and work environment.) She became an expert in this field, training leaders and championing employee-involvement programs.

INFPs have a need for perfection in connection with their personal values. They become frustrated with those who dwell on trivialities. One American INFP living in England tells this story about herself. "One night while I was dining with a friend in a restaurant, my friend looked across the table at me and, with mild irritation said, 'Oh, I see you haven't learned to eat the British way yet.' I had not even been aware that there was a 'British way to eat.' Apparently, when cutting meat, the British do not switch their fork to their left hand and their knife to their right hand; instead, they always hold the fork in their left hand, with the knife in the right. I was annoyed with my friend for suggesting that I change my behavior in observance of what I perceived to be an utter triviality."

INFPs need a purpose beyond the paycheck. They become burned out easily if their job does not fit their value system; they may not feel good enough about what they have achieved and, as a result, may undervalue themselves and their contributions.

In retirement, INFPs need to look back and feel that they have led a worthwhile life that has made a difference. They want time for a variety of activities, including travel. They may also be very attached to their family and enjoy special visits with them. One INFP grandmother writes stories about her grandchildren's visits to her, takes pictures of them, and makes personal booklets for each child. Her stories are exciting and dramatic bedtime entertainment for her grandchildren.

LEARNING

INFPs learn best in flexible situations where they know the teacher takes a personal interest in them. They like to be able to interact with their peers, but not too much so. They want to feel free to dig into subjects that are of interest to them. Having both flexibility and creativity rewarded is encouraging to them. While they may not enjoy deadlines, if they value the assignment, they will meet those deadlines. Deadlines may force INFPs to decide that their work is "good enough" to turn in.

Subjects that hold a great deal of interest for them are learned readily. They will often do extra work in their attempt to learn as much as possible about something of interest. An INFP graduate student got As in all the courses that were the most difficult for others because she was interested in them. She received Bs in what were the snap courses for others, because they had less meaning for her and were therefore not so challenging.

INFPs usually read assignments carefully and then work their creativity into the given framework of the assignment. Thus it may appear that they did not pay careful attention to the details of the assignment in their reinterpretation. It is best if they have teachers who appreciate their unique approach and who do not hold them to the letter of the law.

LABORING

At work, INFPs contribute their creativity, their value system, and their ability to work with others. They are able to see the larger picture and how specific programs fit in. They do not dwell on the trivialities or the details. Their job must be fun, although not raucous, and it must be meaningful to them. They need a strong purpose in their work. They want to be recognized and valued, without undue attention given to them. They may become embarrassed when made the center of attention. As a result, they may undersell their strengths in order to avoid being singled out and made to feel conspicuous. They would rather have their worth be noticed gradually over time.

Work Setting

INFPs like to work with cooperative people committed to the same values that they are. They can become bothered when they see others working at cross purposes, especially when conflict is overt. They do not like competition or bureaucracy. They see what needs to happen in a broad sense and dislike dealing with red tape. They want some privacy and keep a lot to themselves, especially personal information. Calm and quiet appeal to them, as does time and space for reflection. People usually like working with INFPs even though they may not know them well.

Organizing Style

When tasks at hand are important and best done in an organized way, INFPs strive to do so. At times, others are likely to call them hopelessly disorganized. They may lose their keys or forget appointments. Their errand running has no apparent sense of order. It seems as if they go here and there "as the spirit moves them." The INFP teacher may lay the chalk down one place in the classroom and her notes in another, "losing" both while all the time delivering a wonderfully intriguing lecture.

When they do minor household repairs, for example, INFPs may continually lose important tools. If they start sorting through their tools, they are likely to discover five hammers, when one would have been sufficient. However, it is likely that the search for the hammer also turns up other things. Flexibility and adaptability are characteristics of INFPs. In their quests, they may discover many new things to do or creative twists for solving problems.

INFPs may keep objects because of sentimental attachment and have difficulty parting with them. As a result, their attics may be full of things that are intriguing to them but that others may call junk. Because aesthetics may be important to them, they may move their files and bookshelves out of sight.

Practicality is not a driving force for INFPs. Things that traditionally belong together may not be placed together because the INFP does not see it as necessary. One INFP kept the kitchen garbage pail on the back porch rather than by the sink, a more practical location.

INFPs may have trouble finishing what they start because of their perfectionistic nature. When they do finish a project, they may not consider it done "for good." Projects can always be improved upon, revised, and reworked, and therefore INFPs find it hard to bring tasks to closure. Because they are able to visualize the finished product long before it is done, the actual completion is of less importance.

Occupations

To perform well at work, individuals may need to use all of the eight preferences at the appropriate time and when required by the situation. Knowing this, people tend to select occupations that allow them to use the preferences that are most natural to them.

INFPs prefer occupations in which they can be involved in making the world better. Having their heart in their work is important to them. These occupations also allow for an element of creativity and flexibility.

While INFPs can and do enter all occupations, some are more appealing to them than others. According to available research,[1] some occupations (in alphabetical order) seem to be especially attractive to INFPs: counselor, editor, education consultant, English teacher, fine arts teacher, journalist, psychologist, religious educator, social scientist, social worker, teacher, writer, and other occupations that engage their values. These occupations are not meant to be an exhaustive list but serve to illustrate some areas that an INFP might enjoy. If your specific occupation or one that you are interested in is not listed here, think instead of its general characteristics and ask yourself how those fit with your type.

LEADING

The INFP leadership style is subtle, gentle, indirect, and inclusive of others. INFPs do not confront people head-on, but rather work with them and through them to get the job done. Their style is not an aggressive one but is highly persistent; only reluctantly do INFPs assume leadership roles.

They lead with their values in mind, and these guide them. They prefer not to take a hands-on approach with others but to allow them to achieve in independent ways. They are facilitative rather than directive. They encourage others by appreciation and praise. Critiquing others does not come easily to them. One INFP was continually disturbed by her neighbor constantly disciplining his dog in an extremely loud voice. One day she gently asked her neighbor, "Is your dog deaf?" thereby making her criticism in a subtle, indirect manner.

As leaders, INFPs may not confront situations directly, in part because they do not like conflict. Whenever possible, they would rather wait for a situation to work itself out, since they trust that people will work things through. Careful timing is very important in their style. They are often able to wait out refusals and objections from others, and eventually to find a way to get done what they really want. They do not like following all the rules and regulations, but they are not overtly rebellious. They seek to get things done in their own style.

An INFP in a community service occupation listened intently through many meetings to what others were saying. When it came time for her to assume a leadership role, she chose her words carefully, brought in much-needed humor, and made her points conceptually. Since she had not dominated earlier, others were quite willing to listen to her, to see her approach as a fresh new one, and to accept her leadership.

LEISURE

Leisure activities are very important to INFPs, but at times it is difficult for them to separate work from play. The INFP architect may continue drawing in his free time, helping out his family, friends, and neighbors. The INFP psychologist joins professional organizations in which she can continue her specialty.

When a new leisure pursuit is found, INFPs typically do a great deal of research. They may read many books and make several phone calls to dig for information. One INFP felt that learning more about his Scottish heritage would be interesting. This led him to a decision to buy the family tartan. Twenty-five books and five phone calls later in his quest for information about kilts, he agonized over the details. To this INFP, having exactly the right kilt length, weight of cloth, and accessories, was exceedingly important. He was developing an image, and he wanted to make sure it was perfect. Once the interest in Scottish heritage was well under way, he moved on to other pursuits. However, like most INFPs, his interest was not abandoned but rather was slowly built upon. Energies are more involved with new activities, but the old ones are never forgotten. This is unlike some other types, who will completely change directions.

Many of the INFPs' leisure activities are done alone—reading, listening to music, and gardening are some activities likely to appeal to them. Reflection time and the opportunity to make sure things are right are important. INFPs often enjoy leisure pursuits with loved ones as well. When they want to be sociable, they can be exceedingly charming and outgoing. Their flexibility, gentleness, and sense of humor can make them quite popular in social situations.

LOVING

For the INFP, love is a very deep commitment, and one that is not easily attained. They have ideals, and therefore reality may be carefully scrutinized. One INFP said, "I waited until I was thirty before marrying and even then had misgivings about not having found perfection. I later discovered that I can contribute to that ideal, that I don't have to wait for it."

With their ideal firmly envisioned, the first date with that special person is carefully planned and prepared for, and often every aesthetic thing is taken care of. The flowers are in place, the right wine is ordered, and the proper meal is prepared. One INFP, when he was ready to propose, decided he wanted to do so in a place that would be around for many years in the future. He chose a prominent building and found an intimate corner in its restaurant. In this way, he could be assured that he would have privacy, yet that the memories would always be there, because the building would be there. He purchased a special porcelain box in which to place the engagement ring, so that this too would have special meaning; porcelain boxes could be given to his partner on special occasions as a tradition. The ring was no ordinary ring, but one that had been in the family for several generations. All the details and the proper image were in place, not because the details were important but because personal investment in the pursuit of the ideal was the key. (Imagine this INFP's consternation when his intended did not want to go out to dinner that evening.)

INFPs may have difficulty sharing their feelings about others. They keep so many of those feelings inside that they may forget to tell their partner how much they love and appreciate them. They also need reminders of their partner's love.

When things go wrong in a relationship, the INFP takes it to heart but does not readily discuss it with others. They may not be willing to communicate to let others know how they are feeling. When scorned, they are very hurt and may overreact in an almost maudlin way.

LOSING OUT

Each type has the potential to overuse or abuse its preferences. This is likely to happen when individuals are under great stress or pressure. At these times, they may act in ways that are unlike their usual style. The following paragraphs describe some of the ways INFPs may lose out, in addition to some strategies that they can use to get back on track.

One way INFPs may lose out is through focusing on their dreams so strongly that they do not see others' points of view. They do not adjust their vision to the facts and the logic of the situation. They may appear so out of touch that others may describe them as mystical. One INFP was sure she had the perfect system to solve the conflicts of the world. She kept presenting her theory to others, emphasizing how important it was for everyone in the world to get along; but she never offered practical, realistic suggestions for how people could reach that desired state. As a strategy, INFPs may need to "reality check" with others to see if their dreams are useful in actuality and if their plans are workable. They may need to be more action oriented and less reflective.

A second way INFPs may lose out is when they try to please too many people and hesitate to criticize others. They do not say no to others' requests and, as a result, may take on too much. They may inadvertently send a message to people that they are in agreement with them, when in fact they disagree strongly. INFPs need to become aware that some people's needs are actually neglected instead of helped when they attempt to please everyone. INFPs need to develop more tough-mindedness and assertiveness, along with the skills of giving negative feedback. One INFP psychologist found leading assertiveness training workshops for professionals to be good therapy for herself as well.

INFPs may delay completion of projects because they are holding out for perfection. They often spend too much time focusing inward, relying on their own inner resources and thereby delaying action. The author of the Myers-Briggs Type Indicator,™ Isabel Briggs Myers, was an INFP who delayed for more than thirty years publication of her most important work, *Gifts Differing*, because she wanted it to be a "perfect" representation of type theory. As a result, her important message was slow in reaching others. It was only when the ultimate "deadline" came—her impending death from cancer—that she decided it was good enough to publish (but not without a lot of help and persuasion by her son). As a strategy, INFPs need to involve others both for their encouragement and their view of reality. INFPs can commit their ideas to public scrutiny, recognizing that they may not be perfect but that something to start with is better than nothing at all.

A final way INFPs may lose out is when they become overly critical; with everything bothering them, they lash out at others. Everyone around them appears to be irresponsible and incompetent. Concerned that her dinner party be perfect, an INFP may start criticizing her spouse's attire, the cleanliness of the house, the dinner menu, and the way the table is set, even though she had been involved in all of these things. She has lost her ability to look at a situation logically and has let her negative self take over. The criticisms do not come from logic but from some deeply felt and not understood value. She and other INFPs in similar situations may need to step back, relax, and let their natural appreciation come out, not their unnatural critiquing.

When INFPs are back on track, they are using their strengths of valuing individual contributions, dreaming about the future, and genuinely helping others reach their ideals. They can be tireless in the pursuit of their ideals.

IN A NUTSHELL

Hallmarks:[2]

Compassionate
Virtuous
Committed
Creative
Devoted

Reticent
Gentle
Adaptable
Curious
Loyal
Contemplative
Empathetic

Acronym:[3]

I Never **F**ind **P**erfection

Chapter Fifteen

ENFP

ENFPs Chose the Following Preferences:

Extraversion	ENERGIZING	. . . . Introversion
Sensing	ATTENDING	. . . . **iNtuition**
Thinking	DECIDING	. . . . **Feeling**
Judgment	LIVING	. . . . **Perception**

In general, ENFPs are initiators of change who are keenly perceptive of possibilities, and who energize and stimulate through their contagious enthusiasm. They prefer the start-up phase of a project or relationship, and are tireless in the pursuit of new-found interests. ENFPs are able to anticipate the needs of others and to offer them needed help and appreciation. They bring zest, joy, liveliness, and fun to all aspects of their lives. They are at their best in situations that are fluid and changing, and that allow them to express their creativity and use their charisma.

LIVING

ENFP children are "into everything." Their natural curiosity results in children for whom questions were invented. ENFP children make sand piles into castles, sticks into military outposts, and pillows into the seven continents. They often spend long periods of time devising new and original—but not necessarily practical—languages, plays, and scenarios. Many ENFPs enjoy drawing, writing, playacting, and dreaming. They are often chosen as leaders because of their persuasive enthusiasm and their energy for new and different ways of developing things (or getting others into trouble!).

An ENFP child joined an after-school nature club. After the first meeting, she became enthusiastically involved in promoting it to all of her friends. The club leader, who had agreed to work with a group with a maximum size of twelve girls, was astounded to find twenty-five girls at the second meeting, all there at the invitation of the ENFP.

The nature club activities included wildflower field trips. The ENFP enjoyed these trips out in the woods looking for flowers. On one field trip, she discovered a patch of poison ivy amidst the wild flowers. Through past experimentation, the ENFP knew that she was not allergic to poison ivy; in fact, she experienced no reaction at all when she rubbed the leaves on her skin. She wanted to continue her experiment to learn if her friends would get any reaction, so she persuaded the other girls to rub poison ivy over their arms and legs. Two days later, most of them came down with rather severe poison ivy. When confronted about her part in the matter, the ENFP said, "But I was only trying to see what would happen. I never meant any harm. I was just trying an experiment."

ENFP teenagers are agreeable, sociable, outgoing people who like to imagine themselves in the future. They spend many hours wondering and discussing with friends whom they will marry, where they will live, what their children will be like, and what work they will do. They leave no option or possibility unexplored and find it difficult to see themselves in any single job or career. In one breath, they may announce that they want to go to college in India to learn about its people and culture, in the next breath saying how much they want to attend the local college so they can be close to home.

A twenty-one-year-old journalism student went on a family skiing trip to Beaver Creek, Colorado. During his stay, he decided to spend a day skiing at Vail. That evening, he announced to his parents that he would drop out of college because he had found a job in Vail, a place to stay, two new roommates, and a longing for the Vail lifestyle. In the space of this one day, he had changed the direction of his life. While this pattern is sometimes found among young people, it is particularly common to ENFPs, who see opportunities and apply the energy to make those opportunities happen.

Because they see endless possibilities, to select one possibility appears to the ENFP to be too narrow a focus. They hate to be boxed into a career for life and therefore hesitate and resist making decisions. It is unwise for ENFPs to settle down too early, and they make the soundest choices when they delay career and marriage decisions until their middle to late twenties. Often when a decision is made, ENFPs will still leave a number of options open or change their minds as they encounter new information.

Even in their everyday activities, ENFPs often search for the new and the novel. If there is a logical route to work and the ENFP has been driving that way continually, he or she will likely tire of it and look for other routes.

ENFPs are more likely than other types to change from one career to another, demonstrating their versatility in doing so. It is not uncommon to hear stories of ENFPs who have established themselves in a career and who, when faced with the daily routine of maintaining it, leave it to start another. One ENFP founded a private school, surmounting many obstacles in financing it and attracting students and teachers. She took particular care in selecting administrators to ensure the smooth functioning of the school. When the school was in good hands, she was ready for a new challenge. She took some time off to think about her future. Building on her school experience and her deep commitment to children, she decided to go to law school in order to become an advocate for children's rights. Another ENFP started and ran a ski school, became a successful free-lance journalist, and ran a nationally known summer camp.

Adult ENFPs maintain characteristics that might be considered youthful, such as enthusiasm, curiosity, and a zestful outlook on life. As a result, people often enjoy being with them. Many times they are young-in-spirit as they age, perhaps because of their temperament.

ENFPs look forward to retirement as a time that can bring freedom from the restrictions of the work world and ample opportunity to pursue their varied interests. However, if ENFPs become disabled or experience a lack of resources, such as money, they may become despondent because this restricts their ability to quest after new experiences. A worst-case scenario for ENFPs is to live alone and be incapacitated, with few resources and little contact with the outside world. In retirement, it is particularly important for ENFPs to live with or near others who share their enthusiasm for life, variety, and new things to do. Because they focus on possibilities, rather than realities, retired ENFPs often do interesting things that may not be thought possible by other, more "realistic," types. For example, a seventy-year-old ENFP farm wife, after the death of her spouse, joined the Peace Corps in order to realize her dream of experiencing a new culture. She used her farm experience to help others in India.

LEARNING

ENFPs often learn best through a variety of means, such as observing, reading, and listening to and interacting with others. They enjoy the search for new ideas and possibilities, and will put in the time necessary to master subjects they find interesting. One strength is their enthusiasm for the process of discovery. They enjoy survey courses, comparative studies, and disciplines in which there is much to research and explore. They do not like classes that are too structured, that consist only of lectures, and that allow no room for their imagination. They may get caught up in the learning process and consequently need strict deadlines to bring a project to completion. The grade of "incomplete" can plague the intellectually curious ENFP.

ENFPs prefer a learning environment in which the teacher takes personal interest in them, in which there is an opportunity to talk about ideas with their peers, and in which there is a chance to ask questions and develop new ideas. ENFPs particularly like tests that relate one event to another or that involve exploring the future with questions such as "What will life be like in the year 2020?"

A motto that might describe the ENFP as a learner is "There's always another way or another answer." For example, if a teacher asks an ENFP for the best way to get to Rome, the ENFP can devise 101 ways to get there and overlook mentioning the one best way!

The style of finding many sources of information is illustrated by an ENFP who was delighted by her first pregnancy. In order to learn more about this experience, she went to the nearest public library and checked out all twenty-three books on the shelf relating to pregnancy and birth. She called everyone she knew in the medical profession and asked them questions on the medical aspects of her new condition. Additionally, she talked to ten new mothers to find out all she could about their emotional and medical experiences. She enjoyed these hours of research and the new things that she learned.

LABORING

ENFPs often follow a nonlinear career track and nontraditional routes to obtaining knowledge, qualifications, and skills. Occasionally, you will find them doing work that requires more credentials than they actually have. They are able to do this because they have persuaded others of their capabilities. ENFPs are particularly good at the start-up phase of a project or undertaking, and tend to have an idealistic view about how things might be done. When they are committed to what they do, they are enthusiastic to the point of preaching to the entire world about it. For an ENFP, work must be fun and must contribute to something larger than merely collecting a paycheck.

Work Setting

The preferred work setting for ENFPs contains imaginative people focused on human possibilities. ENFPs want a work environment that is both physically and mentally colorful. They prefer a participative and collegial atmosphere in which employees are included in the decision making. ENFPs are less productive where there is disharmony because they pay more attention to the relationships between people at work than they do to the tasks. Their ideal job would offer variety, novelty, challenge, and freedom from tight supervision; it would be idea oriented and imaginative, and would have lively, energetic people enjoying themselves and their tasks.

Organizing Style

To call an ENFP organized is to redefine what is meant by being organized because of their personal approach to it. Most ENFPs will say they are organized, but others might not see them that way. Their desire to be open to the moment tends to outweigh their need to be organized. Usually ENFP work space is arranged haphazardly, with work materials and personal mementos scattered about. ENFPs are able to retrieve information efficiently from the clutter because of the associations they make between the information and the interested individuals.

In terms of the management of time, ENFPs find it particularly difficult to estimate accurately how long an activity will take. Because people's needs are more important than schedules, ENFPs are often late and characteristically full of apologies and guilt feelings for their tardiness. In addition, because ideas often come quickly to ENFPs, they find it only reasonable to expect that their ideas can be worked out just as quickly; most often, however, this is not the case. ENFPs enjoy reading and talking to others about organization and time management, but may implement only a small percentage of what they know.

An ENFP professional trainer who offered a popular seminar on stress management presented the materials differently each time he gave the seminar. This constant change caused his staff much consternation because they had to continually change the agendas, page numbers, and illustrations in the seminar workbook. In desperation, the office manager confronted the ENFP with the dollar costs of the time spent by these constant changes, suggesting that the ENFP develop a standard seminar. While the ENFP understood that this was a good idea, he had a difficult time implementing the new plan. After several months, he began to go back to his original style and needed to be reminded of the deal he had struck with his office manager.

Occupations

To perform well at work, individuals may need to use all of the eight preferences at the appropriate time and when required by the situation. Knowing this, people tend to select occupations that allow them to use the preferences that are most natural to them.

ENFPs prefer occupations that reflect their ideals and that promote harmonious relationships with others. They tend to be attracted to occupations with a service orientation. ENFPs usually find a place in their work life for creativity. They particularly enjoy people-oriented work in which they are able to combine things in new and different ways to benefit humanity. Flexibility and autonomy are important to ENFPs, who may bolt from organizations in which this is not attainable.

While ENFPs can and do enter all occupations, some are more appealing to them than others. According to available research,[1] some occupations (in alphabetical order) seem to be more attractive to ENFPs: artist, clergy, consultant, counselor, entertainer, journalist, public relations worker, social scientist, social worker, teacher, and other occupations that allow ENFPs to use their creativity and insight. These occupations are not meant to be an exhaustive list but serve to illustrate some areas that an ENFP might enjoy. If your specific occupation or one that you are interested in is not listed here, think instead of its general characteristics and ask yourself how those fit with your type.

LEADING

ENFPs are energetic and enthusiastic leaders who are likely to take charge when a new endeavor needs a visionary spokesperson. ENFPs are values-oriented people who become champions of causes and services relating to human needs and dreams. Their leadership style is one of soliciting and recognizing others' contributions and of evaluating the personal needs of their followers. ENFPs are often charismatic leaders who are able to help people see the possibilities beyond themselves and their current realities.

While they vary in their approaches to leadership, ENFPs usually function as catalysts. For example, an ENFP was hired by an organization to head its newly created management-development department. She invited people from all levels of the organization to help her brainstorm and conceptualize the department's mission and its approaches to meeting the organization's needs. Through her enthusiasm, she was able to ignite this committee into endorsing her function. Additionally, she worked with individuals on her committee to determine the correct strategy to present the programs to the organization. Because it was a new function, it was imperative that she find the right spokesperson. She determined to meet personally with the president of the organization, and got his commitment and endorsement of her plans. Within three years, the management-development function became a fully integrated part of the company. This was possible because the ENFP had brought together many individuals, resources, and programs to effectively meet the organization's needs.

LEISURE

ENFPs often have a difficult time separating their work from their leisure. Because they like to have fun while they work and usually arrange their work lives to meet this need, the boundaries between their work and their leisure may not be as clear as they might be for some other types.

Because of their continual search for new things to experience, it is rare for ENFPs to become heavily involved in a single activity; their appetite for involvement is too great. Generally, ENFPs are on the lookout for new things and may come across what is "trendy" before others. They tend to participate early on in those new activities.

ENFPs like travel and reading because these activities open experiences of other times and places. Their reading often brings quiet and reflection time, as well as new material for their dreams. Their travels afford them opportunities to experience different people and cultures.

ENFPs' leisure pursuits often involve learning with other people. Some ENFPs may invite others to join them at plays, films, or in classes. Some enjoy physical activities in which they are able to challenge themselves, release their energy, and maintain their physical fitness. One ENFP became enamored with water polo because it allowed him the opportunity to visit with others, to exercise, and to splash about in the pool—all at the same time. He found four separate clubs offering water polo, so he would not be bored by any one team and so that he could easily fit the games into his busy schedule.

LOVING

For ENFPs, loving is an almost constant state. They are generally involved or in love with someone or something new. ENFPs may have originated the quotation "All the world loves a lover." When falling in love, they explore all the new possibilities in the relationship, and the new person is studied in every way. The ENFP tends to idealize his or her current relationship and will often say that the current one is "the best ever."

It might be argued that each type, when first in love, resembles a garden-variety ENFP, because ENFPs normally behave like people in love. Some of the cultural cliches about falling in love—such as "Falling in love with love," "Head over heels in love," "Love is blind," "All the world loves a lover," and "Throw caution to the wind"—seem to apply to the ENFP. This same boundless affection can be showered upon friends, co-workers, and others. People often feel unconditionally loved by ENFPs, but over time many of these relationships dissipate, as in "When I'm not near the ones I love, I love the ones I'm near."

The father of a popular twenty-two-year-old ENFP was reflecting on his daughter's many suitors. On one evening, she was being escorted by an Australian from the city of Perth; two nights prior to that, she was going out with a Hawaiian from Honolulu; and a month prior to that, she had had several dates with a young man from Tokyo, Japan. Because her dating partners tended to reflect her current interests. When she was into sports, she dated only "jocks"; when she was planning her European trip, she saw several Europeans. Her father knew that she must now be interested in and learning about the Pacific Rim.

ENFPs are delightful, enthusiastic partners who are young in spirit; there is rarely a dull moment with them. They readily note their partner's best aspects. They may overlook obvious details and facts about their partners that might cause other types to be more cautious. As their relationships progress, ENFPs romanticize their partners and make strong efforts to rationalize any discrepancy between the reality and their "ideal."

When ENFPs are in love, they may either overcommit and ignore any unpleasant yet true facts; or they may undercommit, believing that there may be a better love "just around the corner." Therefore, ENFPs may be seen as fickle in their relationships as they search for the "right one."

When and if the flaws in the relationship become too obvious to ENFPs, they may admit defeat, feeling great pain because they have put so much energy into perfecting a particular relationship. When ENFPs are scorned, they overgeneralize about their partners' worst faults. Because ENFPs thrive on new possibilities, when they fall out of love, they rebound quickly.

LOSING OUT

Each type has the potential to overuse or abuse its preferences. This is likely to happen when individuals are under great stress or pressure. At these times, they may act in ways that are unlike their usual style. The following paragraphs describe some of the ways ENFPs may lose out, in addition to some strategies that they can use to get back on track.

One way ENFPs lose out is when they become caught in a state of ideaphoria, a feeling akin to drowning in a sea of ideas, all of which seem equally important and vital. This leaves ENFPs with little focus or direction. They feel an inability to turn off their minds and allow matters to settle. Because ENFPs do not prioritize, they reach information overload.

An ENFP had determined it was necessary to take a vacation for health reasons. Having decided to explore the many possibilities, he went to the travel section of a bookstore to see if anything interesting would be suggested there. He also talked to several other people who had taken restful vacations to find out their ideas. The result of his information gathering was a multitude of options, all of which sounded appealing and attractive. He decided to "sleep on the matter," but spent the night tossing and imagining visits to each of approximately twenty locales. In the morning, the ENFP still did not have an idea of where to go and decided to talk to his neighbor. The neighbor asked the ENFP very specific questions about the costs and benefits, the availability of hotel space, and the actual time available for the vacation. His neighbor's questions helped him to sort through the options.

A possible strategy for ENFPs would be to prioritize their ideas based on their own or others' needs and values. They should pay attention to what is actually required in a given situation. A second strategy is to stop idea-generating activity, pursuing instead some physical activity such as walking or swimming. This allows ENFPs to invest their energy in a more direct fashion.

Another way ENFPs lose out is when they fail to factor in the actual details and facts of a given situation and thereby obscure reality. Sometimes ENFPs will find a particular fact and become obsessed about it, even when it is out of context. For example, an ENFP went to see a physician because of an elbow pain. The doctor's tentative diagnosis included arthritis, muscle strain, or tennis elbow. The possibility of arthritis stuck in the ENFP's mind. Between that visit and a subsequent one for a final diagnosis, the ENFP gathered information about arthritis. He went to a nearby bookstore and purchased several books relating to arthritis. As he was reading through the books, every symptom suddenly seemed to apply to him. He became convinced that he must have arthritis all over his body, not just in his elbow. He began to work out an elaborate plan of exercise, diet, and a possible move to a warm climate to combat his illness. At his next visit to his physician, he learned that he had tennis elbow, not arthritis, and that his imagination had worked overtime.

One possible strategy to help ENFPs deal accurately with reality is for them to write down the facts and details of a particular situation. The written facts may help keep ENFPs from going off on imaginative tangents. Also, they could look at logical consequences, the pros and cons suggested by the facts, establishing how important those facts really are to them or to other significant people in their lives. Only after these steps are taken should ENFPs generate possibilities suggested by the facts.

Because ENFPs are zestful and fun loving, they may not complete important work and meet basic responsibilities. They may squander their energy and inspiration on ill-chosen tasks. Others may tire of working with them because they may have to clean up after ENFPs. ENFPs should choose their commitments carefully and finish what they start.

ENFPs also lose out by overextending themselves. Sometimes they overeat, party too much, or overindulge in "the good life" to the point of saturation. They become overstimulated, over-tired, and, in some cases, overweight. A strategy to deal with overextension and trying to do too much is to realistically evaluate the effects of their behavior on themselves and others, and to screen activities and projects for those most relevant to their current situation.

When ENFPs are back on track, they are using their strengths of enthusiasm, seeing possibilities, and generating new ideas. They can be tireless in the pursuit of new possibilities.

IN A NUTSHELL

Hallmarks:[2]

Enthusiastic
Creative
Spontaneous
Independent
Perceptive
Imaginative
Versatile

Curious
Expressive
Friendly
Energetic
Restless

Acronym:[3]

Every day, New Fantastic Possibilities

Chapter Sixteen

ENFJ

ENFJs Chose the Following Preferences:

Extraversion	ENERGIZING	. . . . Introversion
Sensing	ATTENDING	. . . . **iNtuition**
Thinking	DECIDING	. . . . **Feeling**
Judgment	LIVING	. . . . Perception

In general, ENFJs are lively and enthusiastic facilitators who apply warmth and vision to helping people and meeting their needs. They are aware of people's aspirations and develop plans of action to make those aspirations into reality. They like organization and closure. They are at their best facilitating situations that require interpersonal sensitivity. ENFJs are tolerant and appreciative of others, seeking involvement with them in life's tasks. They are able communicators who are liberal in showing appreciation for others.

LIVING

ENFJ children want life to be cooperative, friendly, harmonious, and lively. They are often responsible children because they like to please others and meet their needs. In doing for others, they usually find satisfaction for themselves. They are upset by conflict or disharmony. They are pleasant, exuberant, and talkative. They enjoy social interaction. One ENFJ recalls her grandmother cautioning her not to tell all that she knew to everyone that she knew. The ENFJ did not realize that she was too vocal until her grandmother pointed this out to her. She felt she was proceeding "naturally" in letting everyone know what was important to her.

ENFJ teenagers are constantly on the go, participating in many, many things. They enjoy a wide variety of activities, not only for that variety but also for the action and opportunity to be with others. If the ENFJ teenager is not involved in something, it is simply because he or she does not have the time or because the activity is of little seeming importance. ENFJs love being involved with friends, clubs, and any activities that let them be with others.

An ENFJ teenager enjoyed playing several instruments but did not particularly like the trombone; however, that was the instrument she played in her school band. When asked why she was playing the trombone, she responded, "That was what they needed. No one else would play it. They needed someone who could read music well, and they knew I would be good, not just another body, so I decided I would help out and play it."

The ENFJ teenager may also get heavily involved in activities relating to school spirit. He or she may be active in pep rallies and in raising funds for school projects such as uniforms for the band or the football team. ENFJs are often voted most congenial or nicest person in their class. Additionally, they may serve as leaders in their school activities. As students, they are able to focus on the interpersonal spirit or nature of the school and to speak eloquently to others about the school's best values. ENFJs encourage not only school spirit but individuals as well. ENFJs are likable because they notice what is good about people.

As young adults, ENFJs set goals early on, both in the personal and professional realms. They follow through diligently and usually attain what they seek. Often the goals they set have to do with making society a better place for people. One ENFJ was very interested in children's education. She began by majoring in elementary education, completing her degree a year earlier than her classmates, in part so she could marry her high school sweetheart. She then supported him through dental school, and taught several years beyond that. She taught part-time when their children were young, and when both children were in school, she proceeded toward her ultimate goal: setting up her own school. She now operates a very successful private religious school that reflects her values.

ENFJs may sometimes feel pulled between financial gain and spiritual gain. For example, one ENFJ was a talented artist who was able to come up with designs for tee shirts and sweatshirts. However, he did not like the financial parts of the business, and really wanted to concentrate on the designs and making people happy wearing his work. He ultimately found a partner who would spend the time on the administrative side of the business so that he could concentrate his efforts on the creative function.

ENFJs enjoy group activities and often rise to positions of leadership, particularly if the group activity is focused around meeting the future needs of people. Many ENFJs take their religious and community values seriously and want others to do the same. Loyalty, commitment, and responsibility are important values to ENFJs, even as children.

In adult life, ENFJs often settle into organizations that have a values orientation, or they will find a spot in an organization that is centered on values or people's needs. ENFJs make responsible spouses, employees, and community members. Because most ENFJs enjoy public speaking and seem to have a way with words, they are often asked to present the position of the groups to which they belong. One ENFJ said she really had to work to present ideas concisely. She was perfectly willing to speak extemporaneously, but was likely to be verbose when doing so.

Some ENFJs report that at mid-life they seek situations for themselves where it is possible for them to turn inward. This often takes a structured form such as meditation, journaling, or in some cases even career changes.

In retirement, ENFJs are likely to want to settle geographically in an area where they have close personal relationships and/or close personal ties to a specific organization. The relationships and values that are important to the ENFJ become even more so in their retirement. Many ENFJs move from paid service work into voluntary service work in retirement. Believing that it is necessary to help others, they fulfill this responsibility gladly. ENFJs feel alive and get much pleasure from meeting the needs of others. In retirement, they may need to take care to meet their own personal needs as well and to "relax and let others serve them." Despite severe health problems in his retirement years, one ENFJ continually responded to his organization's desire for extra help. When asked why he kept appearing as a consultant in the office when he should have been home taking care of his own health, he responded simply, "Because they need me."

LEARNING

ENFJs learn best in structured situations in which they are able to talk about the lesson and interact with their peers. Because they want their teachers to be pleased with them, they attempt to be model students. They are willing to do what is required in order to become personally recognized by their teachers. Because they take criticism personally, they can either be wounded by it or be willing to redouble their efforts in order to change the criticism. ENFJs enjoy classes that have subject matter relating to people, their needs, their aspirations, and their characterizations. Many ENFJs choose the liberal arts because it gives them an opportunity to more fully explore humanity.

ENFJs are good students when the subject matter relates to their strong relationship values and people orientation, and when the teacher is warm and personal. They apply the necessary effort and energy to complete the tasks that they start. ENFJs also like some independent learning and projects. These might take the form of adding their unique stamp to a project. One ENFJ completed a class project on team development in which she inserted examples based on her own personal experiences as a team member. These experiences supplemented the more theoretical materials in the report. She was glad that there was a general structure to the project without rigid specifications on what should be included in the paper.

LABORING

At work, ENFJs contribute their encouragement and facilitation toward workplace cooperation. They are focused on the organization's ideals and operate within those ideals. They focus on how organizations should treat people and communicate these values to others. They enjoy leading and facilitating teams, and like to bring matters to mutually beneficial conclusions. ENFJs bring a sense of camaraderie to all they do.

Work Setting

ENFJs prefer a work setting that contains individuals focused on changing things for the betterment of others. They like an environment that is people oriented, supportive, and organized. They do their best when there is a spirit of harmony, with encouragement given for self-expression. Projects which involve creativity and allow for communication are especially sought after by ENFJs. They like their work to be settled and orderly, but not so much so that it is dull, quiet, unchanging, or unchallenging. Most ENFJs find that an aesthetically pleasing physical work setting contributes to their optimal productivity.

Organizing Style

The ENFJ organizing style is to plan around the particular value or ideal and to supply the necessary energy toward its achievement or implementation. Initially, ENFJs tune in to the people and relationship needs and requirements, developing the appropriate assignments for themselves and others in order to carry out the tasks. It hurts their feelings when others do not follow through as they expected. However, sometimes their expectations are not clear, and others inadvertently disappoint ENFJs.

In the accomplishment of the goal, ENFJs will look at the people available and will assign tasks based on who needs the experience, the exposure, or the development. To a lesser degree, they will assign the task based purely on competency, because ENFJs feel it is more important to help others grow and develop new skills. If others have a particular deadline that needs to be met, the ENFJ will work to meet that deadline so that the other person will be happy.

The work space of an ENFJ is generally fairly well organized. It also contains many items of a personal nature, such as family pictures, children's artwork, and gifts from special friends or relatives.

ENFJs like to stick to a plan. However, they will change based on the personal requests of the individuals affected by the plan, if those personal requests are important to the overall value being served.

Occupations

To perform well at work, individuals may need to use all of the eight preferences at the appropriate time and when required by the situation. Knowing this, people tend to select occupations that allow them to use the preferences that are most natural to them.

ENFJs prefer occupations that reflect their ideals and that promote harmonious relationships with others. They tend to be attracted to occupations with a service orientation. They generally follow policies and procedures as long as those procedures are compatible with people's needs. They prefer things to be organized and decided rather than haphazard.

While ENFJs can and do enter all occupations, some are more appealing to them than others. According to available research,[1] some occupations (in alphabetical order) seem to be more attractive to ENFJs: actor, clergy, consultant, counselor and therapist, designer, home economist, musician, religious worker, teacher, writer, and other occupations that allow them to be of service to others. These occupations are not meant to be an exhaustive list but serve to illustrate some areas that an ENFJ might enjoy. If your specific occupation or one that you are interested in is not listed here, think instead of its general characteristics and ask yourself how those fit with your type.

LEADING

The ENFJ leadership style is a highly facilitative one. ENFJs include others and desire to have a participative environment. They are responsive to their followers' needs and yet are uncomfortable with conflict. They can overcome their discomfort with conflict, however, if dealing with it benefits others. They are well aware of the organization's values and feel uncomfortable when those values are in conflict with their own. They inspire change, and that change is usually related toward some humanitarian purpose. They may enter a committee meeting, for example, with a strong desire to get to know the other members of the group first before they get down to business. They look for ways everyone can get their needs met, not solely to further their own personal agenda. They will make sure something happens, since they do like conclusions. Often, this occurs by bringing together their viewpoint and that of others in a creative, complementary way. The results of these deliberations, however, must be true to their values.

An ENFJ manager had good relationships with everyone on his staff. He not only knew about their work life but knew many things about them personally. When one staff member had a child in the hospital, the ENFJ quickly made some adjustments in that person's assignments to allow time to be with the child. The ENFJ enlisted a co-worker's help to take over the reassigned tasks. He persuaded the co-worker to do the necessary work by saying, "This is what I would do for you, if you were in the same situation."

LEISURE

The ENFJ puts relationships and responsibilities before personal leisure. For example, if an ENFJ's daughter needs a ride to a school event, the ENFJ will readily do so before preparing for an important meeting. Their time can be imposed upon easily; however, they need to guard against excessive responsiveness to avoid reaching overload.

ENFJs particularly enjoy reading novels and seeing movies in order to see how the characters play out the life issues and questions presented in the story; it gives them an opportunity to see how others live and get along. They enjoy discussing their reading and may join book groups in order to do that. They like going to movies and plays with others and like to comment on the plot and characterization. They are close observers of others' behavior.

Because ENFJs value relationships, they are willing participants in organizations, particularly if the focus is on helping others or meeting others' needs. Therefore, many ENFJs join religious or community-oriented groups whose focus is to work for better understanding between people. ENFJs like discussion and an opportunity to talk about values and philosophical topics. Many do not like activities in which there is a great deal of competition or in which someone or something could be hurt. Generally, leisure-time pursuits for the ENFJ do not include operating or fixing things. Most ENFJs shy away from serious involvement with tools or materials.

They take the needs and desires of others seriously and will sometimes put their own needs second to fulfilling those of family, job, or community. ENFJs are often spokespersons for community or employee causes.

LOVING

For the ENFJ, love means flowers, poetry, candlelight dinners— in other words, romance with a capital R. When they first fall in love, they fall in love with an ideal perspective of what the relationship will be, and they fall deeply, head over heels. ENFJs value commitment and loyalty, and look for it from their partner. They typically enjoy activities with their partners that allow them to discuss the relationship and focus on what each person truly believes. When commitments are broken, ENFJs become upset because they see the breakup as a personal reflection on them and because they have idealized the relationship. Since they are willing to put the time and effort into the relationship, they expect it will continue on as it was from the very start. Relationships have their ups and downs; the downs, however, are particularly hard on the ENFJ, who does not manage disharmony well.

An ENFJ woman was married twenty years to a lab director. She was initially attracted to him because he was scholarly and because he wanted his work to contribute overall to the well-being of others. She idealized him and their relationship, overlooking some of his other characteristics. His need for being alone, for little interaction with people, and for working on scientific experiments became wedges in the relationship. The ENFJ hungered for more verbal displays of affection, more affirmation, and more time together in the relationship. Because the ideal never met the reality, and because the ENFJ was able to idealize only so long, the relationship ended. This was especially difficult for the ENFJ, who valued loyalty, steadfastness, and commitment.

When scorned, ENFJs may be resentful, spiteful, and deeply hurt. Because they are acutely aware of emotional matters, they take the breakup of a relationship especially hard. They are willing to discuss the ending of the relationship with only a few others because they feel a sense of blame and shame for the relationship not working out.

LOSING OUT

Each type has the potential to overuse or abuse its preferences. This is likely to happen when individuals are under great stress or pressure. At these times, they may act in ways that are unlike their usual style. The following paragraphs describe some of the ways ENFJs may lose out, in addition to some strategies that they can use to get back on track.

For ENFJs, one way of losing out is to become blindly loyal to others or to causes that may not be deserving of the ENFJ's consideration. Because they take their causes seriously, they may feel disillusioned when the causes and the values they represent are challenged or found to be undeserving. When their values do not meet current needs and realities, ENFJs can be thought of as old-fashioned.

As a strategy, ENFJs may need to recognize other people's limitations and guard against unquestioning and undeserving loyalty to causes. This may include paying attention to current needs, logical consequences, and situational requirements. ENFJs may want to come to a new and different level of awareness about their values and, at times, reassess them.

An ENFJ adult educator had a value of individual and personal attention to students that caused her to limit her class enrollments to ten people. The education coordinator asked if it would be possible to double the class size to twenty, making it more affordable to the community education program and to the participants as well. The ENFJ objected vehemently because she believed that in a class of twenty, individual and personal attention would be greatly sacrificed. Because she held firmly to this value, she felt it necessary to resign as the teacher of this course. Later, the ENFJ was asked to reconsider and return to teaching the course because so many people were impressed with her inspired teaching and wanted to take the course from her. When she approached her decision from this new perspective— of people needing to hear what she had to say—rather than from a cost-saving perspective, the ENFJ reconsidered, compromised, and held the class with fifteen participants.

ENFJs also lose out when they avoid conflict and confrontation and, as a result, sweep problems under the rug. They may overlook disagreeable facts, particularly if those facts will lead to arguments with others. ENFJs may need to learn that conflict can be useful to relationships because it can clear the air and give each party new information that has the potential to move the relationship to a deeper plane. When conflict is managed productively, new dimensions in the relationship can be explored. ENFJs would do well to remember that resolving conflict can benefit people and help them to grow.

ENFJs may ignore task requirements in favor of people relationships. While people may require careful attention, work-related issues may also need the ENFJ's attention. One ENFJ did not realize how much telephone time he spent with his clients discussing mutual personal issues, compared with the time he devoted to their business needs. Finally, when one client had reached her limit, she interrupted the ENFJ and in exasperation said, "I think we've talked enough about you and me. Now, please, let's get down to business!" As a strategy, ENFJs may remember that paying attention to the job requirements is a useful way to help others. Keeping their personal comments to a minimum during business hours may keep the ENFJ on track.

Another way ENFJs lose out is when they take criticism personally and become illogical. This happens when the ENFJ is experiencing great stress. One ENFJ was in charge of entertaining foreign dignitaries for his firm. He had an idea of how one occasion should be. His big picture included how the meeting room should be decorated and what specific food should be served. He had communicated his requirements in great detail to the banquet manager. He was certain that things would go well because of his advance planning. Later, he overheard two of his guests complaining about the size of the room. The ENFJ took this as a personal criticism and lost his composure. He took the banquet manager aside and picked on every possible detail, including the shape of the crystal wine goblets. The ENFJ became agitated and illogical as the time of the banquet approached. His unusual behavior was especially noticeable to the guests who were arriving. Under normal circumstances, the ENFJ was generally appreciative of others and their work.

A possible strategy in such situations would be for ENFJs to communicate neither blame nor criticism but instead to state very clearly what their needs are. Using "I" messages such as "I need this banquet room to be arranged the way we planned, immediately!" may have helped the ENFJ calm down and manage the crisis. Additionally, they may need to be flexible and make necessary adjustments in their plans.

When ENFJs are back on track, they are using their strengths of being attentive to the needs of others, understanding and interpreting values, and working enthusiastically and harmoniously. They can be tireless in the pursuit of integrity.

IN A NUTSHELL

Hallmarks:[2]

Loyal
Idealistic
Personable
Verbal
Responsible
Expressive
Enthusiastic
Energetic
Diplomatic
Concerned
Supportive
Congenial

Acronym:[3]

Everyone Needs Fulfillment and Joy

Chapter Seventeen

INTJ

INTJs Chose the Following Preferences:

Extraversion	ENERGIZING	**Introversion**
Sensing	ATTENDING	**iNtuition**
Thinking	DECIDING	Feeling
Judgment	LIVING	Perception

In general, INTJs are strong individualists who seek new angles or novel ways of looking at things. They enjoy coming to new understandings. They are insightful and mentally quick; however, this mental quickness may not always be outwardly apparent to others since they keep a great deal to themselves. They are very determined people who trust their vision of the possibilities, regardless of what others think. They may even be considered the most independent of all of the sixteen personality types. INTJs are at their best in quietly and firmly developing their ideas, theories, and principles.

LIVING

The independent and individualistic INTJ manner appears early in life. As children, INTJs are often inwardly focused on their thoughts of the way the world is or ought to be; they enjoy day-dreaming. They can be quite stubborn when information relayed to them by authorities, such as parents and teachers, contradicts what they believe. They are sure of their own belief system. One INTJ said her mother described her as "the great debater" by age four. She argued logically for what she wanted, to the point that her mother repeatedly said that her daughter should be an attorney, which is precisely what the INTJ did not do.

INTJs are compelled to establish their own rules, boundaries, standards, and style. An INTJ growing up on a dairy farm devised a system to milk the cows in an expeditious way. It was designing the milking system that intrigued him, not the milking itself. While milking cows can be a mundane task, this INTJ made it interesting by devising a novel way to get the milking done.

Often at an early age, INTJs make a commitment to furthering their education. The life of the mind is very important to them. Examples abound of INTJs from economically or intellectually impoverished circumstances setting goals for themselves to continue in education, often earning the highest degree possible. For one INTJ, it was not enough to excel all through school and receive her Ph.D. She felt it necessary to obtain another master's degree and a Ph.D. in a related discipline. Her internally focused quest for information and knowledge was most important to her. There is always more to learn and challenge the INTJ.

INTJ teenagers may be seen as serious and reserved young people who are labeled as bookworms or "brains" by others. They set internal standards of achievement for themselves and often do well academically. Being sociable is a standard that they rarely think is worth their time and energy. They will engage in a social activity only if it achieves a purpose for them, that is, if they learn something. The INTJ teenager may be somewhat slow to date. Once attracted to someone, he or she sticks with that individual as long as that other person meets their standards.

As young adults, INTJs are focused on attaining their inner goals and standards. A young married INTJ living at a far distance from a university wanted to pursue his law degree. He arranged his work schedule so that he was able to make the long commute, and that solitary time was spent thinking and mentally organizing his busy life. His degree took a great deal of planning, energy, and commitment. At times, he appeared so single-minded that his family felt left out. He was focused on getting that law degree and therefore seemed remote to others. INTJs are inclined to lose themselves in their interests, whether they are related to work, school, or a hobby.

One INTJ homemaker found herself on the wrong track for a while because she focused on a less than complete vision for herself. She was very devoted to her family and made her homemaker role into a broad one. She attended many committee meetings to help out in the community. She came home greatly exasperated after one of those meetings, saying, "They never get anything done. All they do is socialize!" She took stock of herself and decided that what she really enjoyed was creating artistic designs, not socializing. With the encouragement of her family, she started a design business. She enjoyed isolating herself and creating designs far more than attending committee meetings that had little meaning to her and wore her out.

In adult life, INTJs may set a particular course based on their theory of what ought to be. They work extremely diligently to accomplish what they feel is important. Work is not "work" to them in the traditional sense. They enjoy what they do and see it as a challenge. They are not easily dissuaded and may regard others' needs and wants as an impediment to attaining their objectives. Others may be unhappy with the distance and preoccupation of the INTJ.

INTJs may find bureaucracy distasteful because of the need to abide and live by other people's visions or systems and not their own. For this reason, INTJs may become fed up and seek new projects in their organizations or even leave to start their own businesses. They want to follow their own visions and theories and make their mark on their world.

INTJs tend to be frugal with their time and resources unless the time or resources involve something they can support on principle. An INTJ parent was very generous in paying for his children's education because he valued education. However, he regularly shopped at second-hand stores for his children's clothes and gifts. Of course, other INTJs may opt to do it differently.

INTJs' adjustment to retirement depends upon the amount of success they have had in living their lives according to their vision and in making those visions into reality. An INTJ research scientist enjoyed his work so much and kept feeling he was so close to a breakthrough that he would not retire. He continued being busy; however, his work schedule became increasingly flexible as he traveled more to visit grandchildren and to attend scientific meetings. Overall his focus continued to be on his work. Another INTJ was not so clearly focused. She lived alone in a small apartment. She did not like the "confusion and fuss" of her more outgoing and sociable neighbors. "These women talk all the time about things that are really inconsequential. Their small talk gets on my nerves," complained the INTJ. In the same discussion, however, the INTJ also lamented the fact that she had no one to talk to. She had not nurtured relationships with people with whom she could discuss things that were of interest to her. Her existence was made richer by the discovery of a college professor several years her junior who could talk about books and ideas and "other important things."

LEARNING

INTJs learn best when they can design their own approach and when they are able to absorb themselves in an area that interests them. They tend to focus on systems, theories, and constructs relating to universal truths and principles. They prefer challenging teachers, ones who meet INTJs' standards. High grade-point averages and test scores tend to characterize INTJs, who like rigorous academic work. Learning needs to be a creative process. Rote memory can be dull and boring for the INTJ.

INTJs are diligent in pursuing new ideas and thoughts, and they exert effort to master a given subject. This makes INTJs particularly adept in most school situations. If a teacher, however, does not meet their needs, INTJs tend to bypass them and set off on their own course of study.

Because of their resourcefulness, thirst for knowledge, and inner needs, INTJs tend to find ways of acquiring knowledge. They gravitate toward libraries, public lectures, courses, and other learners and teachers—sources that offer them information and direction.

An INTJ thoroughly enjoyed his school work, often reading more books than were required. However, his mother was exceedingly frugal and did not want him to waste electricity by reading late into the night. Because he so valued this quiet, uninterrupted, solitary time, he devised a way of rigging his blankets and table lamps so he could continue reading without anyone finding out.

Ideal assignments for INTJs are those in which they can construct a theoretical model to explain something in life. INTJs might be intrigued by assignments like the following: developing theoretical constructs about how soldiers behave in warfare, how parents relate to their children, how cells fight cancer, or how spirituality can be attained. They like intensive introspection and deep probing into a subject that interests them. An INTJ decided to write a book on the uses of authority. She did not consult any of the major theoreticians on the subject but rather isolated herself and drew upon her own internal understandings and inspirations. The result was a well-received book on the subject.

LABORING

At work, INTJs use their conceptual strengths to analyze situations and then develop models to understand and anticipate future needs. They are highly determined individuals who follow through relentlessly to reach their goals, develop their competence, or work out their own ideas. They will continue on with their plans, even in the face of adversity and data that might suggest to other more practical types that their goals are no longer feasible. By nature, INTJs are independent individualists. They see their visions so clearly that they are often surprised when others do not see things the same way. INTJs are strong at critiquing and as a result tend to notice the negatives. To them, a job well done should be reward enough in itself. They may neglect to comment favorably on others' contributions.

Work Setting

INTJs prefer a work setting that contains decisive and intellectual people focused on designing future strategies and visions. They prefer a task-oriented work environment with space for privacy, time for reflection to delve deeply into something, and opportunity to exercise creativity. They value competence in themselves and others. INTJs seek autonomy and often have little need for a team approach, unless that approach allows for generating ideas and critiquing and (changing) the status quo.

Organizing Style

INTJs tend to be relentless reorganizers who are seldom satisfied with the way things are. One of their strengths is seeing the broad-range implications of day-to-day processes and procedures. Their long-term, theoretical vision establishes their *modus operandi*. They organize themselves, and they work alone, often without consulting others.

While INTJs are usually quite focused on the bigger picture, there is more variability as to how well they relate to the details. Some INTJs are almost compulsive in their organizational style, and they take care of every piece of paper that crosses their desk immediately. One INTJ had a file for each family member that contained newspaper articles and cartoons he thought they might enjoy. When he had collected enough of them, he would send them to the particular family member. Others let certain things pile up that are not in their areas of interest or are not predetermined priorities. For example, an INTJ computer analyst was exceedingly organized in tracking the latest research on his topic and in keeping his voluminous files carefully catalogued. However, he never recorded checks he wrote nor did he ever balance his checking account. These details were not important to him.

Outcomes are important for INTJs. They set up methods to meet their goals. For example, an INTJ wanted to send her children to expensive colleges and started saving small amounts of money in the early years of her career in order to ensure that when the day came, her children, as yet unborn, would be able to attend the best colleges.

Occupations

To perform well at work, individuals may need to use all of the eight preferences at the appropriate time and when required by the situation. Knowing this, people tend to select occupations that allow them to use the preferences that are most natural to them.

INTJs tend to seek occupations that allow them to change the status quo and to design models to express their vision creatively. They desire autonomy and room for growth. They prefer to work in a place in which the future can be planned and where they can work for change in an organized manner.

While INTJs can and do enter all occupations, some are more appealing to them than others. According to available research,[1] some occupations (in alphabetical order) seem to be especially attractive to INTJs: computer systems analyst, electrical engineer, judge, lawyer, photographer, psychologist, research department manager, researcher, scientist, university instructor, and other occupations in which long-range vision is essential. These occupations are not meant to be an exhaustive list but serve to illustrate some areas that an INTJ might enjoy. If your specific occupation or one that you are interested in is not listed here, think instead of its general characteristics and ask yourself how those fit with your type.

LEADING

In INTJ terms, leadership means a person who is willing to conceptualize, design, and build models, strategies, and systems to attain organizational goals. INTJs act strongly and forcefully in the field of ideas and work hard to make them become reality. They are tough-minded and drive themselves and others. They are more task than relationship oriented, and may need to learn to say an appropriate word of thanks to others.

INTJs are people who enjoy reorganizing and will take on entire systems when necessary. They may get so deeply involved in a task that they respond to little else in their work or home environment. Once a decision or a goal is conceived, the INTJ moves toward that decision and is not willing to stop. Effective INTJ leaders are those who are willing to involve others in their models, realizing that congenial relationships are necessary to achieve their goals. To enhance their impact, INTJs need to use persuasive and political skills to make their ideas realities.

For example, an INTJ was the science and technology director for a small organization. He foresaw problems in the intellectual and educational obsolescence of the scientists who reported to him and, therefore, devised a plan for his entire organization to keep his scientists professionally vital. This plan was crystal clear to the INTJ, but not to those in his organization. He recognized the resistance and took what he considered to be a step backward by involving others in his plan. In that way, others began to understand his ideas and became more willing to institute his program.

LEISURE

Nothing seems to be haphazard about INTJ leisure-time pursuits. These individuals tend to select leisure activities that fit into their global perspective of themselves or their model of what a person ought to do with leisure time. They seldom leave leisure to chance. An INTJ will often select one or two seasonal pursuits and be consistent and disciplined in taking part in them. For example, an INTJ male religiously played tennis three times a week in the warm weather, and in the winter participated in cross-country skiing, also three times a week. This sporting activity was important to him because he believed it was what kept his body in good shape and his mind focused and clear for his work.

INTJs tend not to get into fad activities, including fashionable clothing. If physical exercise is important to their view of themselves, they will select a sport and continue with it on a schedule regardless of what others are doing. In fact, one INTJ refused to become a jogger or a Nautilus weight lifter because those were fads. Biking had been her sport, but she didn't like when it too became a fad. One seventy-five-year-old INTJ has been swimming every afternoon for the past fifty years. If INTJs like reading as a leisure activity, they will choose an author and read every work by that author, plus literary criticisms and reviews. However, one INTJ stated that she did not read literary criticisms because she preferred her own judgment of the work.

INTJs often combine business with pleasure. The daughter of an INTJ did not ever recall a family vacation in which her father had not attended a seminar or conference at the same time. She viewed that as a normal part of everyone's vacation. Once, her father attended a ten-day conference in Prague, Czechoslovakia, and the family went along for a vacation. The conference headquarters were located one block away from a famous medieval clock. The family of the INTJ had thoroughly enjoyed seeing this clock "perform" and were quite shocked upon leaving town to discover that their father had never bothered to see it. He found far more enjoyment in discussing his ideas with other scientists.

LOVING

For INTJs, love means including someone in their vision of the world. INTJ men tend to be attracted to partners who enjoy living their lives with an outward vitality and zest. Perhaps it is to compensate for their internal, visionary focus that they often find partners who are more outgoing and may even run interference to help the INTJ deal with the day-to-day world. INTJ women, however, may seek someone more like themselves.

INTJs tend to have a model in mind of how their relationship ought to be. This is less a romantic vision than it is an idea that relates to how the relationship functions in a unique or special way. An INTJ man raising several small children married an outgoing woman who also had several small children. He visualized how his children, his academic lifestyle, her children, and her profession would blend into his view of the perfect family.

When reality and the distinct personalities of the seven children involved did not meet his model, he became very frustrated. Others did not see the whole in the same way he did.

INTJs tend to withhold their deep feelings and affections from the public and sometimes even from the object of their affections. They can be intensely loyal and caring, even though this is not always expressed in words. INTJs can be generous with their gifts if the gift fits their vision of what ought to be appreciated by their partner. For example, an INTJ was happy to put his spouse through school and willingly paid her registration and book fees. However, when it came time to allotting money to go to the movies, he felt quite differently.

When scorned, INTJs retreat to their own world and may share none of their feelings with others. They may assume that there is a right way for a relationship to end and look for that. They act on the outside as if nothing has happened to them when indeed much has. They may lash out with criticisms of their former loved ones. It may take them a while to recover.

LOSING OUT

Each type has the potential to overuse or abuse its preferences. This is likely to happen when individuals are under great stress or pressure. At these times, they may act in ways that are unlike their usual style. The following paragraphs describe some of the ways INTJs may lose out, in addition to some strategies that they can use to get back on track.

One way INTJs lose out is when their future visions are not based on actual facts or current realities. They may have difficulty letting go of impractical ideas. Sometimes their ability to see and predict what might take place in the future takes precedence in their lives, and they seem to be living in the present in an almost detached fashion. They may keep their vision so much to themselves that they neglect to involve others in its implementation.

One INTJ company president had a strong belief about the direction the company should follow. However, market realities intervened, and his plans were inappropriate. Unfortunately, he would not give up. He was very surprised the day he learned that he had been replaced by the board of directors. As a strategy, INTJs may need to learn when to give up on impractical ideas and to solicit the input of others to help get them back on track. Just because a model or a vision exists does not mean it is the correct way to proceed. Course correcting may not be an affront to the INTJ's competence but rather appropriate in the larger context.

INTJs may ignore the impact of their style on others. Often they do not care what others think. With their more impersonal and independent view of life, they may believe others also function best in an impersonal environment. People may see them as unyielding, detached, and so logical that they may be afraid to approach or challenge them. One INTJ surrounded himself with people he believed worked the same way he did. He was surprised when his boss commented to him that his style was alienating his staff. He had not solicited their opinions nor encouraged them to speak up and disagree with him. As a strategy, INTJs need to take the time to foster their relationships and consider their impact on others; they should not assume that others are in agreement. They need to make sure that they have shown appreciation to others and allowed for the niceties in human interactions.

INTJs may have a specific model in mind and critique others who do not fit that model. For example, INTJ parents may decide early on that their children are to attend their alma mater. The INTJ may ignore the facts that the children do not have the same academic interests, the requisite grades, or the desire to attend that university. They may become resistant to their children's desires to be different. As a strategy, INTJs may need to allow their children (and others) their own choices. The goal of the INTJ is improvement. However, their suggestions are often received as criticism. It would serve the INTJ well to show appreciation to others based on merit, not just on the fit with the INTJ's model.

Another way INTJs can lose out is to become obsessed with unimportant details. Their need to control all possibilities results in them being unable to focus on what is really necessary. For example, an INTJ had the position of conference planner. When the site of one of the events changed, she wrote the change on each of the 200 tickets that had been printed. She could have simply posted a sign directing people to the new site only a half block away. Stepping back from the situation, looking at the total picture, and checking with others about possible alternatives to handling the details often help.

When INTJs are back on track, they are using their strengths of recognizing new possibilities, setting goals for the future, and developing novel and ingenious solutions for problems. They can be tireless in the pursuit of improvement.

IN A NUTSHELL

Hallmarks:[2]

Independent
Critical
Systems minded
Visionary
Demanding
Global
Logical
Original
Firm
Theoretical
Private
Autonomous

Acronym:[3]

It's Not Thoroughly Justified

Chapter Eighteen

INTP

INTPs Chose the following Preferences:

Extraversion . . . . ENERGIZING . . . . **Introversion**
Sensing . . . . ATTENDING . . . . **iNtuition**
Thinking . . . . DECIDING . . . . Feeling
Judgment . . . . LIVING . . . . **Perception**

In general, INTPs are known for their quest for logical purity, which motivates them to examine universal truths and principles. They are constantly asking themselves and others the questions "Why?" and "Why not?" Clear and quick thinkers, they are able to focus with great intensity on their interests. They appreciate elegance and efficiency in thought processes and require them, even more so, in their own communications. They may be seen as unwilling to accept what everyone else regards as truth. While often low key in outward appearance and approach, the INTP is "hard as nails" when challenging a truth. INTPs do not like to deal with the obvious. They are at their best in building conceptual models and developing unusual and complex ideas.

LIVING

As children, INTPs are inwardly focused, often enjoying their own thoughts more than the company of others. One INTP child, after moving to a new neighborhood, spent the entire spring in his house, reading. When summer vacation started, one of the neighborhood children came over and asked his mother if he was ever going to come out and play. It had not occurred to the INTP that he was not already playing. However, he did set aside his books and join the neighborhood children.

The INTP is full of questions, sometimes voiced, most often not. INTP children often challenge and even stump their elders. A young INTP asked his grandmother, "Why is the moon broken?" after he had observed that the moon changes form.

INTP children enjoy fantasy, mysteries, inventing, thinking and doing things that may be somewhat atypical for other children of their age, and they sense their uniqueness early on. If INTPs are fond of books or games, it is likely that their choices will not be the "current rage." If an INTP is fond of music, it is likely to be of an unusual sort. A teen-age INTP found enjoyment in the music and philosophy of the rock group the Grateful Dead. He liked their lack of commercialism and their acceptance of all individuals, even different ones.

INTPs tend to either respect and go along with society's rules, or to question and rebel against them. Their response to these rules depends on how the rules might affect them. When INTPs do not like the rules, they are quick to find the flaws in the rule makers' thinking, regardless of their status, position in the hierarchy, or renown. When driving home late at night, one INTP felt silly stopping at stoplights when there was no one else around. She would usually not wait for the light to change before she proceeded on her way.

An underachieving but academically capable INTP teenager was told to attain at least a C average. However, he was far more interested in designing and building a ramp for skateboarding. Cleverly, he figured out how much work was necessary to attain the C average, did the work, and presented his parents with a report card filled with Cs. This C average frustrated his parents because they knew he was capable of better work. The INTP, however, responded to the letter of the law while maintaining his own interests and therefore thought he should not be admonished about his grades.

As young adults choosing careers, INTPs either set a course and work toward it quietly yet forcefully or continue to resist and rebel against society's expectations and "irrational rules." One INTP who found her niche in artificial intelligence attained several academic degrees, worked in a major artificial intelligence research center, and married a man who shared some of her unusual interests. Because of the steadiness of her interest in artificial intelligence and society's need for research on it, this INTP was able to make a fine contribution.

Other INTPs, however, rebel against society's rules about education, marriage, family responsibilities, and work, because they seem irrational. These INTPs lead lives of quiet rebellion as a result. They turn from one idea and interest to the other and from one job to another, all in search of illusive logical purity.

INTPs may either focus in depth on a major interest or move from one interest to another without showing others—friends, colleagues, and bosses—their reasons why. It is the process, the quest, that has been most interesting to them. Once they have found the answer, they do not often share it because the answer is obvious, and documenting the obvious is redundant. This attitude includes a tendency not to respond or speak up in groups, because the INTP feels that what he or she was going to say seems *so obvious* that no one would want to hear it. To the INTP's chagrin, someone else often speaks up, says the obvious, and gets the recognition for it. This particular behavior may be frustrating to the INTP, as well as to those with whom they interact.

As INTPs mature, they continue their quest for logical purity, but now it includes more balance in their activities. An INTP professor, well established in his career, balanced his life with hobbies that were highly intense and adventuresome. In the space of five years, he was involved in motorcycling, snow-mobiling, cultivating tropical fish, setting up a state-of-the-art stereo system, sailing, and learning to use a personal computer.

To an observing bystander, the hobbies may seem unrelated. Typical of INTPs, this professor showed internal consistency in his hobbies: unrelated to his academic interests, they involved total concentration and attention; they were thoroughly explored and their nuances worked out, at which time the INTP moved on to his next hobby; and he shared each hobby with his significant other.

For many types, retirement signifies external changes in behavior and in lifestyle. For the INTP, however, external life is seen as incidental; internal life is "where the action is." Therefore, while external changes may occur, INTPs are less likely to change what is really important to them, what is going on in their internal world.

Thus, in retirement, INTPs often continue the activities that were important to them in their working life. It may be difficult for others to see where the working life stopped and retirement has begun. Just because INTPs no longer go to work does not mean that their minds are no longer at work.

LEARNING

The INTP is a relentless learner in areas that hold his or her interest. They often seem "lost in thought," and this characteristic appears very early. INTPs enjoy the life of the mind and the learning process, regardless of whether that process takes place in a formal sense. They are often characterized as life-long learners. One INTP physician commented that periodically he thinks of returning to graduate school in an entirely different area than medicine because he so loved being in school. INTPs focus broadly and conceptually, rather than superficially and emotionally.

In school, well-rounded INTPs work on their assignments with a great deal of inward energy and interest that is usually not apparent to others. INTPs tend to connect unrelated thoughts. As learners, they are able to find logical flaws in the thinking of others. They analyze these flaws and find ideas for further study. They go to great depths in their analysis. A young INTP taking an honors course in religion read the Old and New Testaments three times in their entirety in order to get the full sense of the history contained in the Bible.

INTPs regard their teachers as equals and as individuals to be challenged. Competence in a teacher is important to INTPs, who are more likely to do their best when they see their teachers as competent.

In taking exams, INTPs prefer theoretical questions. When INTPs view a test, teachers, or subjects as irrelevant, they may respond as follows: "I know what I need to know about this topic; I may even know more than my teacher. The teacher made this test, and this test is dumb. Therefore, my teacher is dumb, and I will not do the test." Because of such reactions, the INTP's academic record may include successes or may be filled with failures.

LABORING

INTPs contribute a logical, systems-building approach to their work. They like being the architect of a plan, because of the scheming and thinking involved, far more than being the implementer of that plan. Implementation tends to be drudgery. They are content to sit back and think about what might work, given their view of the situation. INTPs may ignore standard operating procedures. The hours that they spend are not what is important to them, but rather the completion of their thought process. When their projects are of interest to them, they can become mesmerized and may even work through the night. When their projects are not intriguing, their work is considered drudgery, and the INTP finds it difficult to stay motivated.

Work Setting

The preferred work setting for the INTP contains independent thinkers focused on solving complex problems. The INTP enjoys a work environment that fosters independence and self-determination, that allows for privacy and quiet, and that is flexible and unstructured. They avoid meetings when possible. INTPs like to set their own goals and, if possible, choose how they are to be rewarded.

Organizing Style

INTPs prefer to organize ideas rather than situations or people. They can be relentless reorganizers of thoughts and concepts. They do not, however, seek to structure the outside world of activities and people unless they must. They are recognized as people who are able to contribute conceptually about how to organize, but they may not directly apply these organizational concepts to their own lives.

The work space of the INTP is generally cluttered with papers, books, objects, or prototypes that are important to their interests and thoughts. One INTP reported that he clipped journal articles and devised a filing system for them but never actually got to the point of getting things filed. It is difficult for an INTP to throw out things that may have a possible future relevance and, generally, many things have that possibility. When faced with the possibility of having to throw journals or books away, INTPs are often left with a sense of loss or discomfort because they feel that they may throw away things of critical importance.

An INTP mathematician was moved into a new job in human resource development. In order to become familiar with his new discipline, he clipped and saved every article pertaining to it. Because of the many periodicals in this field, his office began to resemble a paper warehouse. After two years, it was necessary for him to move his desk into a corner, which was the only available space left in his office. Only after some urging from his peers did he see a need to externally organize his work environment. He threw out *some* of his files.

Occupations

To perform well at work, individuals may need to use all of the eight preferences at the appropriate time and when required by the situation. Knowing this, people tend to select occupations that allow them to use the preferences that are most natural to them.

INTPs usually find a place in their work for using their logical and structured thinking. They enjoy work that allows them to abstract, to generalize beyond the data, and to build models. Flexibility is desired because INTPs like to "do the job when they want to do it and as they want to do it." They also prefer occupations in which the hierarchy is minimal and not important. This attitude stems from their firm belief that, to be legitimate, a hierarchy should be built on the competency of individuals who are logically placed according to their talents.

While INTPs can and do enter all occupations, some are more appealing to them than others. According to available research,[1] some occupations (in alphabetical order) seem to be especially attractive to INTPs: biologist, chemist, computer programmer, computer systems analyst, lawyer, photographer, psychologist, researcher, surveyor, writer, and other occupations that allow INTPs to use their logical thinking in appropriate ways. These occupations are not meant to be an exhaustive list but serve to illustrate some areas that an INTP might enjoy. If your specific occupation or one that you are interested in is not listed here, think instead of its general characteristics and ask yourself how those fit with your type.

LEADING

As leaders, INTPs focus on logic and principles, leading others by the strength of their ideas. They are able to analyze problems and goals conceptually and apply logical systems thinking to meet organizational needs. Generally, INTPs do not seek traditional leadership roles, preferring autonomy for themselves and others. They do their best when leading other independent, idea-focused people. INTPs relate to others based on their expertise, not their position or status in the hierarchy. As leaders, INTPs tend to interact intellectually rather than emotionally and appeal to their followers using their logical thinking rather than personal examples.

A group of human resource trainers met to discuss the future of a training program that they had developed. There were a number of problems with the program, including marketing logistics, competition from other vendors, and uniformity of quality. Even with these problems, most of the trainers were determined that the program should continue to be offered with only slight modifications.

One of the trainers, an INTP, stood up in the middle of the meeting and challenged the entire premise of the training program. He said that external trainers could manage it better and that the market for their training was close to saturation. Given all the existing quality problems with the program, he believed that continuation was outside the training department goal of providing a high-quality program.

In previous meetings, this INTP had been quiet and somewhat removed from the discussions. After his own private reflection, he saw the flaws in the organization's logic. "Let's not do any more training," he argued convincingly. He clarified the issues for everyone and helped them look at the future in a more objective way. The other trainers, unaccustomed to the INTP's directness, were amazed at the clarity and convincing nature of his counterproposal. In four minutes, he had shifted the whole concept from providing training to engaging outside vendors to do it.

Once the conceptual shift had occurred, the INTP had little interest in carrying out the redirection of the department. He returned to his usual role as "thinker." Once INTPs master a concept, they are ready to move on to new territory. They do not have a strong need to carry out their concepts.

LEISURE

Leisure tends to have two dimensions for the INTP. One dimension reflects their depth, concentration, and focus on conceptual matters. The other dimension reflects a need for risk-taking activity in the external world.

The INTP likes ample time alone to read, to think, to play with computers, or to watch television. Television viewing may be purposeful or may be used as a background while the INTP is busy processing information internally. Sometimes they find these inner activities more fascinating than the company of people. This is particularly so with computers. INTPs usually take to them like "ducks to water." What seems to appeal to INTPs is the quiet and deep involvement with the logical ordering of information that computers demand.

INTPs may develop their interests in great depth and use their logic for focus. An INTP was intrigued by the plot and characterization of Agatha Christie's novels. She decided to read every Agatha Christie book in print. Then she compared original editions of the Christie mysteries with current paperback editions. Next, she read criticisms of those works and viewed available films relating to Agatha Christie. Generally, INTPs have little desire to read "best-sellers," probably because they look skeptically at public or majority opinions. They prefer to trust their own judgments.

INTPs may engage in physical challenges, sometimes putting their lives at risk. INTPs, ready to take a risk, might climb mountains (especially where technical rock-climbing skills can be used), skydive, or raft down white-water rivers. In urban settings, INTPs purposely go to the most dangerous parts of town to "hang out and experience the thrill of being there."

INTPs often play games that require thought, such as bridge, Monopoly, and poker, choosing such games because risk taking and strategizing are a part of them. They may play golf or other sports in which there is a potential for strategic thinking. When playing games, they do not want too much small talk, nor do they pay unnecessary attention to details. While others talk, INTPs may find their mind wandering to wordplays and puns, which more closely resemble their form of "cocktail party humor."

LOVING

For the INTP, love has three distinct phases: falling in, staying in, and getting out. These phases relate to their thinking preference and its need for order and sequence.

An INTP characterized falling in love as a stage of complete loss of rationality that may last a year or less. When an INTP falls in love, he or she falls hard—an "all or nothing" phenomenon. At this stage, INTPs are likely to be very lively, almost giddy, in their new love. The experience rushes over them and carries them along. They do not structure or control it but simply enjoy and experience it. During this stage, INTPs do many loving things, such as writing poetry, reading to the loved one, and buying gifts that have special meaning. They are curious about their loved one and are able to overlook his or her flaws. Even quirky faults are enjoyed because they are something new to experience and examine. They may bravely ignore the realities of distance, weather, and time to be with the loved one. One INTP risked life and limb in the most devastating snowstorm of the decade to spend ten minutes with his new love.

As relationships progress to the staying-in-love phase, INTPs begin to evaluate their structure and form. They may withdraw at this point because they are moving toward their more customary inward style. Outward demonstrations of affection lessen, and the giddy state changes. Interactions are more matter of fact, perhaps even impersonal. INTPs take their commitments to their partner seriously; however, they may not discuss these commitments at any length with their partner or with other people, because their commitments seem so obvious to them.

The third phase, falling out of love, which may not always occur, results from an analysis of the real expectations and needs of the relationship. Often an undefined line is crossed that neither partner knows about ahead of time. However, the INTP knows after the line has been crossed, and then the relationship deteriorates or ends. If INTPs recognize their emotions and needs as valid, they are able to sever relationship ties fairly cleanly. However, if they misjudge their own needs and those of their partner, the breakup can be messy, perhaps affecting other aspects of their lives for a long time. If the INTP shares some common (usually intellectual or conceptual) interests with the former loved one, the relationship continues but on a different level. When INTPs have a reason to continue relationships, they do.

LOSING OUT

Each type has the potential to overuse or abuse its preferences. This is likely to happen when individuals are under great stress or pressure. At these times, they may act in ways that are unlike their usual style. The following paragraphs describe some of the ways INTPs may lose out, in addition to some strategies that they can use to get back on track.

INTPs may lose out in focusing their attention on the inconsistencies of others; they may therefore be perceived as continually acting in a negative way. They may appear aloof and fault finding, and are surprised when others don't readily warm up to them.

An INTP was astounded to learn that his spouse took personally his logical, impersonal comment "The roast is burned!" He was merely calling attention to a poor result and wanted to help determine its cause. He thought that maybe the recipe was incorrect, the stove was overheating, the roaster pan was inappropriate, or the meat thermometer was unreliable. He had made his statement with the best of intentions—to find the cause of the burnt roast. He did not consider that his wife may have made an error and may have taken his comment personally. In fact, he did not tell her about any of his internal analysis; he only talked about his conclusion. If he had included her in his internal thinking process, she might have understood his comments better and might not have taken them so personally.

Some possible strategies for the INTP include being friendly and showing appreciation to others. From an INTP perspective, this may feel like "going overboard." They may find benefit in taking the necessary time to learn more about others, both personally and professionally, and in learning the skills of small talk. Only after establishing a relationship and learning to share their thought processes can INTPs appropriately direct their critical analysis toward others.

Another way the INTP may lose out is by focusing on the minor inconsistencies in a plan or project. INTPs may call these out at the expense of others' feelings, teamwork, or the completion of the project. They may prevent a project from proceeding because of a slight problem in one step. INTPs may need to learn how and when to challenge themselves and others in a positive way and when to let go of a minor logical inconsistency in favor of an overall plan. Because the points they focus on are sometimes so minor, their thoughts can appear convoluted and unfathomable to others.

Being competent is very important to INTPs, yet they can be their own worst critics. They hamstring themselves looking for the exact answer in their attempts to represent their ideas perfectly. One INTP, a Ph.D., after turning his critical thinking upon himself, felt that he was a fraud. He had achieved much career success but confided, "My confidence still does not fit with my skills and achievements. I can always see the flaws in my own performance and can think of ways to make an even greater contribution. I can't listen to praise because I know I could have done so much better." The hypersensitivity toward himself was not shared with others. He turned inward to an even greater degree, finding that his performance always came up short when compared to his standard of perfection. This focus on his own flaws caused him to feel depressed. A possible tactic for him and other INTPs in similar situations is to discuss his feelings with other people who might provide a more realistic assessment.

INTPs lose out when their emotions, the least accessible parts of their personality, take control. They may experience unmanageable emotional outbursts and appear hypersensitive. The friend of an INTP suggested that she might think about updating her college hairstyle to a more professional look. The INTP looked at her friend and screamed, "Why are you always picking on me and criticizing the way I look!" The friend was overwhelmed at the intensity of the response to her "helpful" and well-meaning suggestion.

Possible strategies for situations like these would be for INTPs to learn to become more aware of their personal emotions and feelings. Emotions should not be ignored just because they are illogical. Exploration of their emotions may benefit INTPs because they reveal potential areas for growth.

When INTPs are back on track, they are using their strengths of analysis, finding flaws, and standing firm on principles. They can be tireless in the pursuit of logical purity.

IN A NUTSHELL

Hallmarks:[2]

Logical
Skeptical
Detached
Reserved
Speculative
Self-determined
Precise
Original
Theoretical
Independent
Autonomous
Cognitive

Acronym:[3]

It's Not Theoretically Possible

Chapter Nineteen

ENTP

ENTPs Chose the Following Preferences:

Extraversion . . . . ENERGIZING . . . . Introversion
Sensing . . . . ATTENDING . . . . **iNtuition**
Thinking . . . . DECIDING . . . . Feeling
Judgment . . . . LIVING . . . . **Perception**

In general, ENTPs are known for their quest of the novel and complex. They have faith in their ability to improvise and to overcome any challenges that they face. They are highly independent, and value adaptability and innovation. They may be several steps ahead of others in encouraging and valuing change. ENTPs hate uninspired routine and resist hierarchical and bureaucratic structures that are not functional. They need freedom for action. With their entrepreneurial tendencies and broad understandings, they push against all odds to further their projects. They are at their best in changing circumstances in which they can develop conceptual models and devise strategies to effectively navigate through change.

LIVING

ENTPs are lively children who question established truths and norms, dream and scheme, and develop unusual ways of doing traditional childhood things. The ENTP child is oriented toward doing the unique, which may mean taking risks and outwitting parental, school, and societal authority. Tell an ENTP child that some behavior is inappropriate for his or her sex, and the ENTP will develop even more commitment to it. They enjoy creating projects and following interests that are unusual and different.

ENTP children enjoy inventing new toys, dances, and languages. Because they are outgoing in their personality style, they often engage other children in their projects and assign them particular roles to play. One ENTP recalled how she designed a float for a local 4H parade. She persuaded her cousins to join her, and they came up with an unusual treatment of a baby buggy, attaching everyday household objects to it. The buggy, which ended up looking like a pirate ship, won a prize for the most unusual float.

ENTPs rarely accept things just as they are. They like to test or explore to see new meanings and relationships. One ENTP recalled an instance in kindergarten in which he discovered a better way of handling the snack time. Each kindergartner was given two crackers—one saltine, one graham. They were not allowed to have two of one kind. The ENTP thought a "better way" would be to trade with someone else to get two of the same kind. The ENTP remembered not being able to reasonably persuade his kindergarten teacher. "The rule was the rule" for her. So much for ingenuity in kindergarten. The ENTP decided not to carry this any further, stating that he did not do any "under-the-table cracker deals." He simply ate his crackers and remembered writing off his teacher as "dumb."

When things do not go as ENTPs want, they use their ingenuity and cleverness to bring people and situations around to their point of view. In her freshman year of college, one ENTP disliked the big city where her school was located and the long bus commute between school and home. She wanted to come home each weekend to be with her friends and family. She felt she needed a car to make the trip more pleasant and devised a strategy for that end. Because she knew her parents valued education, she told them that she would drop out of school unless they bought her a car. Just as she had planned, her parents purchased a car for her; she continued her weekend commute and stayed in college until graduation.

As young adults, when ENTPs choose a career for themselves, they tend to set flexible goals that allow them to incorporate new information and accommodate to new circumstances when they come along. It is hard for ENTPs not to be able to explore the "road not taken." Their byword is "keep your options open." Sometimes this flexibility can look like indecision to outsiders. For example, an ENTP decided to be a medical doctor. Because she was not given much encouragement or financial support from her parents, she opted instead for psychology. She entered a Ph.D. program in psychology and did her internship in a medical school, where she could be in a medical setting and vicariously enjoy that experience. After she obtained her Ph.D., she used the title "Doctor" even though it was not customarily used by other psychologists in her community. When she started her own practice, she focused on work with medical teams, hospital administrators, and other health-related professionals. In this way, she maintained her medical interest and made the optimal use of her interests and circumstances. It is not uncommon for ENTPs to have more than one career focus.

As adults, ENTPs take advantage of opportunities. Because of their ability to see relationships and connections between seemingly unrelated things, they are able to realize the potential in many things. When they see an opportunity that others have missed, they set action-oriented strategies that allow them the greatest flexibility to achieve the results they want. While they may adapt in their methods of obtaining results, they will remain persistent in their objectives. Many ENTPs are enterprising in nature; even when they are inside organizations, they may act like entrepreneurs as they look to maximize opportunity. Because they like autonomy, ENTPs usually find ways to manage their work as they see fit.

The worst job for them is working for someone who demands considerable rule following or tries too often to tell or order, rather than make suggestions to the ENTP. They find the options in the rule book and do what they think will bring the results they want. Sometimes ENTPs find trouble when they skirt the usual protocol or hierarchy of an organization. One ENTP who works in human resources for a large corporation finds that having to enforce the policies and procedures of the organization is often frustrating and confining. There always seem to be exceptions to every rule or guideline. She hates, most of all, to be called "bureaucratic or rigid" by managers, because that is how she least sees herself. Most line managers do find her responsive and easy to work with because she does not get bogged down in the bureaucratic red tape.

ENTPs do not take well to those who impose arbitrary authority. They accept "coaching" from the experts if they value their competence. Competence is a key word for ENTPs; in order to be respected by an ENTP, one must be competent in his or her field.

One ENTP accepted a position as a long-range planner within a large financial corporation that allowed her a great deal of autonomy and flexibility to act. Since she was quite insightful, she noted changes in the wind for her department and moved to an investment position when another department sought her out. In her new position, she encountered some resentment because she did not have the "official" background and qualifications (an M.B.A.) for this job. She did not let this bother her, however. She jumped right in and brought to the department a new awareness of how things could be. It was not long before she was noticed by her superiors as having novel ideas and implementable plans to carry them out. Her "different" way of doing things resulted in her being asked to consider a promotion to start a new department based on her ideas about how to generate more private investment.

Throughout their careers, ENTPs want their work to be enjoyable, with interesting possibilities for applications. Additionally, having their work widely acclaimed and accepted as a unique contribution would be highly gratifying for ENTPs. They also weave in vacations whenever possible and want a flexible work schedule.

In retirement, ENTPs want to continue following their inspirations and having fun. While they may not have planned financially for retirement, most ENTPs have given ample thought to what they will do at that point in their lives. ENTPs have many dreams and ideas of what they want to do in retirement. For most of them, life feels too short for all their interests and dreams. One ENTP said, "There is no such thing as 'retirement.' I only imagine another stage of life. In fact, that is one of my dreams—to be a character actor when I get older."

Security is not necessarily a key motivator for ENTPs, especially when they are young. Thus, their financial well-being in retirement may be unpredictable. Having made career changes throughout their lives, many ENTPs may not have spent enough time in any one organization to benefit from a complete retirement package.

One ENTP, to gain more flexibility and autonomy, bought a small company. Growing the company to the point where it took care of all of his personal financial needs, he opened a division that was strictly research oriented and focused on the cutting edge of his field. Even though he found people to run his company and its new division, he still remained involved in all of it. When it came time to retire, he discovered that what he really wanted to do was have his current employees run his ongoing businesses so that he could be free to buy and make profitable two new businesses that were faced with challenging financial problems. Even in his retirement, this ENTP needed to use his ingenuity. His desire for challenge, newness, variety, and change had not abated with his advancing age.

LEARNING

ENTPs are relentless learners. When the subject matter interests them, they are able to find meaning in whatever they are studying. Knowledge is important to them, but they may not feel the need to show this to their teachers and therefore may be somewhat lackadaisical about assignments and tests. However, when ENTPs find other students to compete or match wits with, they become dedicated to doing well in their assignments.

ENTPs use their enthusiasm and energy to get others involved in their learning. They learn through give-and-take discussions and by questioning and challenging others. They are quick, verbal, and logical, preferring to use their skills in interactions with others. ENTPs look at the logical foundations in others' thinking and build on them to develop their own conceptual systems.

ENTPs want to be taught concepts rather than facts. Models are important to them, providing an overall context or backdrop in which specific details can be subsumed. They typically absorb their teacher's material and present it in a framework that ties all of the elements together.

As learners, ENTPs like to challenge their teachers and classmates and enjoy competitive learning tasks through which they can show their conceptual versatility. ENTPs may enjoy independent study in which they can pursue an area of interest, using their own time frame and their own methods. Highly structured learning, in which students must memorize facts that do not fit together into a whole, is generally not to their liking. ENTPs do best with theoretical questions and essay exams in which they can relate one idea to another. The essence of an ENTP learning environment is "critical analysis of process and change in an applied setting."

LABORING

ENTPs contribute an innovative, versatile, and enterprising approach to work. They view limitations as challenges to be overcome and look for new ways to do things. They need to find a niche for themselves in order to be free to maneuver. They prefer the start-up phase of a project rather than the follow-through or maintenance phase. Once the project is designed, they prefer to turn it over to someone else. They take initiative and inspire others toward greater accomplishments and challenges. In meeting these challenges, they generate conceptual frameworks that they use to determine their courses of action.

Work Setting

The preferred work setting for ENTPs contains independent thinkers working on real ways to solve complex problems, often by applying conceptual models. ENTPs enjoy work environments that favor change, are flexible, reward risk, and focus on competency. ENTPs seek autonomy for themselves and encourage it in others. They want things at work to have only as much structure and bureaucracy as is necessary in order to allow for creativity.

Organizing Style

ENTPs prefer to organize logically and strategically toward the accomplishment of something different or innovative. An ENTP may listen to a lecture and devise a conceptual framework from it to illustrate its key points.

The work space of an ENTP may not exhibit an easily understood sense of organization. However, ENTPs tend to have a rational system to organize those things that are important to them. This organization may not always be visible to other people, but the ENTP is not bothered by that. "As long as it works for me" is their major criterion.

Because ENTPs are focused on the big picture and future happenings and because they organize according to their concepts, they may overlook simple, basic details necessary to accomplish a project. Details are viewed as relatively unimportant in relation to the overall model or concept. For example, an ENTP national sales manager planned a sales meeting to update her staff. She presented a straight-forward model of the interactions between the home office and the field. In working on her model, she focused all her energy on these interactions and overlooked information that the sales representatives needed to accurately fill out the new customer order forms. When questioned about the forms, she was able to draw on her ability to spontaneously meet situational requirements, and answered all of the sales representatives' questions smoothly and accurately. ENTPs can improvise well, and they come to rely on this attribute.

Occupations

To perform well at work, individuals may need to use all of the eight preferences at the appropriate time and when required by the situation. Knowing this, people tend to select occupations

that allow them to use the preferences that are most natural to them.

ENTPs usually find work that involves an analytical, entrepreneurial, and creative focus. They tend to tolerate ambiguity well. They want to be in situations in which they can take intellectual risks and meet challenges. To perform in their best fashion, they prefer flexibility and versatility. While they like status and titles, they ultimately want to be judged on their innovative accomplishments. They take advantage of changing circumstances and work those circumstances into their plans. As a result, they function effectively in chaotic times.

While ENTPs can and do enter all occupations, some are more appealing to them than others. According to available research,[1] some occupations (in alphabetical order) seem to be more attractive to ENTPs: actor, chemical engineer, computer analyst, credit investigator, journalist, marketeer, photographer, psychiatrist, public relations worker, sales agent, and other occupations that allow them to be innovative. These occupations are not meant to be an exhaustive list but serve to illustrate some areas that an ENTP might enjoy. If your specific occupation or one that you are interested in is not listed here, think instead of its general characteristics and ask yourself how those fit with your type.

LEADING

ENTPs seek leadership roles that allow them to make their mark and have impact. They may develop theoretical models to address individual and organizational needs. They are able to apply logical systems thinking and use compelling reasons for whatever position they take. They encourage independence in their followers and act as catalysts between people and systems. ENTPs can be skilled in generating enthusiasm for a new approach. They may like a certain amount of the limelight, and they tend to adopt a "sink or swim" approach to training staff. They will describe the big picture, pointing others in the right direction and assuming the rest will follow. They discourage dependence on the part of their employees, and they encourage initiative. As managers, they tend to allow a great deal of freedom to others and do not typically work in a hands-on approach.

An ENTP insurance executive moved through the sales ranks to the position of vice-president of a large insurance company. He had a reputation for being able to attract new clients with his forward-thinking approach to insurance products and services. Because of his ability to forecast market trends in addition to customer needs, the company developed new and innovative insurance products. For his sales force, he purposely selected high-powered, outgoing, and bright people like himself. Most of these employees enjoyed the flexibility and autonomy he granted to them. His major concern, however, was his organization's handling of all the details in their contracts and the specific requirements of their customers. Because he knew he tended to overlook the "nitty gritty" details, he relied heavily on his internal office staff to monitor these aspects of the work. While people on his staff were frequently bewildered by his many changes in contracts and products, they appreciated his ability to generate so much income for the company.

LEISURE

Leisure tends to be wonderful for ENTPs. They are great at playing and constantly seek new outlets for their energy. They like to take risks and to explore. If their play has to have a structure, ENTPs prefer one that is freeing. An open calendar for the weekend is quite appealing to them.

Because they are constantly scanning their environment for things that are new and novel, they are often "in on the latest things." They like the involvement of others in their leisure activities, and they especially like dreaming up and taking charge of their own leisure time. To allow for maximum flexibility, actual details are often worked out during the leisure time itself. ENTPs do not like things to be planned by the day or to the hour.

Travel is often important to the ENTP because it allows the opening up of new vistas and horizons and new ways of conceptualizing life. One ENTP planned a trip to Bermuda. Once she arrived there, she did not have any specific plans other than going to the beach and seeing a few of the tourist spots. She enjoyed the physical challenges of riding the surf and the competitive sports and games at the local club. Many ENTPs are involved in experiences in which they can test themselves physically, allow their minds to focus on a physical task, and find the relaxation that comes from doing something different. ENTPs enjoy reading because it offers them quiet and the opportunity to reflect. Reading also allows their active minds to fantasize further. They often read between the lines and anticipate the outcomes.

LOVING

For the ENTP, falling in love occurs when they feel that there is a good fit with the other person. Often within the first meeting, ENTPs will know whether the relationship has any "real potential." ENTPs may find it difficult to commit to anyone until the right person comes along. During this period, ENTPs explore the possibilities of social companionship and the various kinds of closeness until they can be certain that they have looked at all of the possibilities. Because of this, they are not likely to settle down early. When they do become involved in a relationship, they generally want to maintain as much independence and freedom as their loved one can tolerate. Their mates may need to have high self-esteem and to be independent themselves in order to accept the ENTP need for freedom and novelty.

Often when an ENTP selects a partner, it is on the basis of the fit between the partner and the overall conceptual framework of what the relationship might be like. An American ENTP engineer explained how he met and married an attractive and sweet woman from Germany. Her "kinder, kuchen, kirche" (children, kitchen, and church) behavior and her pleasant personality matched his concept of the ideal partner. She had the attributes of the perfect wife who shared his life's goals, the ideal mother who would raise fine children, and the devoted community volunteer who matched his own commitment. His intuition that they would have a mutual meeting of needs was accurate because his wife took joy and pride in these activities.

For ENTPs, falling out of love, which may not always occur, results when their vision of the relationship does not square with reality. Sometimes they will select someone who offers stability and comfort and ENTPs later will become bored with the stability. When scorned, ENTPs use their powerful and broad-reaching analysis to explain the reasons why the relationship was not good in the first place; additionally, they may become competitive with their former partner and work hard to win. ENTPs do not like to lose at anything they undertake.

LOSING OUT

Each type has the potential to overuse or abuse its preferences. This is likely to happen when individuals are under great stress or pressure. At these times, they may act in ways that are unlike their usual style. The following paragraphs describe some of the ways ENTPs may lose out, in addition to some strategies that they can use to get back on track.

Being competent is very important to ENTPs. Looking stupid or ignorant is one of their greatest fears. However, they may overlook some of their own conceptual flaws. Because they rely on their concepts, they may think that their actual performance is as good as their original concept. An ENTP designed a six-factor model to explain parenting. The model was brilliant in conception, but in reality it missed several key points that all parents know. In focusing on the global view, this theorist over-looked some of the basic points. The parenting strategy had several fine points, but the ENTP required that others buy the whole strategy, not just those parts that worked for them. For that reason, what appeared to be a potentially useful model was less well regarded.

Because ENTPs enjoy dreaming up new models and working them out logically on their own, they may believe that they have the perfect answer to a given situation. They may be unappreciative of others and become competitive when others challenge them. This may place them in the position of believing that they alone have "a corner on the truth." Being resistant to the input of others, they may find that people do not readily embrace their scheme and may even sabotage its implementation. A possible strategy for the ENTP is to acknowledge and validate the input of others and to double-check their ideas and inspirations for flaws. Giving an inspiration a day to rest and then checking it again usually allows ENTPs to spot real flaws and make the inspiration fit better with reality. ENTPs may need to learn how to engage others by really listening and gathering data on their needs and points of view before laying on "the perfect solution."

Another way ENTPs lose out is when they forget about current realities and get caught up in their conceptual models. As a result, they may overextend themselves. Because ENTPs easily make connections and see new possibilities, they often forget how long it may take in real time for these ideas to work out. Their sense of timing may be hampered by their enthusiasm and complete involvement in their current interest. As a result, ENTPs may commit to too many projects and too many deadlines, some of which will eventually suffer. As a strategy, ENTPs may need to set realistic priorities and time lines, perhaps even doubling the amount of time they originally think something will take. ENTPs may not necessarily take deadlines seriously, since they are seen as arbitrarily imposed by others. They may need to learn which deadlines are the important ones to keep. In addition, learning to pay attention to the actual facts and the here-and-now may be important to their overall success.

Finally, ENTPs may find it difficult to adapt to standard operating procedures. Policies are viewed as guidelines, not absolutes. They are there to be broken whenever extenuating circumstances so demand. ENTPs are especially adverse to situations that require the exact following of policies. They value their "maverick" thinking and may struggle more than necessary to gain support for their projects. ENTPs may need to learn how to work within the system, using its policies, procedures, and structure to better further their work. Or ENTPs could decide to leave the system and develop their own policies, which they can control themselves.

When ENTPs are back on track, they are using their strengths of seeing the possibilities, making connections and associations, and finding new and novel ways to proceed. They can be tireless in the pursuit of complexity.

IN A NUTSHELL

Hallmarks:[2]

Enterprising
Independent
Outspoken
Strategic
Creative
Adaptive
Challenging
Analytical
Clever
Resourceful
Questioning
Theoretical

Acronym:[3]

Each New Thought Propels

Chapter Twenty

ENTJ

ENTJs Chose the Following Preferences:

Extraversion . . . . ENERGIZING . . . . Introversion
Sensing . . . . ATTENDING . . . . **iNtuition**
Thinking . . . . DECIDING . . . . Feeling
Judgment . . . . LIVING . . . . Perception

ENTJs take charge quickly and deal directly with problems, especially in situations that involve confusion and inefficiency. They provide structure to the organizations to which they belong and design strategies to accomplish their personal and organizational goals. They develop broad, action-oriented plans, and supply the necessary energy and momentum to see that these plans are accomplished. ENTJs are "take charge" people who organize their own and others' external environments. They do not take "no" for an answer; instead, they use their resources to find a way to meet the challenge. They are at their best in using their analytical and strategic thinking.

LIVING

ENTJ children need to have goals for everything. These goals may be related to achievements such as swimming the fifty-yard freestyle one second faster than they did the previous year, getting a straight-A report card, or winning the school math contest. ENTJ children tend to take charge of themselves and others. They are motivated to organize their world to meet some logically derived objective. They seek power and control. They want to have an impact. Because of their desire to take charge, ENTJs are often leaders. They are not content to just be members of the group. Conflicts may exist when authority figures exercise too much control and deprive ENTJs of their need to be in control of themselves. ENTJ children desire structure and order in their lives. When a given structure is acceptable to them, they will go along with it; when it is not, they challenge and attempt to change it.

ENTJs enjoy an active and diverse lifestyle. They are likely to be in extracurricular activities and often function as the team captain, the president, or the leader. They pursue leadership roles very directly and have difficulty following others unless those individuals demonstrate more competence than they themselves have. Even then, it may be tough for the ENTJ to follow along.

ENTJs are constantly looking for the most strategic way to organize and accomplish a task. They are mindful of how much effort they want to give to a task and the consequences of using their time that way. For example, a teenage ENTJ was told by his father to clean the garage. The ENTJ had other things he wanted to do and determined how to accomplish the cleaning quickly so he could have the rest of the morning for his own activities. While the ENTJ was getting his lunch, his father came by and asked him why he had quit before he had cleaned the garage. The ENTJ said, "Go check the garage. I did it first thing and then went horseback riding." To the father's surprise, the garage was spotless. He knew it had taken considerable organization to clean the garage in less than one-third the time he had estimated.

ENTJs see life as a series of strategic moves and, as a result, are likely to commit to a career goal early, often in their teen years. They determine their overall goals and objectives and what it will take to accomplish them. For ENTJs, the critical thing seems to be their understanding of the things they are doing. Whatever they do must make sense to them according to their logic or they have difficulty doing it. They are well aware of the factors they want in their career, such as prestige, status, and money, and the most expeditious ways to attain them.

An executive vice president of a large company grew up in impoverished circumstances on a farm. Even as a child, he realized the need to obtain an education to better his life. He had to find his own way because he knew his family could not afford to pay for his college education. He decided to enlist in the army knowing he would be eligible to attend school on the G.I. Bill. From all the possible majors, he selected marketing because it appeared to him that there would be positions available that offered both good starting salaries and a chance for advancement. Upon graduation, he was hired immediately into a sales and marketing position by his present company. He focused his drive and energy toward the goal of being an executive vice president by age forty-five. He reached this goal at age forty-four. In looking back, he realized that even as a young adult, he had been confident of his capabilities. He found the means to capitalize on them and applied himself to get where he wanted to go. That he was ahead of schedule by a year was even more rewarding to him.

In mature adulthood, ENTJs are often in leadership positions in their work organizations. They go after what they want with gusto. They set their sights high and work hard. Work and its related activities may become their lives. When joining community and service organizations, they do so as an element of the overall plan. For example, an ENTJ was active in his church in part because it led to business for his firm.

In some instances, ENTJs will change a course of study or take a step back organizationally in order to gain a new skill or to position themselves for greater advancement. Usually this change is carefully chosen because its potential for future gain outweighs its short-term setbacks. ENTJs do few things by chance. Changes that are made must fit their overall strategy.

ENTJs may find retirement unsettling, boring, and difficult because it may bring with it a loss of the power that they had during their working years. Often they make arrangements so that they do not have to retire, preferring to "die with their boots on." Because ENTJs are hard drivers and are goal oriented, they become restless with inactivity and with nothing of consequence (in their view) to do. Thus, they may shift from their current work activities to other arenas in which they can take charge. For example, after retiring, the ENTJ businessman described above became a consultant to struggling new businesses.

In retirement, ENTJs may find it easier to do what they want to do when they want to do it. This may mean that they are unwilling to put up with people whom they had to deal with in their work life. They will maintain true friendships but will ignore those acquaintances who are not enjoyable to them. Maintaining their autonomy is one of their major retirement goals. They may need to learn to rely on others as circumstances dictate, even if this is hard for them to do.

LEARNING

ENTJs see education as one of the major ways of getting ahead. They are willing to learn about the past and what is but always with the mind-set of how that information affects their future. They especially enjoy critiquing and solving problems. They apply their logical systems view to the issues they deal with. They want to change things to fit their concept of what should be. ENTJs learn best through a variety of instructional methods, including lectures and group activities. Without variety and action in the classroom boredom sets in. They like teachers to be well organized, and they seek to organize their own work carefully. Outlines, diagrams, and flow charts supply the essence of organization to their work.

ENTJs like to debate and view problems from all sides. They are comfortable critiquing and analyzing, and do not mind intellectual conflict in the classroom. Other types of students may find a teacher's critique unsettling, but the ENTJ welcomes direct feedback. Negative feedback may be painful if it relates personally to their competence. They view their mistakes as an opportunity to learn more about how to conduct themselves better the next time.

As learners, ENTJs like challenge, and they enjoy organizing to meet that challenge. They may have a general study plan laid out, with test dates and paper deadlines noted. If a subject can be mastered by 100 hours of study, the ENTJ will set up a schedule and work to attain the goal within that time. However, their aim is to do it in even less time, and they feel pride in exceeding their standards by either exerting less effort or less time.

LABORING

At work, ENTJs contribute a wealth of energy directed toward their goals and those of the organization. ENTJs often become their jobs. Their sense of identity is closely tied to how they carry out their responsibilities. They are curious about new ideas and theories, evaluating them in terms of their goals. They are efficient, and deal directly with problems caused by confusion and inefficiency. They prefer to be in charge, operating with logic and decisiveness. They are willing to sacrifice short-term goals in favor of the long-term and are especially adept in tough times. ENTJs are often fiercely competitive, strategic, and task focused.

Work Setting

ENTJs prefer a work environment that contains results-oriented, tough-minded, and independent people focused on complex organizational issues. These goal-oriented individuals demand efficiency from both the systems and people with whom they work; however, they are open to new ideas and strategies that will help them to solve problems and reach their goals. They seek work that is challenging and in which there is a direct payoff for their efforts.

Organizing Style

ENTJs usually determine what they want globally and organize themselves to attain that. They continually scan their external environment looking for opportunities to position themselves or their organization for advancement. They set goals, priorities, and deadlines, and marshall the necessary resources. It is rare to find an ENTJ who does not have an effective time-management system, which may include a master schedule, calendars, and "to do" lists.

One ENTJ, recently appointed to a managerial position, decided to reorganize the office staff. Previously, seniority and loyalty were the basis of staff assignments. However, from the viewpoint of the ENTJ, it seemed logical to match assignments to strengths. She constructed a matrix of the competencies of each staff member and the projects that needed completion the next year. Then she assigned employees to projects for which they were most qualified. She created a time line with strict accountabilities for each person and set up appointments at appropriate intervals with her staff to check progress toward goals. She had no need to meet with them daily or to receive regular memos providing updates. Her system provided her with as much information as she needed.

Occupations

To perform well at work, individuals may need to use all of the eight preferences at the appropriate time and when required by the situation. Knowing this, people tend to select occupations that allow them to use the preferences that are most natural to them.

Occupations that require tough-mindedness, goal direction, and a global perspective tend to attract ENTJs. They use logic and analysis to form conclusions, to organize themselves and others, to give direction, and to take charge.

While ENTJs can and do enter all occupations, some are more appealing to them than others. According to available research,[1] some occupations (in alphabetical order) seem to be especially attractive to ENTJs: administrator, attorney, consultant, credit investigator, labor relations worker, manager, marketing personnel, mortgage banker, personnel professional, systems analyst, and other occupations that allow them to use their strategic sense. These occupations are not meant to be an exhaustive list but serve to illustrate some areas that an ENTJ might enjoy. If your specific occupation or one that you are interested in is not listed here, think instead of its general characteristics and ask yourself how those fit with your type.

LEADING

It has been said that ENTJs cannot *not* lead. One ENTJ recalled that as a child she interpreted her need to lead as somehow being negative. It was not until her thirties that she appreciated the value of her leadership role.

ENTJs are quick to take charge and are quite decisive about whatever they consider to be logically necessary. They are action oriented, energetic, tough-minded, and direct. They like to run as much of the organization as they can and are willing to take on new and different assignments, especially when those assignments involve complex problems and long-range planning.

ENTJs may ask others questions to help them think through what a problem is really about and to force them to look beyond their initial response. Many ENTJs find that asking questions helps others understand and find the reasons why a particular behavior or situation exists. In this process, ENTJs work with others to mold their future.

One ENTJ, who was promoted to president of his company with a mandate to get it on the move again, inherited a staff of thirteen. Within a month of his promotion, he had transferred twelve of the thirteen employees to new positions. He said, "I found out quickly that twelve members of my staff were not going to work out, so I moved them to other positions in the company and brought in people who would do the job the way it needed to be done. I know that if it's not going to work with people, it's not going to work. However, I always treat my people well, and I found all twelve of them new positions." While it was a tough decision, which had to be made for the long-term effectiveness of the company, the ENTJ believed he had acted humanely in accordance with the task he faced. ENTJs take charge quickly, have a vision of what will work in their organization, make tough, even unpopular decisions, and take the necessary actions.

LEISURE

ENTJs are not naturally oriented toward leisure time for leisure's sake. For them, the best leisure activities have a purpose, such as developing business, maintaining health, or critiquing ideas. Fun is struggling through or thinking about a problem. A party becomes enjoyable and worth attending when there is intense conversation about an idea, when there is a group effort to work through or make sense of a complex issue, or when there is a need to understand a concept.

They can be competitive and enjoy using strategy or force to win. An ENTJ participated in a softball league with a variety of people, including some customers of his company. He was the captain of his team, and he enjoyed using his athletic prowess to compete and to win. He felt that being the leader of a winning team reflected well on his business skill.

ENTJs have difficulty with having nothing to do, and they know it. To test himself, one ENTJ deliberately set a goal of sitting still for ten minutes. After one minute, he was already fidgety and thinking about what he would do next. He ended his experiment after four minutes because he could see no point in continuing further. It was one of the few times when it was okay for him to lose.

ENTJs like to be involved in constructive activities that are regularly scheduled. For example, one ENTJ enjoyed playing the piano every night after dinner because he found it extremely challenging and disciplined. He would work on interpretations of Bach and experiment with the music of new composers to understand their style. Another ENTJ talked about her intense concentration and enjoyment of golf. She made it into a scientific game, thinking strategically about which club to use, based on wind direction and course difficulty. Golf provided her with a way to measure her athletic performance vis-á-vis a predetermined standard and to monitor her progress toward playing well.

ENTJ parents have an overall vision for appropriate family leisure activities and the part they will play. They may carry over their own achievement orientation to these activities. They especially like situations that are organized and structured and ones in which they and their family members can demonstrate skill.

An ENTJ mother, who enjoyed ballet herself, set a goal for her daughter to become a ballerina with a major ballet company. Throughout her daughter's childhood, she scheduled her daughter's lessons and used her salary to pay for the best teachers and equipment. She chauffeured her daughter to various lessons and practice sessions, keeping her focused on the ultimate goal. When her daughter was selected by the ballet company, the mother was jubilant. It was a fitting reward for the effort and focus both had put in.

LOVING

For the ENTJ, love needs to fit into the overall picture and may become subservient to their larger goals. Love is always within the context of what the relationship is. One ENTJ stated, "I don't 'allow' love to course freely through my body. God forbid that it should control me rather than I control it!" Love means a match between the ENTJ's needs and what the partner provides. The loved one is, in a sense, an extension of the ENTJ's vision, preferably acting in a supportive, not competing, role. ENTJs tend to make rigorous demands of love. While they may fall in love easily, they maintain that love only if the other person is willing to accept the ENTJ's directness and need for independence. One ENTJ said, "I am really demanding in my love. I expect my partner to keep her commitments to me, particularly when she says she will do something. If she does not do it, I am extremely angry. I don't need a lot of reinforcement, and I don't often give it. I have to remember to do special, loving things. I find it best to schedule a date night to keep me focused at least once a week on our relationship."

Because attractiveness is a part of our culture and an initial standard for many relationships and because ENTJs like to do better than the standard, they particularly take note of attractive people. Given their competitive nature, ENTJs often wonder if they can "win the heart" of the attractive other. It becomes almost a game for them. However, they may not always take action on their observations. They prefer partners who complete their own image of success and attractiveness. The accomplishments or attractiveness of the partner should not overshadow or interfere with those of the ENTJ.

The partner of an ENTJ can expect a hard-working and industrious provider who may use the fruits of his or her labor as an expression of love. ENTJs may not be as verbally communicative of their loving feelings as other types. An ENTJ fast-track career woman married a jovial, laughing, fun-loving construction contractor. In their courtship, she discovered that she particularly liked his manner of poking fun at her, her business dress, and her climb up the corporate ladder. He called her business suit her "full metal jacket" and provided a necessary bit of humor to offset her serious and hard-working career-mindedness. While many outsiders did not understand how the two of them got along, she felt the relationship was just what she needed.

ENTJs expect to have their needs met in relationships, while maintaining their independence. When the partner can no longer do that, it is logical for the ENTJ to sever ties and to move on. However, when ENTJs are scorned by others, they may feel a passionate devastation and a strong sense of loss that is seldom shared with others. However, this sense of loss and gloom generally lasts only a short period before they are ready to move on.

LOSING OUT

Each type has the potential to overuse or abuse its preferences. This is likely to happen when individuals are under great stress or pressure. At these times, they may act in ways that are unlike their usual style. The following paragraphs describe some of the ways ENTJs may lose out, in addition to some strategies that they can use to get back on track.

One way of losing out for ENTJs has to do with their directness in pursuing a goal. They may decide too quickly. Sometimes they are surprised and dismayed by the rapidity with which they make judgments. They may not even be aware of having come to a conclusion until they start acting on their decision. They then become impatient when things are not done according to their plan and time schedule. When this happens, they tend to overstructure, overcontrol, and dictate how things ought to be done.

As a strategy, ENTJs need to keep their overall goal in mind and understand that there may be a variety of paths to its attainment, one of which could be better than the one they chose. This strategy also includes factoring in the needs of others and gaining their input and commitment to the plan.

ENTJs may overlook practical considerations and constraints in favor of driving forward to their long-range goals. This may include discounting the input of others, ignoring common-sense advice, or pushing to extremes. They may do so much and with such intensity that they become overzealous. By busily concentrating on what might happen next, they may miss what is currently happening. They often see little need for new information and, as a result, may make momentous mistakes because they have not considered enough options, let alone enough facts.

As a strategy, ENTJs could check the practical, personal, and situational resources available to them before they plunge ahead. This check needs to include their own internal personal resources, in addition to their external resources.

Another way ENTJs lose out is when their emotions "take control of their personality." This occurs when they have ignored or suppressed their feelings too long. They may find themselves overreacting emotionally or responding inappropriately to situations because they have not paid adequate attention to their inner feelings along the way. To fully accept their feelings, they have to understand and make sense of them, which takes time since their feelings have to undergo logical analysis. This may occur when they feel their competence is questioned, especially by someone whom the ENTJ respects. However, under stress, they may misinterpret the criticism as an attempt to control them, and thus overreact. When ENTJs explode, they may astound themselves and others by the intensity of their response to seemingly trivial situations. The impact of these behaviors on others can be damaging to their interpersonal relationships.

An ENTJ was in charge of a particularly difficult project at work. All of his careful plans seemed to be blocked by people with little foresight. His supervisor noticed what was going on and called him in to discuss the project. The ENTJ mistook the manager's help as a criticism of his competency. He responded emotionally, with anger, rather than listening long enough to see what his supervisor actually intended.

In situations such as these, ENTJs need to sit back, count to ten before acting, and factor in their emotional state. Their generally unacknowledged feelings can be important data to consider in difficult times.

ENTJs are often so task focused that they may overlook others' needs. Because they see the goal so clearly, they may not consider people's input and feelings as they move onward. As a strategy, ENTJs need to factor in the needs of others and take the time to appreciate their contributions. This is especially true when they are dealing with people who are less powerful than they are (their children, for example).

When ENTJs are back on track, they are using their strengths of global analysis, strategic thinking, and standing firm on principles. They can be tireless in the pursuit of the goal.

IN A NUTSHELL

Hallmarks:[2]

Logical
Decisive
Planned
Tough
Strategic
Critical
Controlled
Challenging

Straightforward
Objective
Fair
Theoretical

Acronym: [3]

Executives Need Tough Jobs

Conclusions

We hope you will find that knowing about your LIFEType enhances your self-awareness and your appreciation of others. It should help you be more knowledgeable about individual differences and, as a result, make it easier for you to communicate more effectively, approaching problems in a healthy and productive manner.

While type theory teaches that people are born with natural preferences, external influences can cause individuals to use preferences other than their natural ones. For example, family and parental pressure can cause a person to act like their parents or other family members, even though their natural preferences are different. Work may require individuals to behave differently than they actually prefer. When people are in periods of stress or growth, they may experiment with new and more difficult behaviors.

It is important to keep in mind that all types are worthwhile and equal in value. While type preferences illustrate a style of behavior, they do not limit people to only that style. Sometimes people need to strategize and deliberately use preferences that do not come as naturally to them. For example, sometimes Extraverts need to take the time to introvert and reflect. At times, Introverts need to extravert and act. From time to time, Sensors need to dream and consider other possibilities, while iNtuitives may find it valuable to consider facts and look at practicalities. Thinkers sometimes need to consider human values and the ramifications of their behavior on others, and Feelers need to use logic and analysis. Judgers need to remain open and tolerant of new ideas, while Perceptives at times need to close on their ideas.

Good "type development" means that people use their own preferences well and know when to strategize and use the other preferences appropriately. It does not mean that they will use all preferences equally well.

As you have seen, your LIFEType does not describe you entirely or precisely. Each person is unique, in spite of the patterns he or she shares with others.

Type theory has been well documented, with hundreds of scientific studies verifying its utility. If you want to learn more about your type, we suggest you take the inventory called the Myers-Briggs Type Indicator™ (see page 277), refer to the bibliography at the end of this book, and contact the type-related organizations listed.

We wish you the best of LIFETypes!

Notes

CHAPTER ONE.
The Extravert and Introvert Preferences

1. Myers, Isabel Briggs, and Mary H. McCaulley, *Manual: A Guide to the Development and Use of the Myers-Briggs Type Indicator* (Palo Alto, CA: Consulting Psychologists Press, 1985), 244–246.
2. Myers and McCaulley, *Manual: A Guide to the Development and Use of the Myers-Briggs Type Indicator*, 244–246.
3. Myers and McCaulley, *Manual: A Guide to the Development and Use of the Myers-Briggs Type Indicator*, 45–47.
4. Hirsh, Sandra K., and Jean M. Kummerow, *Introduction to Type in Organizational Settings* (Palo Alto, CA: Consulting Psychologists Press, 1987), 5.

CHAPTER TWO.
The Sensing and Intuition Preferences

1. Myers and McCaulley, *Manual: A Guide to the Development and Use of the Myers-Briggs Type Indicator*, 246–248.
2. Myers and McCaulley, *Manual: A Guide to the Development and Use of the Myers-Briggs Type Indicator*, 246–248.
3. Myers and McCaulley, *Manual: A Guide to the Development and Use of the Myers-Briggs Type Indicator*, 45–47.
4. Hirsh and Kummerow, *Introduction to Type in Organizational Settings*, 5.

CHAPTER THREE.
The Thinking and Feeling Preferences

1. Myers and McCaulley, *Manual: A Guide to the Development and Use of the Myers-Briggs Type Indicator*, 248–250.
2. Myers and McCaulley, *Manual: A Guide to the Development and Use of the Myers-Briggs Type Indicator*, 248–250.

3. Myers and McCaulley, *Manual: A Guide to the Development and Use of the Myers-Briggs Type Indicator*, 45–47.
4. Hirsh and Kummerow, *Introduction to Type in Organizational Settings*, 5.

CHAPTER FOUR.
The Judgment and Perception Preferences

1. Myers and McCaulley, *Manual: A Guide to the Development and Use of the Myers-Briggs Type Indicator*, 250–253.
2. Myers and McCaulley, *Manual: A Guide to the Development and Use of the Myers-Briggs Type Indicator*, 250–253.
3. Myers and McCaulley, *Manual: A Guide to the Development and Use of the Myers-Briggs Type Indicator*, 45–47.
4. Hirsh and Kummerow, *Introduction to Type in Organizational Settings*, 5.

CHAPTER FIVE. ISTJ

1. Myers and McCaulley, *Manual: A Guide to the Development and Use of the Myers-Briggs Type Indicator*, 261–263.
2. Hirsh and Kummerow, *Introduction to Type in Organizational Settings*, 15.
3. *MBTI News* 7/2 (Spring 1985): 18.

CHAPTER SIX. ISTP

1. Myers and McCaulley, *Manual: A Guide to the Development and Use of the Myers-Briggs Type Indicator*, 263–265.
2. Hirsh and Kummerow, *Introduction to Type in Organizational Settings*, 15.
3. *MBTI News* 7/2 (Spring 1985): 18.

CHAPTER SEVEN. ESTP

1. Myers and McCaulley, *Manual: A Guide to the Development and Use of the Myers-Briggs Type Indicator*, 265–267.
2. Hirsh and Kummerow, *Introduction to Type in Organizational Settings*, 15.
3. *MBTI News* 7/2 (Spring 1985): 18.

CHAPTER EIGHT. ESTJ

1. Myers and McCaulley, *Manual: A Guide to the Development and Use of the Myers-Briggs Type Indicator*, 267–269.
2. Hirsh and Kummerow, *Introduction to Type in Organizational Settings*, 15.
3. *MBTI News* 7/2, (Spring 1985): 18.

CHAPTER NINE. ISFJ

1. Myers and McCaulley, *Manual: A Guide to the Development and Use of the Myers-Briggs Type Indicator*, 269–270.
2. Hirsh and Kummerow, *Introduction to Type in Organizational Settings*, 15.
3. *MBTI News* 7/2 (Spring 1985): 18.

CHAPTER TEN. ISFP

1. Myers and McCaulley, *Manual: A Guide to the Development and Use of the Myers-Briggs Type Indicator*, 271–272.
2. Hirsh and Kummerow, *Introduction to Type in Organizational Settings*, 15.
3. *MBTI News* 7/2 (Spring 1985): 18.

CHAPTER ELEVEN. ESFP

1. Myers and McCaulley, *Manual: A Guide to the Development and Use of the Myers-Briggs Type Indicator*, 272–274.
2. Hirsh and Kummerow, *Introduction to Type in Organizational Settings*, 15.
3. *MBTI News* 7/2 (Spring 1985): 18.

CHAPTER TWELVE. ESFJ

1. Myers and McCaulley, *Manual: A Guide to the Development and Use of the Myers-Briggs Type Indicator*, 274–276.
2. Hirsh and Kummerow, *Introduction to Type in Organizational Settings*, 15.
3. *MBTI News* 7/2 (Spring 1985): 18.

CHAPTER THIRTEEN. INFJ

1. Myers and McCaulley, *Manual: A Guide to the Development and Use of the Myers-Briggs Type Indicator*, 276–278.
2. Hirsh and Kummerow, *Introduction to Type in Organizational Settings*, 15.
3. *MBTI News* 7/2 (Spring 1985): 18.

CHAPTER FOURTEEN. INFP

1. Myers and McCaulley, *Manual: A Guide to the Development and Use of the Myers-Briggs Type Indicator*, 278–280.
2. Hirsh and Kummerow, *Introduction to Type in Organizational Settings*, 15.
3. *MBTI News* 7/2 (Spring 1985): 18.

CHAPTER FIFTEEN. ENFP

1. Myers and McCaulley, *Manual: A Guide to the Development and Use of the Myers-Briggs Type Indicator*, 280–282.
2. Hirsh and Kummerow, *Introduction to Type in Organizational Settings*, 15.
3. *MBTI News* 7/2 (Spring 1985): 18.

CHAPTER SIXTEEN. ENFJ

1. Myers and McCaulley, *Manual: A Guide to the Development and Use of the Myers-Briggs Type Indicator*, 282–284.
2. Hirsh and Kummerow, *Introduction to Type in Organizational Settings*, 15.
3. *MBTI News* 7/2 (Spring 1985): 18.

CHAPTER SEVENTEEN. INTJ

1. Myers and McCaulley, *Manual: A Guide to the Development and Use of the Myers-Briggs Type Indicator*, 284–286.
2. Hirsh and Kummerow, *Introduction to Type in Organizational Settings*, 15.
3. *MBTI News* 7/2 (Spring 1985): 18.

CHAPTER EIGHTEEN. INTP

1. Myers and McCaulley, *Manual: A Guide to the Development and Use of the Myers-Briggs Type Indicator*, 286–288.
2. Hirsh and Kummerow, *Introduction to Type in Organizational Settings*, 15.
3. *MBTI News* 7/2 (Spring 1985): 18.

CHAPTER NINETEEN. ENTP

1. Myers and McCaulley, *Manual: A Guide to the Development and Use of the Myers-Briggs Type Indicator*, 288–290.
2. Hirsh and Kummerow, *Introduction to Type in Organizational Settings*, 15.
3. *MBTI News* 7/2 (Spring 1985): 18.

CHAPTER TWENTY. ENTJ

1. Myers and McCaulley, *Manual: A Guide to the Development and Use of the Myers-Briggs Type Indicator*, 290–292.
2. Hirsh and Kummerow, *Introduction to Type in Organizational Settings*, 15.
3. *MBTI News* 7/2 (Spring 1985): 18.

Bibliography

Bibliography: The Myers-Briggs Type Indicator. Gainesville, FL: Center for Applications of Psychological Type, Inc. Computer listing, revised at each printing.

Hirsh, Sandra Krebs. *Using the Myers-Briggs Type Indicator in Organizations.* Palo Alto, CA: Consulting Psychologists Press, 1985.

Hirsh, Sandra Krebs, and Jean M. Kummerow. *Introduction to Type in Organizational Settings.* Palo Alto, CA: Consulting Psychologists Press, 1987.

Jung, C. G. *Psychological Types.* Princeton, N.J.: Princeton University Press, 1971.

Kiersey, David, and Marilyn Bates. *Please Understand Me.* Del Mar, CA: Prometheus Nemesis Books, 1978.

Lawrence, Gordon D. *People Types and Tiger Stripes.* 2nd ed. Gainesville, FL: Center for Applications of Psychological Type, Inc., 1982.

Myers, Isabel Briggs, and Mary H. McCaulley. *Manual for the Myers-Briggs Type Indicator: A Guide to the Development and Use of the MBTI.* Palo Alto, CA: Consulting Psychologists Press, 1985.

Myers, Isabel Briggs. *Introduction to Type.* Rev. ed. Palo Alto, CA: Consulting Psychologists Press, 1987.

Myers, Isabel Briggs, with Peter B. Myers. *Gifts Differing.* Palo Alto, CA: Consulting Psychologists Press, 1980.

To learn more about your LIFETypes, you may want to contact the following organizations that promote the understanding and ethical use of psychological type:

Association for Psychological Type
9140 Ward Parkway
Kansas City, MO 64144

Center for Applications of Psychological Type
2720 N.W. 6th Street
Gainesville, FL 32609

Consulting Pyschologists Press, Inc.
3803 E. Bayshore Road
Palo Alto, CA 94303